avant-garde

jazz

musicians

university of iowa press Ψ iowa city

DAVID G. SUCH

avant-garde

jazz

musicians

performing 'out there'

University of Iowa Press,

Iowa City 52242

Copyright © 1993 by

David G. Such

All rights reserved

Printed in the United States

of America

Design by Richard Hendel

All photos by the author

Printed on acid-free paper

Library of Congress Cataloging-in-
Publication Data

Such, David G.

Avant-garde jazz musicians: performing
"out there" / by David G. Such.

p.   cm.

Discography: p.

Bibliography: p.

Includes index.

ISBN 0-87745-432-9,

ISBN 0-87745-435-3 (pbk.)

1. Jazz—History and criticism.

2. Jazz musicians.   I. Title.

ML3506.S93   1993

781.65'6—dc20   93-3753

CIP

MN

97 96 95 94 93 C 5 4 3 2 1

97 96 95 94 93 P 5 4 3 2 1

To all artists,

educators, and folks

who envision a more

peaceful world

contents

acknowledgments

In the preparation of this book, I am indebted foremost to all the musicians and listeners whose names herein are mentioned. Without their cooperation and hard-earned trust, none of this would be possible. I would also like to thank Mark Gridley for generously sharing his opinions and extensive knowledge; Chuck Braman for his helpful editorial suggestions; and Tom Owens for his willingness to review my transcriptions. There are many others to whom I am thankful for their input. These include Jon Pareles, James Lincoln Collier, Dan Morgenstern, Bob Rusch, Paul Berliner, Leonard Feather, James Porter, Jacqueline DjeDje, D. K. Wilgus, Kwabena Nketia, Lewis Porter, Verna Gillis, Rod Harrison, Robert Georges, and the Sort of Quartet. I would also like to express my appreciation to the Institute of American Culture, University of California, Los Angeles, for their kind support and to the guys at Rhino Records in West Los Angeles for their diligence in locating essential but hard-to-find LP recordings. Lastly, I am grateful to my grandmother, Verona Sadinsky, whose simple but perceptive insights never allowed my ego to exceed my abilities while preparing this book.

avant-garde

jazz

musicians

o n e

introduction

The origins of out jazz, more commonly called avant-garde or free jazz, extend back to the mid and late 1950s. During this time, Charlie Mingus and Ornette Coleman were the first out performers to experiment freely with alternative approaches to group improvisation. Their efforts stimulated a great deal of controversy that virtually divided the jazz community. Though over the years musicians and critics have grown to tolerate out jazz, the music today still attracts much negative criticism. When examined closely, the basis of these criticisms appears to rest awkwardly upon misunderstandings about the music and the motivations of the performers. Consequently, the role of out music in the development of jazz remains ambiguous.

In addressing these issues, this work focuses not only upon a number of different musicians and their respective approaches to performing out but also upon how certain cultural and personal factors have influenced the music. By penetrating the music and worldviews of out performers in a comprehensive manner, I hope to resolve some of the more controversial issues surrounding out jazz and to make the music more understandable to jazz fans and scholars. This will also help to clarify the role of out music in the development of jazz.

I have opted to use the label *out jazz* in lieu of more familiar synonyms such as avant-garde or free jazz whose accumulated meanings over the years have become confounded. Out jazz evolves from metaphors like "out of this world" and "far out." For the listener, these terms are a reaction to some of the salient features of the music. For the performer, the term *out* often describes startling moments when the musicians strive to extend the normal boundaries that characterize most forms of Western music and most styles of jazz.[1]

Out Jazz and Western Music

Many of the distinctive features of out jazz begin to surface when contrasting it with some forms of Western music, from which it deviates so dramatically.[2] From nursery songs to a Bach sonata, the most pervasive and influential component in many forms of Western music is functional tonality. In the West, functional tonality refers to the way in which tones in music are ordered according to prescribed functions.

Consider, for example, the function of the leading tone, or seventh degree, of a scale. It is near in pitch to the tonic, or first degree, of the scale on which a melody often begins and ends, and it produces a dissonant tone when sounded simultaneously with the first degree note. Aware of this tendency, composers often exploit the dissonance of the leading tone to anticipate the sounding of the tonic. In addition, the tonic enjoys functional relationships with other tones in a scale or grouping which also contribute to the listener's expectations, and they establish in part the parameters of style. Eric Salzman adds,

> Every musical event has a "function" or a functional role which relates it to what has come before and what will happen next. The basic psychological principle here is expectation; the basic musical technique

is that of direction and motion. Out of this grow the characteristic ways in which musical lines will rise and fall and the ways in which simultaneous musical lines will relate to one another in harmonic patterns. The idea of expectation suggests the use of resolution and non-resolution; of so-called dissonance and consonance; of intensity and relaxation; of cadence, accent and articulation; of phrase and punctuation; of rhythm and dynamic; even of tempo and tone color.[3]

Prior to the turn of the century, Western classical composers began to abandon functional tonality. In Richard Wagner's Prelude to *Tristan und Isolde* (1859), the composer shifts emphasis among several tones that weaken the listener's awareness of a primary tonal center. In the early part of the twentieth century, Anton von Webern, Alban Berg, and Arnold Schoenberg advanced this principle further by taking steps to ensure that no one tone within a grouping of tones serves as the tonic. Sometimes called serial composing, this approach establishes random relationships among these tones. The end result, of course, is a piece of music that sounds dissonant or "chaotic" to most listeners accustomed to hearing functional relationships among tones. Webern's "Five Orchestra Pieces," Op. 10 (1913), for instance, is athematic, avoids functions among tones, and lacks motivic development.

The techniques of serial composing, forwarded by Schoenberg, did not have a direct bearing upon jazz until the early 1950s.[4] During this time, George Russell, Gunther Schuller, Jimmy Giuffre, and others endeavored to fuse serial techniques of composing with jazz. The Modern Jazz Quartet performed pieces that incorporated instruments such as flutes, cellos, and violins, found mostly in Western classical music. Gunther Schuller coined the term *third stream jazz* to describe any combination of classical music and jazz.[5] The results were not always successful, in the sense that a true blending of both styles was achieved, though the Modern Jazz Quartet came closest to realizing a satisfying balance. By broadening the technical resources in jazz and introducing a variety of means of breaking away from functional tonality, the influence of third stream jazz upon out performers is apparent. Charlie Mingus, in his 1954 LP recording *Jazz Experiment*, for example, reveals an interest in contrapuntal techniques and forms other than the repeating chorus.

Another compositional approach favored by some modern European and American classical composers which has had limited impact on American out jazz is aleatory composing. This technique exploits randomness of tonal material as its primary goal. Thus the ordering of tones is not based on functions but instead on the principle of indeterminacy. Improvisation is often dictated within notated kinds of compositions (e.g., musical graphics, frame notation, action notation). During the formative years of out jazz in Europe, a small group of West German musicians utilized aleatory approaches by composers such as Alois Zimmermann. In America, however, this approach has had few supporters. In contrast, American out jazz musicians approach improvisation mostly without the use of notated materials. For example, though he cites the influences of Béla Bartók and Olivier Messiaen, American jazzman Cecil Taylor's piano performances are improvised without precomposed materials.

Whereas aleatory approaches among some European contemporary art composers exploit randomness of tonal material as a primary goal, out jazz musicians living in New York City believe that no matter how improvised a performance becomes or how much it deviates from the constructs of functional tonality, unifying bonds of an emotional nature are present. These play a significant role in shaping musical content. In order to express in sound the wide range of emotions that collective improvisation allows, primary relationships are established among individual tones and elements, including texture, dynamics, and mode of playing (attack and vibrato), which Western classical composers traditionally regard as secondary to functional tonality.

Out Jazz and the Jazz Continuum

Out jazz tends to lack three major ingredients basic to hard bop (and a number of other styles of jazz), which has been the dominant jazz style since the mid-1950s. These are (1) melodic lines that conform to a chord structure, (2) swing feeling, and (3) adherence to either a twelve-bar or thirty-two-bar form. When soloing, hard bop performers shape their melody lines to preset chord changes. Tunes are often written in twelve-bar or thirty-two-bar forms. Drummers keep a steady rhythmic pulse. However, wind players sometimes play their melodies slightly ahead of the pulse in order to create tension between melody and rhythm. This in turn renders an effect called swing feeling, which is the sensation that the rhythmic pulse rushes forward; in reality, it stays constant.

In the mid-1950s, the first musician to challenge these conventions was Charlie Mingus. In some of his compositions during this period he experimented with variable rhythms and the free-form, collectively improvised approach. This refers to a situation in which all or some of the performers in a group, including the lead melody and rhythm section instruments, improvise at the same time. It is free-form in the sense that what the players are playing is not based on a preset form, such as the standard twelve-bar or thirty-two-bar forms; thus form evolves from function.

After Mingus, the next significant figure to contribute dramatically to out jazz was Ornette Coleman. Like Mingus, Coleman also experimented with collective improvisation. However, Coleman's most significant advancement was to liberate the melody from preset chord changes. Whereas hard bop performers closely contour their melodic improvisations to a preset chord structure, Coleman devised an approach that allowed performers more autonomy in constructing their improvisations.

In 1959 Coleman debuted with his group at New York City's Five Spot Café. Though his debut was mostly triumphant, two things weighed heavily against him. First, Coleman was new to the New York City jazz community, and his technical skills on the alto saxophone were not yet fully developed. Second, detractors felt that Coleman also lacked a basic knowledge of harmonic ideas, which they believed was the reason he played in the manner that he did. Nevertheless, Coleman's contributions have withstood the test of time and the careful scrutiny of his peers.

In the early and mid-1960s, out jazz performers such as Cecil Taylor, John Coltrane, and Albert Ayler began to assert their influence upon the New York City jazz community.[6] Of these three musicians, Coltrane generated the most controversy. His deep commitment to broadening the directions for musicians to take and his technical mastery over his instrument attracted a great number of followers. Especially because Coltrane had mastered the hard bop style and even expanded its stylistic parameters, his influence crossed over more style, age, instrumental, and ideological boundaries in the New York City jazz scene as a whole than did his out predecessors Ornette Coleman and Charlie Mingus.

Because many out performers had grown deeply dependent upon Coltrane for their sense of direction, his death in 1967 caused his followers to lose their sense of purpose and identity. Many of them either abandoned their instruments or returned to the fundamentals of bebop and hard bop. For example, Archie Shepp, a close associate of Coltrane who played with him in numerous collectively improvised contexts, reverted to playing hard bop and blues-based compositions.

Coltrane's followers who continued to play learned an important lesson about innovation and imitation in jazz. Briefly stated, it is unlikely that some true innovators such as Coltrane or Ornette Coleman set out consciously to transform the face of jazz. Their innovations proceed from a very personal, even idiosyncratic approach to absorbing and interpreting musical materials. In order for out jazz to grow in new directions, musicians like Dewey Johnson and Frank Lowe had to realize that the problems of melodic, harmonic, and rhythmic restrictions imposed by hard bop were not all to be solved by a single musician such as Coltrane. In other words, musicians who merely imitated Coltrane had no really firm base to stand upon and did not contribute alternative solutions to these musical problems.

Current Problems of Factionalism among Out Jazz Musicians

Out performers gradually accepted the challenge of evolving their own strategies for increasing expressivity and freedom in their music. As a result, styles of musical performance among out musicians living in New York City began to diversify. This trend, which continued through the 1970s and 1980s, led to the formation of isolated camps or factions of out musicians. Each camp is organized around a central figure who is generally the leader of a performing group.[7] Although these camps are perhaps not as closed to outsiders as were the bebop cliques of the 1940s, members of such camps tend to cultivate in-group bonds which are reinforced whenever leaders of a camp hire the same sidemen for a performance, tour, or recording date. Despite such divisions, however, there is an atmosphere of toleration and acceptance among the camps.

The camps are formed by members whose approach to performing and philosophy are compatible and mutually supportive. Musicians from one camp who seek to perform with members of another may find their approaches incompatible. Saxophonist Daniel Carter, for example, would not be inclined to ask saxophonist Jemeel Moondoc, whose style of performance leans toward a more conventional approach, to perform in a free-form, collectively improvised setting. During a performance, the differences of musical expectations and attitudes could confound the music. Of course, this situation does not exist to the same degree among hard bop performers, who share a common repertoire of tunes and expectations that allow them to perform with one another without having to radically alter their style.

A critical debate among musicians exists today as to whether this situation serves the best interests of the out jazz community as a whole. Daniel Carter, for example, sees the division of musicians into factions as a sign of weakening bonds among performers which he feels need rebuilding. If the community had the same goals and approach to performing, Carter believes it could become a powerful voice aimed at presenting a social message.

Bassist Earl Freeman, after returning to New York City from Europe, observed that most out musicians have become too preoccupied with their own approach to performing. He comments,

> Each faction in the avant-garde has its own direction and center point. They are all off into a different thing.
>
> . . . It's hard to say who are the important influences in the music, who are the real leaders in the music, not in the sense of Coltrane or Coleman in the sixties. I wrote a poem called "The Death of the Hero." We don't have any real heroes anymore in that sense. I came to that conclusion over five years ago. It's like up to every man to develop the sense. They are finding out that the self is not always workable. Therefore, you got groups or cults working, like Sartre's [*sic*] quote, "No man is an island." You have to join something or be with something, I suppose.[8]

According to Freeman, a solution to the apparent problem of factionalism is for more musicians to engage in a unified style of performing, such as the free-form, collectively improvised approach. This approach can accommodate an indefinite number of musicians and tolerate great diversity among individual performers while imposing the least number of restrictions. Theoretically, bringing together a greater number of musicians in this manner reduces the need for separate camps.

Drummer Milford Graves, who began performing in the out scene in the early 1960s, argues in a similar fashion. He posits that part of the reason these camps have formed is because today's newest generation of out performers, who were too young to have witnessed the early and perhaps most important stages in the development of out jazz, lack an overall sense of

Milford Graves at his home in Jamaica, New York

perspective and direction.[9] According to Graves, unity at this time could be achieved only if surviving key figures of that early era (e.g., Archie Shepp, Bill Dixon, Pharoah Sanders) would return and actively lead the out community. Graves adds,

> You are getting these guys now, twenty-two years old, this is fine, but what they need is these guys who were around in the sixties who needed to cool out for a minute and come back and redirect this thing now. . . . The music is really not happening now. I can listen to it and appreciate what some guys are doing. But when you really get down to taking care of business, it's not happening from what was started in the sixties.
>
> . . . There is no one out there who is a true innovator force. I listen to them on records or radio. I listen to horn or drum players and I say these guys don't see what is really happening. I just did a percussion album with [Andrew] Cyrille, [Don] Moye, [Kenny] Clarke, and we got Max [Roach] to do the liner notes and to unify it. Kenny is seventy

years old, so we thought we could try to unify this. . . . We're trying to regroup and this is what is happening.[10]

However, the trend toward diversity in out jazz is probably too entrenched to be reversed at this time. Furthermore, to suggest that out performers conform to a single, unified style of musical performance undermines the spirit that guided the first innovators. That is, the purpose of playing out is to cultivate individual expression without imposing upon it prescribed frameworks of any kind. Therefore, the formation of camps is a logical development, and the opposing views and differences in styles of musical performance among musicians represent positive growth. Thus camps are not necessarily a threat to the survival of out jazz.

The problem of finding suitable outlets for performance, however, poses a more serious threat. Even after more than thirty years of visibility, the out group is still stigmatized by the dominant hard bop group and by club owners and producers as a subgroup on the periphery of the New York City jazz community. The fact that out musicians have continued to pursue this style of performance attests to their strength, dedication, and determination.

The Out Jazz Controversy

Most of the criticisms leveled against out jazz generally focus on features in the music that are "cacophonous" and too difficult for average listeners to comprehend. Out jazz, with its rapidly played flurries of tones, squeaks and squawks, collective improvisation, variable rhythms, and so forth, aggressively challenges most listeners' expectations and can burden them with too many complex bits of information. As a result, listening to out jazz may seem a difficult and unpleasant chore, especially if the emotional content of the music is harsh and intimidating.

Because swing feeling is considered by some to be one of the most important constants throughout the development of jazz, its absence in out jazz is often interpreted as a major flaw. For example, in 1961 critic John Tynan referred to John Coltrane's music in the following terms:

It is my old-fashioned notion that there should be discernible rapport and working unity between soloist and rhythm section, that each should complement the other, transforming individual effort into a collective blend delivering what I have come to expect of good jazz—that

elusive element, swing. Coltrane and Dolphy seem intent on deliber-
ately destroying this essence, this vital ingredient. They seem bent on
pursuing an anarchistic course in their music that can but be termed
anti-jazz.[11]

Despite Tynan's claims to the contrary, Coltrane's group with Eric Dolphy often played compositions using swing feeling in the traditional sense. Dolphy
counters, "[My music] swings so much I don't know what to do—it moves
me so much. . . . I'd like to know how they [the critics] explain 'anti-jazz.'"[12]

    Another criticism that plagued out musicians, especially in the 1960s and
1970s, was that some performers often took over twenty minutes to complete a solo improvisation. Musicians argued that such inordinate lengths of
time were necessary to explore fully their musical objectives. Critics were
less tolerant, suggesting that out performers were overly self-indulgent.
Commenting on John Coltrane's style of musical performance, André Previn
remarked, "From now on I'll take any saxophone player's word for it that
he can play 6,000,000 notes per bar, have the fashionable unbearably ugly
sound, play what they call superimposed changes, which in plain English
means wrong, and make tracks [on a commercial recording] that are never
any shorter than 10 minutes."[13]

    Feeling that the problem warranted a solution, critics suggested that out
musicians should take greater care in editing their solo improvisations,
whereas others felt that out musicians should rehearse before performances
in order to remove redundant sections from the music. This, however, presents a troubling paradox. From an artistic viewpoint, how is it possible to
rehearse free improvisation and expect to duplicate the same results for a
performance?

    In the 1960s, some musicians were also critical of inexperienced newcom-
ers who were given opportunities to record with major out performers. For
instance, hard bop performers castigated Dewey Johnson and Frank Wright
when John Coltrane asked them to record with his group in 1965. Rather
than first establishing a reputation among hard bop performers as proficient
exponents of the hard bop style, Johnson chose instead to explore out approaches to playing the trumpet. When Coltrane hired him, many hard bop
musicians questioned Johnson's lack of experience, unproven technical abilities, and right to accept Coltrane's offer.

    In more recent times, critics have found new bones to pick. For example,
the authors of *The New Grove Gospel, Blues and Jazz* posit that "it seems

unfortunate that with a few exceptions . . . most American musicians have chosen to ignore its [European free jazz] discoveries, especially considering that free jazz in the USA has made few real advances since the early 1970s."[14] In the 1980s, I believe that out musicians did make important advances, though apparently not as dramatic as some critics who favor the European scene would prefer. In all fairness, one must consider that European listeners support out jazz to a greater extent than do American listeners. Perhaps with equal support, American out jazz musicians would prosper as well.

After thirty years, one might expect the attacks against out jazz to soften. Yet while reflecting on the history of out jazz, critic John McDonough writes,

> Jazz had never produced a music in which fakes [e.g., Ornette Coleman and Cecil Taylor] could move so easily and undetected among real musicians.
>
> . . . [Critics] honored its raw, unprocessed "energy" and "passion" as if these elements constituted artistic achievements. They proclaimed its importance before the "experiment" was done.
>
> . . . Free jazz, with its ideological subtexts of black liberation, third world primitivism, and spiritualism, continues to exist in the outer world of 20th century eccentrics.[15]

McDonough's comments regarding Coleman and Taylor, however, are overshadowed by a large number of major musicians and writers who have acknowledged the musical achievements of both artists. Because McDonough is unwilling to expand the parameters of "artistic achievements" to include music that exhibits "passion" and "energy," he sees little value in compositional approaches that render more freedom to the improviser. Thus he overlooks the significant ways in which out jazz enables musicians to express a much broader range of emotions than what the parameters of hard bop allow.

Part of the negative reaction toward out jazz also stems from its poor showing in the commercial market. While some very talented jazz-rock and modern hard bop performers like Wynton Marsalis have gained wide appeal (aided by the promotional machinery of large recording firms), out music remains mostly obscure. I believe that if out jazz were promoted somewhat more, it would attract a large enough audience to be profitable for both musicians and producers.

In emphasizing the negative, many critics overshadow the valuable achievements of Charlie Mingus, Ornette Coleman, John Coltrane, Albert Ayler, Eric Dolphy, and Cecil Taylor, who have broadened the boundaries that formerly restricted jazz soloists. By carving inroads into uncharted domains of improvisation, these musicians have glimpsed beyond the traditional performer's roles and the conventional usages of form and tonality. Because of out jazz's spontaneity and flexible parameters, events occur in out performances that could not happen in any other music or under any other circumstances. Thus out performers have provided a viable alternative to hard bop.

The Study of Out Jazz

Only a few books have dealt comprehensively with out jazz. Some of these focus primarily on the music and ways in which performances, involving several instruments improvising collectively at a feverish, nonmetric pace, can be notated. Despite dense textures of chaotic sounds that appear on the surface of out performances, Ekkehard Jost, in his work *Free Jazz*, demonstrates their dependency on precomposed structures.[16] Using schematic diagrams, Jost cleverly discloses formal features in the music of John Coltrane, Cecil Taylor, Archie Shepp, and others. For example, he illustrates the thematic and improvised sections of a musical performance as well as the tonal center or mode on which a particular section is based. Though Jost claims that the music cannot be divorced from the social and psychological context in which it was created, he fails to emphasize the interdependence of the musicians' worldviews, context, and the music itself. This is not surprising, since Jost's book is based almost entirely on materials gathered from recordings and literature.

Unlike Jost's work, Valerie Wilmer's work *As Serious as Your Life* incorporates a great deal of contextual data, much of which she has collected first-hand.[17] Devoted exclusively to out performers, this study explores the backgrounds and attitudes they share as a group. This is done, however, to the exclusion of musicological considerations. There are no comparative transcriptions to suggest shared stylistic features among the performers considered in her study. Though she discusses many ideological issues in the text, there is little to suggest how these may shape a particular musician's style of musical performance.

John Litweiler's publication *The Freedom Principle: Jazz after 1958* fits somewhere in between the above approaches. Litweiler outlines the important stylistic changes marking the transition from bebop to out jazz. When translating into words what he hears in the music, however, his passages either paint a poetic image of the music or construct a wall of complex and confusing terminology which is unsupported by illustrations or additional explanation. When examining selections of Ornette Coleman's music, for example, he remarks: "The tension of indeterminate tonality is now often replaced by the certainty of cadential modulations; his solos contain extensive sections of sequences; much of his music conveys a modal atmosphere."[18] Furthermore, Litweiler's probing into the shared belief systems and values among out performers rarely gains adequate depth.[19]

In contrast to the above examples, the approach utilized in the present work attempts to strike a suitable balance between out music itself and the cultural domain. The cultural domain includes the contexts and economic pressures that affect out musical performances. It also involves the study of how broad sociohistorical movements such as civil rights, postindustrialization, and urbanization shape the beliefs and attitudes of out musicians. In turn, these beliefs affect how out performers view their music and the ways in which they respond to their environment (e.g., how they act and speak in musical and nonmusical situations). In this regard, out jazz is highly symbolic, since it reflects the musicians' views of the world.

The present study, however, is but a modest step toward realizing fully all the dimensions of the cultural and musical. In taking this step, I am compelled to draw upon methodologies from several fields of study, since no single discipline is completely equipped to handle this enormous task. Thus I stray across boundaries that traditionally distinguish the concerns of folklorists, ethnomusicologists, anthropologists, and jazz scholars. Part of my interest in using a multidisciplinary approach is also spawned by advances in areas such as psychobiology which raise basic questions about our ability to perceive musical sounds and to transform these into ideas about music.

My methodology for collecting the material for this work also differs somewhat from the above authors. Though both Litweiler and Wilmer conducted interviews with musicians whom they discussed in their respective books, neither joined in performances with these musicians. Since the late 1970s I have made several long visits to New York City, where I performed on alto saxophone or flute (including the Western flute, Middle Eastern *ney*, and Chinese *ti'tzu*) in formal concerts with Daniel Carter, Michael Keith,

Earl Freeman, and Dewey Johnson or in informal gatherings of musicians at Dennis Charles's apartment on the Lower East Side of Manhattan. This helped to establish a rapport with musicians leading to high degrees of trust and openness. Furthermore, as a performer I also grew acutely aware of the nuances in the music as well as the kinds of cues and impulses that out performers respond to in free-form, collectively improvised settings.

t w o

labels and out jazz

The problem of labeling out jazz stems in part from the ways in which people generally perceive the term *jazz*. Soon after it entered into popular usage around 1917, jazz became an ambiguous term whose origins were unclear.[1] Since then the term has come to engender almost as many concepts as there are people who use it. For example, it has been employed loosely to describe any kind of syncopated rhythm, even if it appears in a performance of music written by a classical or modern composer. Or it may also be used to describe an ornate object or style of dress (e.g., "that's a jazzy-looking hat").

The term is also used to refer broadly to many separate substyles in the development of jazz, many of which differ greatly from one another in terms of function and form. Not all fans and critics agree as to what substyles should be included under the jazz label. So-called moldy figs argue that only the early substyles, which retain certain folk characteristics, constitute true jazz. For example, both early New Orleans jazz and Chicago jazz borrowed many elements from the African-American folk music continuum, such as the blues. Both musics were performed and learned using the aural-oral mode; that is, musicians learned their parts by listening and duplicating what other musicians played. Furthermore, musicians mostly performed in communal settings such as picnics and parades, or they performed for relatively small audiences in honky-tonks and bars. However, by the early 1930s, the popularity of Chicago jazz had waned as big bands began to flourish across the country. Unlike the early New Orleans and Chicago jazz styles, big bands attracted large numbers of dancers and adopted mostly prewritten arrangements.

From the musician's point of view, labeling may present certain problems. For example, because jazz has often been stigmatized as music suitable only for honky-tonks and bars, many musicians shun the term while claiming that it emphasizes the musician's role as entertainer rather than as serious artist. Tenor saxophonist Archie Shepp concludes, "I think the connotations of the word [jazz] are generally pejorative, as perceived by most . . . Americans. I think the term has many deep sociological and economic implications. Therefore, I think it's a very special word—I'm not sure when people use it if they're calling me a 'nigger,' or what exactly."[2] Of course not all share this extreme view. Dizzy Gillespie counters:

> Jazz is all right for want of a better name. . . . It doesn't detract from the importance, the seriousness, or the dignity of our music. It surely didn't bother Duke Ellington; or Louis Armstrong, they say he's a jazz artist; or Dizzy Gillespie. If the music were named anything else, I think I'd have just as much respect as I get now from my colleagues and contemporaries. I get just as much credit as I'd receive if I were playing another kind of music.[3]

Another reason musicians may shy away from labels is that they often perpetuate the false notion that the musicians to whom these labels refer conform their music strictly to the standards defined by the labels. In other words, by emphasizing similarities among artists, the labels downplay each individual artist's own style. When haphazardly used by writers, labels are potentially misleading and harmful.

Consider briefly the case of pianist Thelonious Monk and his highly individualistic usages of rhythm, dissonances, and sparsely sounded chords. Although Monk performed with several of the leaders of what today is termed bebop, his music challenged many of the musical expectations associated with bebop. Some forty years thereafter, his approach remains fresh and clearly distinct from all others. Thus the only apt label for Monk's music is "Thelonious Monk's music."

Labeling Out Jazz

Descriptions of out jazz which I elicited from out performers contrast dramatically. Multi-instrumentalist Ken McIntyre calls it "healing" music, whereas trumpeter Dewey Johnson commented, "It is just someone trying to speak his peace, and he isn't well known." Baritone saxophonist Charles Tyler defines it as a mixture of bebop, avant-garde, and anything else one wants to add to it. Bassist William Parker believes that an out performer is anyone wanting to change the world for the better. Milford Graves once labeled his music "Ba-be," an onomatopoeic designation for the tones he played on the drums. Dennis Charles adds, "[Out jazz] is a combination of everything. It's art. It's beautiful. It opens my head up. It keeps me from being complacent. Don Cherry came through the door this morning and started singing an African tune he had heard when he was in Africa and then an Indian tune. He started dancing around. . . . The music breaks down all the barriers, such as playing chord changes. Cecil Taylor used to tell me to just play."[4]

In the early 1960s, widely varying perspectives on out jazz were also to be found in the labels that writers and critics created for this new music. Because each musician's style of playing differed significantly, no one label was agreed upon that could conveniently fit the entire group. Subsequently, writers forwarded a plethora of terms, sometimes indiscriminately. These labels are as inventive and divergent as the music itself. A few examples follow:

free bop	jazz modernists
free jazz	black classical music
today music	the new thing
the new wave	post- or neobebop
avant-garde jazz	out jazz
action or energy jazz	fire music

Charles Tyler performing on baritone saxophone at Soundscape

Dennis Charles with Rrata Christine Jones performing at Soundscape

Some insight into what out jazz is can be generated by looking at what it is not. Each of the above terms emphasizes certain features that may typify some performers but also disguise the musical and attitudinal diversity of the labeled musicians.

Free Jazz Labels

"Free" or "free-form jazz," for instance, suggests that few guidelines are established in the music to instruct the musicians in what they will play during a performance. Each musician in the out group, however, varies in his or her treatment of form and freedom in improvisation. Whereas some use improvisation to shape form, others prefer to have form dictate improvisation. Composer and violinist Billy Bang, for example, writes out most of the parts that each instrument will play during the theme sections of a given composition. During sections of solo improvisation, soloists then tend to base their melodic lines on the motives that were precomposed in the theme section.

Other out performers adopt a different approach which imposes fewer restrictions on improvisers. In situations when the musicians engage in collective improvisation, improvisational freedom may take precedence over form. Thus melodic material, as it is being generated through collective improvisation, determines form. Such musicians, who often use no precomposed melodies or formal arrangements, may begin a performance without knowing in advance how the music will sound.

As described above, the free-form, collectively improvised approach is perhaps the most demanding upon the musicians, since they have little or no pre-established guidelines and they must be conscious of creating both the melodic content and the form. During a performance, success depends upon the abilities and skills of the musicians to interact with the other musicians. The musicians must be open-minded and versatile enough on their instruments to express instantaneously a broad range of ideas. Reflecting upon Daniel Carter's style of performing in the free-form, collectively improvised approach, bassist Earl Freeman points out that a chord progression "gives the musicians a sense of direction. . . . In Daniel's music *you* create your own sense of direction. You make your own orchestral arrangements and guidelines. Daniel's playing is about energy and intensity with gusto. It demands a love energy and creativity and improvisations; it's really demanding. You have to create all the time."[5] Since so many factors affecting the performance lie outside the performer's immediate control, these become high risk performances. Soprano saxophonist Steve Lacy warns, "To play free in public is dangerous. Unless it's magic, it's just research, I still do it; I work with students that way. . . . But we don't do that in public."[6] Though this type of approach comes closest to eliminating many of the restrictions traditionally imposed on the improviser in jazz, it also amplifies the contextual, psychological, and emotional factors that affect performers and subsequently the outcome of the performance.[7]

Steve Lacy suggests that in the 1960s more out performers used the free-form, collectively improvised style than they do today. He explains:

I had a group in 1966 with Enrico Rava and Johnny Dyani and Louis Moholo [documented on *The Forest and the Zoo*] and we played completely free music: we dropped the tunes, the rhythm, and the harmony, one by one, until we were completely free of all those things. But after a year, it all started to sound the same—it wasn't free anymore. So we started to structure the free, started to put limits on it. That was the beginning of the whole period that's flowering now—the post-free, the poly-free, controlling what we learned in that '60s revolution. We use that material as an ingredient—but with fences all around it.[8]

Tenor saxophonist Frank Lowe adds:

After Coltrane did his thing, a lot of people jumped on Trane's shit who had taken the music into another sphere at that point. They played orgiastic and freaked and freaked. That was a dead end. The Art Ensemble of Chicago came along with an alternative. They took the shit into another level that was organized. It was organized "outness." It was done in different degrees. It was disciplined, organized freedom which was just as out. When the shit goes out completely, it ain't happening.[9]

Since the 1960s, many out styles of performing have attempted to combine both form and freedom in improvisation. For instance, multi-instrumentalist Charles Tyler describes how he blends freedom and form in his style of musical performance. He explains: "I use definite melody lines or story lines. But after that I let the musicians go for themselves as long as they don't drift too far away from the general melody line. Most of the time I don't set certain changes. . . . I never count one-two-three-four go and that's it. . . . The improvisation is not structured as long as no one gets too far away from the general idea."[10] Trumpeter Earl Cross also outlines how he applies certain controls when playing out. He comments:

I've had bands that were in a free style of music. We would have a way of communicating between us how to control this music. We might do this with the personnel. If we like this cat's sound but he don't like to play changes, at a certain point we might play some weird styles of changes. At this point, use him, us, or the orchestra to play this particular element of music. Then we might use it against controlled sound. We put control on it by establishing that something is going to last only so long. A steady rhythm might last ten bars. Or it will last until the conductor says it will last.[11]

Out Labels and the African Background in Jazz

Labels for out jazz that tend to stress its African or African-American origins (e.g., "black classical music," "black jazz," or "black folk music") raise questions concerning the degree to which out jazz, or all jazz for that matter, is influenced by European or African sources. In fact, this debate extends nearly throughout the entire spectrum of African-American music. In the late nineteenth century, for instance, arguments ensued over whether black spirituals stemmed from African music or the Anglo-American folk-song tradition.[12] Some writers claimed that Negro songs were "mere imitations of European compositions," whereas others set out to refute such claims by presenting evidence for the African origins of the same songs.[13] After the turn of the century, the debate intensified when George Pullen Jackson claimed that call-and-response patterns, repetition, and syncopation in about half of all Negro spirituals were ascribable to the camp-meeting hymns sung by whites.[14] He met strong opposition among others who claimed Africa as the ultimate origin for these same features in Negro song.[15]

The popular and grossly oversimplified notion about the development of jazz is that its rhythm is of African origin and its reliance upon Western harmony and counterpoint is of European sources. What about aspects of the music other than rhythm and harmony? For example, most writers believe that multiple meter, call-and-response patterns, syncopation, and the falsetto break were carried to the New World by blacks and reintroduced throughout the various styles of jazz from New Orleans to bebop.[16]

The origins of blue notes, or microtonal flatting (especially of the third and seventh degrees of the scale), in jazz, however, are more difficult to determine—especially since microtonal flatting is reported in Anglo-American folk music, with which black slaves had contact. Microtonal flatting also appears in the music of some African groups but not in others. For instance, it occurs in Muslim music of the Savannah regions of West Africa, but it is missing in the rainforest areas of the Guinea Coast. Thus, if the African-American usage of microtonal flatting stems from the African background, how does one explain the fact that not all African slaves arriving in the New World were bearers of this tradition? William Tallmadge forwards a credible solution to the problem. He states:

> When the savannah slaves arrived in this country, they found a musical culture which, instead of suppressing their own inflected musical practice, actually sustained and reinforced it. Later arrivals from the rainforest areas of the Guinea Coast, even though they came in overwhelming numbers, were unable to dominate and suppress the combined tonal practice of the white-English and Scotch-Irish folk singers and savannah Negro slaves. Rather, it worked the other way. The later arrivals adopted the inflected tonal system of the Muslim slaves and white folk singers.[17]

The origins of early jazz remain clouded due to the lack of detailed historical records identifying the borrowing and adaptation of musical traits during the 1800s. However, it is clear that African-Americans founded jazz and that its origins are traceable to both the African and European homelands. What is not always obvious is how the majority of elements in jazz which are assumed to be African in origin have been retained and adapted over successive generations.

Most out musicians, however, do not consciously attempt to trace through history the African origins of out jazz. African music, however, does play an important role for some out musicians who seek to infuse their own music with greater expressivity. For example, tenor saxophonist Frank Lowe is aware that some styles of African music use tuning systems much different from the Western tempered system. He considers the latter system to be no better or worse than those found in Africa or elsewhere. Instead, they are relative to one another. Thus Lowe is unafraid to incorporate numerous pitches that fall outside the Western tempered scale in order to expand the emotional range of his music. Lowe posits that they are "out of tune" only if measured against the Western tempered scale, despite the fact that these tones may not necessarily be derived from a specific African scale.

This openness toward world music and African music in particular further helped to extend the musical resources available to out performers. For example, multi-instrumentalist Don Cherry learned to play the *doussn 'gouni*, an African chordophone, and utilized it in performances with the group Codona. Vocalist Leon Thomas, who recorded with Pharoah Sanders in the late 1960s, practiced a yodeling technique that was inspired by African Pygmy vocal styles. In 1969 tenor saxophonist Archie Shepp and drummer Sunny Murray made a live recording of their performance at the Algiers Pan-African Festival (Actuel 529 351). On this recording, a variety of Algerian musicians accompanied them using indigenous musical instruments.

Another aspect of out jazz that seems traceable to African musical sources and cultural life is the use of the aural-oral mode of communication. In most African communities, music is learned orally; that is, youngsters are taught to perform the drums by observing and imitating the patterns that their teachers demonstrate. Similarly, out bassist Charlie Mingus often rehearsed his bands by singing or playing his sidemen's parts on the bass. Pianist Cecil Taylor also adopts this approach in rehearsals with his group.

Another manifestation of the aural-oral mode of communication in out jazz and in the other styles of jazz as well is the heavy reliance upon improvisation. Approaches to improvisation differ, depending on the style of jazz. For example, a hard bop soloist creates a melodic line that is coherent with preset chord changes. Out jazz performers, however, may incorporate the free-form, collectively improvised approach, which they view as an extension of traditional approaches to improvisation in jazz.

Labels Based on the Politicization of Out Jazz

The terms *black jazz*, *black classical music*, and *fire music* have certain political connotations.[18] They were coined in the 1960s as a response to social and racial attitudes that prevailed during this turbulent decade. Nationwide discontent, expressed by African-Americans toward discrimination, erupted into violent confrontations with the dominant society. As the awareness of African-American nationalism spread, many felt the need to characterize African-American accomplishments as a continuation of African aesthetics rather than mere imitations and adaptations of white American culture. Thus African-Americans took the lead in defining the boundaries of their culture, though its ties to the dominant society remained implicit.[19] This attitude carried over into more popular domains of African-American culture as well. For example, the slogan "black is beautiful" was coined out of a growing interest in everything African, including fashions, names, languages, philosophies, and so forth.

Two other broad social movements whose social and political philosophies were in some ways aligned with the civil rights movement also shared the spotlight in the 1960s: the antiwar movement and the counterculture revolution. In the antiwar movement, forthright and sometimes violent contempt for the Vietnam War was voiced among a growing number of leftist, white middle-class college students who also supported the doctrines of the civil rights movement. In the counterculture revolution, another cross section of the middle-class white population questioned their parents' middle-class values and the work ethic. Instead of actively becoming involved in trying to change the system using political means, they chose instead to "drop out." In other words, these youths refused to accept the conventional roles in which society expected them to live and behave. Subsequently, they opted to experiment with alternative modes of communal living and alternative states of drug-induced awareness.[20]

Archie Shepp

In the 1960s and 1970s, one of the most provocative out musicians to actively promote the politicization of out jazz was tenor saxophonist Archie Shepp. However, Shepp's role in politicizing out jazz remains highly controversial. His views are clearly racist, and they are shared only by a minority of out musicians. However, because the media presented Shepp as a key spokesperson for the music, his views gained widespread public exposure.

Shepp was born in Fort Lauderdale, Florida, on May 24, 1937. He studied dramatic literature at Goddard College and in 1959 completed his BA degree. Soon afterward, Shepp moved to New York, where he played alto saxophone in local dance bands. He soon met John Coltrane, who greatly influenced Shepp's style of musical performance. From 1960 to 1962 Shepp played with Cecil Taylor. He was also a co-leader in two groups, one with Bill Dixon and one called the New York Contemporary Five, which included John Tchicai and Don Cherry. Around 1964 Shepp began to lead his own groups, which featured talented sidemen such as Roswell Rudd, Beaver Harris, Bobby Hutcherson, and Grachan Moncur III. From 1969 to 1974 he served on the faculty of the black studies program at the State University of New York (SUNY). In 1974 he left SUNY to accept a faculty position at the University of Massachusetts, where he was eventually promoted to associate professor. Shepp claims that Duke Ellington, Max Roach, and Charlie Mingus were important influences who fused music with sociopolitical opinions. Shepp's political views were also inspired by writers, including Langston Hughes, Richard Wright, and Ralph Ellison.

Throughout the 1960s, Shepp articulately voiced anger and resentment toward the dominant society, which he blamed for racial policies that discriminated against African-American musicians, especially those playing out jazz. Commenting on the economics of music, Shepp contends, "Music for a nigger *is* a hobby! White folks make a lot of money playing black music. A nigger will never make a dime; if he makes a dime, he's lucky. But that's good, because this country is giving up less and less. I'm opposed to what I see, and I'll go on record as being opposed to what I see being done to my people!"[21] Shepp also posits causal relationships between jazz and certain political and social attitudes. In defining the jazz tradition, he argues that . . . jazz is "self-expression. . . . And a certain quality of human dignity despite all obstacles. Despite the enslavement of the black man and then his oppression. And each of the great players has had so distinctive, so individual a voice. There is only one Bird, one Ben Webster, one Cootie Williams."[22]

It is not hard to imagine how some listeners to Shepp's music might interpret the brash squeals and vocallike screams emanating from the high registers of the saxophone as anger, which he attempts to project against the discriminatory racial and economic policies of the dominant society. Furthermore, while performing on stage, he has been known to point his saxophone at the audience in an aggressive manner. He has stated that this gesture can represent both a Freudian symbol and a machine gun.[23]

The Role of Writers in Politicizing Out Jazz

One of the most significant writers to address the sociopolitical implications of out jazz is LeRoi Jones. Jones's influence in the out jazz scene began in the early 1960s. During this time he produced several out jazz concerts at Marzette Watts's loft in Greenwich Village. Milford Graves recalls that Jones sometimes read his own poems before or between performances. According to Graves, these poems often depicted the music in political terms which probably influenced the way in which many of the musicians perceived the music.[24]

In his classic work *Blues People*, Jones tests the hypothesis that African-American music reflects changes in African-American culture that occurred as the African-American's status evolved from that of slave to citizen.[25] Throughout the development of this theme, Jones forwards many incidental challenges against the integrity and values of the dominant society. Though he is successful in pointing out the need to look at jazz in relation to social and historical data, he is unable to draw clear boundaries separating culture and music, which become diffuse entities. He also fails to consider the influence of factors other than the social and historical on the development of African-American music. For instance, according to Jones, the development of bebop was mainly spawned by separatist attitudes among its innovators.[26] However, Jones offers little convincing proof to support the notion that bebop musicians consciously altered their music to fit a political attitude. He also neglects to regard the development of bebop as a means of expanding musical resources, which at the time had grown limited.

Since the publication of *Blues People*, two other authors have devoted considerable attention to the nationalistic aspects of out jazz. In his book *Black Nationalism and the Revolution in Music*, Frank Kofsky clearly places out jazz in the context of the black political extremist movement.[27] He conjectures, "Today's avant-garde movement in jazz is a musical representation of the ghetto's vote of 'no confidence' in Western Civilization and the American Dream—that Negro avant-garde intransigents, in other words, are saying through their horns, as LeRoi Jones would have it, 'Up your ass, feeble-minded ofays!'[28] In another related study, Ben Sidran calls out jazz "confrontation music," which he considers to be an expression of the civil rights movement and of the resentment black musicians fostered toward racism and the economic policies of the entertainment industry.[29]

None of the above authors is successful in systematically demonstrating how broad social components (e.g., the civil rights movement or resentment toward racism) shape particular aspects of musical performance. If causal relations between the musical and social are posited, it is necessary to ask whether it is race, religion, economic background, or some other aspect of culture that determines how music is performed. In turn, how do these factors affect the melody, pitch, or ways in which music is organized? In their works, these authors isolate the components of music and culture to such a degree that they reach abstract proportions which are far removed from the everyday reality in which they operate. A leap of faith is not sufficient to negotiate the gap between a sociopolitical condition when viewed as a determinant of musical structure.

Frank Kofsky and Ben Sidran also fail to consider how the decision-making process of the individual fits into all this. Could not preferences in music and the interpretation of music be equally the result of an act of free will or imagination? Some listeners, especially in the West, are prone to attribute emotions to certain sound patterns.[30] Other listeners may express an aesthetic preference for music on the basis of its visual or verbal imagery or even upon its moral implications.[31] In other words, the motivation for interpreting out music politically is merely one of many possible responses.

In retrospect, the politicization of out jazz was achieved by a relatively small number of outspoken musicians whose opinions were effectively amplified by an equally small number of writers. This probably did more damage to the music than good, since even apolitical out performers became stigmatized as political activists. Additionally, the politicization of out jazz alienated potential listeners who did not share these views. As a result this inhibited opportunities for out jazz to reach a wider audience during the beginning stages of its development.

By regarding certain features in out jazz as solutions to musical problems rather than a reaction to social elements, it is possible to avoid many of the above problems. This does not preclude the fact that the social and cultural have a bearing upon out jazz. However, it does suggest that the social and musical are processes that operate epiphenomenally; that is, they may parallel each other but may not always be causally connected.

The possibility even exists that out jazz may have been influenced by cultural and social configurations that encompass developments in other arts. Modernism, for instance, reflects feelings of alienation in the face of rising technology and the decline of humanism in postindustrial societies. In painting, the attributes of modernism are manifested by a shift from the faithful reproduction of images to the conventions of painting, that is, texture, structure, and medium.[32] Similarly, many out jazz musicians give greater priority to texture, which may supersede melodic or rhythmic considerations.

Other Labels for Out Jazz

Though nearly thirty years have passed since Ornette Coleman arrived in New York City, current usages of the terms *avant-garde, contemporary, the new thing*, and *the new wave* imply that the music is novel. These terms also suggest that out performers are on the cutting edge of jazz; thus they are shaping its direction. This is far from the case. Most jazz writers and critics currently consider trumpeter Wynton Marsalis to be the most influential exponent of jazz. Marsalis, who in 1984 won Grammy Awards for both a jazz recording and a classical recording, avoids playing out jazz. Instead, he performs mostly in the hard bop and bebop idioms, which predate out jazz. Thus these writers position out jazz on the periphery of developments in hard bop.

The above labels for out jazz furthermore imply that the music has evolved in a unilinear fashion from immediately preceding jazz styles, such as hard bop, to its present complex form. However, because of its heavy reliance upon collective improvisation, out jazz seems to enjoy closer ties with the early styles of New Orleans Dixieland jazz (ca. 1917) than with most others. In addition, the use of unusual instruments is common to both styles of music. Whereas some out performers may incorporate non-Western instruments into their performances, some early New Orleans jazz performers played the kazoo and washboard. Sometimes they even performed on instruments constructed from household materials.

Action or *energy jazz* also appeared in print to describe features of out jazz, such as dense textures, high degrees of interaction among performers engaged in collective improvisation, and rapidly played passages of notes. Released in 1972 by the Impulse recording label, *Energy Essentials* (ASD 9228) is a collection of performances by out musicians which were recorded between 1961 and 1971. Some of the selections, such as Albert Ayler's "Holy Ghost," seem to meet the above criteria; many others do not.

In referring to the highly personal approaches to performing among avant-garde jazz musicians, the expression *out jazz* carries fewer connotations. Some performers adopt the free-form, collectively improvised approach, whereas some may combine features of hard bop with techniques of playing out. Regardless of the stylistic diversity among performers in the out group, some unity is achieved among them, since all tend to deviate to some degree from hard bop and most forms of Western music, and all tend to lessen the restrictions imposed upon the soloist and accompanying instruments.

three

jazz styles and the precursors

of performing out

Because out jazz tends to lack swing feeling and functional tonality, many jazz historians perceive the music as a radical departure from most other styles of jazz. Hence, they often assign it a peripheral and diminished role in the overall development of jazz. However, the musical innovations leading to the so-called avant-garde movement of the 1960s are not as radical as they may appear on the surface. Instead, they represent the logical culmination of certain stylistic trends in the development of jazz, such as the need to expand musical resources.

The Jazz Continuum and Stylistic Change

The treatment of out jazz in the manner outlined above has a lot to do with how jazz historians generally model the development of jazz. For instance, in most textbooks on jazz, historians divide the development of jazz into separate stylistic periods, which they form by isolating the distinctive elements of each style and tracing their origins through individual musicians.[1] Historians tend to describe each style as though it had a life of its own; that is, they identify its growth, period of peak popularity, and decline.[2] In this manner, one can compare different stylistic periods and performers.

However, this model engenders a few problems. First, it suggests an evolutionary development; that is, the model represents the development of jazz from less complex forms such as early New Orleans jazz to more complex ones such as bebop. In so doing, however, it exaggerates differences among the substyles while masking important areas in which they overlap. For instance, bebop and hard bop share more features in common than not. They borrow from the same repertoire of tunes, and both types of performers handle rhythm and melodic phrasing in similar ways. Thus it is more appropriate to think of the development of jazz in terms of dominant traits that are recast a little differently in each of its many styles.

Hard bop and bebop are sometimes considered separately, which illustrates that the differentiation of styles constitutes no more than drawing arbitrary lines at given points along a continuum. The same also applies to labeling performers. It would be a great disservice to Lester Young if one were to label him strictly as a big band saxophonist, since he continually sought to broaden his style of musical performance throughout his career. For example, Young performed in the small group settings of the 1930s; on occasion, he also performed with bebop musicians.

Because the above model for the development of jazz mainly attributes stylistic change to purely musical considerations, it also overlooks certain cognitive components of behavior. For example, the processes of composing and performing music involve a countless number of decisions that performers make on both the conscious and unconscious levels. Leonard Meyer summarizes: "What remains constant from style to style are not scales, modes, harmonies, or manners of performance, but the psychology of human mental processes—the ways in which the mind, operating within the context of culturally established norms, selects and organizes the stimuli that are presented to it."[3]

Such processes operate in situations when jazz musicians assimilate different musical styles. In other words, as jazz musicians come into contact with other styles of musical performance, they may borrow certain features and adapt these to fit their own styles of musical performance. Since the 1940s, jazz musicians increasingly began to look to non-Western music as sources for new ideas. For example, Charlie Parker and Dizzy Gillespie incorporated into their music African-influenced rhythms from Cuba such as the mambo. Furthermore, in the 1950s, Bud Shank and Oscar Peterson recorded tunes using the Brazilian samba rhythm.

The practice of assimilation plays a central role throughout the development of the African-American folk music continuum as well. In the 1700s, for example, African slaves brought to the New World lived amidst the pressures of the dominant European culture. Unable to fully sustain their African musical traditions under these conditions, they began to borrow and adapt features from the music of the dominant culture. In fact, some African slaves became skilled in playing European dance tunes on Western instruments.

Aural-oral modes of perception are also important factors of stylistic change in the jazz continuum.[4] These, too, are rooted in African culture, in which ideas and knowledge are communicated using mainly nonwritten forms such as speech. In improvised jazz, the aural-oral mode encourages the direct expression of the performer's inner emotions and creative impulses through musical sound. To ensure the vitality of this process, jazz tends to incorporate highly flexible and relatively noncomplex rules governing performance. This is precisely what enables musicians like Eric Dolphy to extract sounds from the environment and transform them during a musical performance. Saxophonist Ornette Coleman comments, "Regardless of race or nationality, if you are not trying to compare your values with those of other people, but are interested in expressing musically something that you have in your mind and not trying to get anyone's approval—then jazz seems to be the most honest and freest form of taking the opportunity to see if you can express something."[5] Along these lines drummer Elvin Jones adds, "A solo can take any form the artist chooses; he can use any form he wants within the framework of the composition. It goes back to getting away from the rigidity that jazz had to face when it was primarily dance music."[6] Jones's comments also suggest that when the rules grow too complex or too staid and fresh expression is inhibited, some musicians may seek alternative ways to organize improvisation.

Such flexible parameters in jazz encourage high degrees of individuality.

For instance, listeners learn to recognize particular performers based on the way they shape their melodic improvisation, attack tones, or apply personal inflections to timbre, pitch, and vibrato. Alto saxophonist Johnny Hodges (1907–1970), who intermittently played in Duke Ellington's band from 1928 to 1970, was noted for his unusually deep and lush tone and his technique of gliding from note to note.

The Roots of Early Jazz

The origins of jazz extend back as far as the sixteenth century, which marks the beginning of the institution of black slavery. Traders forcibly took slaves from West African tribes in areas stretching from Dakar through the Gold Coast and from Dahomey to Nigeria and brought them to the New World. In their new environment, African slaves retained some of their native musical traditions, whereas others were suppressed or altered.

Tracing African musical influences throughout the development of African-American music and jazz calls for speculation as well as caution. One problem is the lack of any reliable historical data that indicate what West African music sounded like between the sixteenth century and the 1950s, that is, the time between the arrival of West African slaves to the New World and when ethnomusicologists first began to conduct intensive field research in West Africa.[7] Comparisons between early forms of African-American and West African music have to be made under the assumption that the latter remained relatively stable over this period. Hence, West African societies would have had to remain relatively free of outside pressures that might have significantly altered their music.

Ethnomusicological data since the 1950s betray a number of stylistic differences as well as similarities in the music of West African tribal groups. Similarities include the way in which music functions as accompaniment for communal activities such as work, ceremonies, and rituals. The most dominant approach to musical performance involves group singing, which is often organized using antiphonal patterns. West African melodic scales tend to be pentatonic and composed of pitches that vary in relation to the tempered Western scale. Drumming styles also persist based on multiple, overlapping rhythms that render dense textures, syncopation, and contrasting meters—for example, three beats sounded against two beats.

During the acculturation process, slaves adopted European musical traits, such as instrumentation, the diatonic scale, standard meters, and popular song forms. However, their approach to using these reflects the influence of their African background. For instance, slaves tended to lower the third, seventh, and sometimes fifth degrees of the scale. Called blue tonality, this practice is found in many forms of African-American folk music and is traceable to West Africa.[8]

Toward the end of the nineteenth century, numerous genres of African-American music coexisted. These had secular and sacred as well as urban, folk, popular, and classical roots. For instance, the spirituals—a sacred tradition—enabled slaves to project their spiritual aspirations and hopes. Secular forms included work songs, plantation songs, social songs, banjo and fiddle music, ragtime, a brass marching band tradition, and the blues. To some degree, all retained African influences, such as the falsetto voice, the attainment of ecstatic states of arousal, and the presence of a ground beat.

Early New Orleans Jazz

Around the turn of the century, jazz most likely evolved from the blending of African-American folk music such as ragtime and blues with various popular musics.[9] Historians generally credit New Orleans as the birthplace of jazz, though some claim that early styles of jazz emerged independently throughout certain areas of the South and Midwest.[10] Nevertheless, New Orleans boasts certain advantages. It was geographically located near several slave states and attracted runaway and freed slaves, who brought their music with them. A large French and Creole population that favored European dance music also inhabited New Orleans. Thus the presence of these musics in one location suggests that some degree of musical exchange probably occurred.

The most likely forerunner of the early jazz band in New Orleans was the marching band, which generally performed at social gatherings (e.g., picnics and funerals). A typical New Orleans marching band used mostly instruments borrowed from the European military marching band tradition. New Orleans marching bands generally played quadrilles, polkas, marches, hymns, and popular songs.

Between 1900 and 1915 these bands steadily incorporated stylistic features of the blues and ragtime, including blue tonalities, slurring, bent notes, growls, and a loosening of the melody from the ground beat. They also began to reorganize the rhythm of rags and marches into four beats per measure rather than two beats per measure. Furthermore, these bands applied uneven accents and durations to the beats, thus introducing an early stage in the development of swing feeling in jazz.

Although early New Orleans jazz was first recorded in 1917, the most important exponents of the style did not record until 1923.[11] These musicians include King Oliver, Freddie Keppard, Louis Armstrong, Jelly Roll Morton, Sidney Bechet, and Bennie Moten's orchestra.

Joseph ("King") Oliver (1885–1938) was born and raised in New Orleans, where he absorbed many different types of music. Around 1916 he moved to Chicago and quickly began to exert a tremendous impact upon the local scene. His group, called the King Oliver Creole Jazz Band, was composed primarily of musicians from New Orleans and featured a young cornet player named Louis Armstrong.

The King Oliver Creole Jazz Band's 1923 recording of "Dippermouth Blues" offers a good example of the stylistic developments in early New Orleans jazz. In this recording, the two cornets, or frontline instruments, play the melody in a kind of heterophonic-polyphonic manner. The clarinet plays a harmony part above the melodic line, whereas the trombone plays the most important note in each chord change.[12] In the early New Orleans jazz style, drummers kept a simple time pattern.[13] The banjo played the chord changes, usually in a flat-four rhythm, that is, one strum per beat, with four even beats per measure, and no one beat accented more than another. There is also a noticeable swing feeling to the performance and the use of blue tonalities.

The heterophonic-polyphonic style of collective improvisation in New Orleans jazz differs from out styles of collective improvisation in that the former is shaped according to key, prerehearsed melodic patterns and the rhythmic structure. This is evident in Louis Armstrong and the Red Onion Jazz Babies' 1924 recording of "Cake Walking Babies from Home." Music example 1 illustrates the degree to which soprano saxophonist Sidney Bechet's embellishment of the primary melody differs from cornetist Louis Armstrong's interpretation. Immediately after the vocal chorus, the soprano sax line seems entirely independent of the cornet's primary line in measures 96–99. In the next two measures, however, it begins to conform more closely with the pitches and melodic contours of the cornet. The trombone part is less active; during brief pauses by the other lead instruments it plays lines that are far different from those of the cornet and soprano sax.

Example 1. *Excerpt from "Cake Walking Babies from Home," illustrating heterophonic and polyphonic textures among the lead section instruments*

Between 1925 and 1928, Louis Armstrong's Hot Five and Hot Seven recordings represent a significant departure from the heterophonic-polyphonic style of early New Orleans jazz. For example, Armstrong's 1928 recording of "Sugar Foot Strut" demonstrates a tendency toward increased solo improvisations which follow the chord changes more closely.[14]

In Chicago during the 1920s, many white musicians adopted the early New Orleans style, which was labeled Chicago jazz. These include Nick LaRocca, Paul Mares, Bix Beiderbecke, Eddie Condon, Frank Teschemacher, Pee Wee Russell, Max Kaminsky, Wingy Malone, and others. These musicians in some cases brought to the music a superior instrumental technique and a greater emphasis on solo improvisation. In comparison, their African-American counterparts performed in a less inhibited manner while incorporating swing feeling to a greater extent.

Big Band and Small Group Jazz

In the 1920s the number of jazz orchestras began to increase dramatically, especially in New York City. Consisting of ten to fifteen pieces, these bands primarily functioned as entertainment for large crowds of dancers. They can be divided into two groups: sweet bands and swing bands. Sweet bands such as Paul Whiteman's band were mostly composed of white musicians who played in a reserved style. The bands were not loud, nor did soloists use growl techniques, which were popular among early New Orleans jazz performers. Furthermore, these bands used swing feeling in an understated fashion.

In contrast, African-American-led bands highlighted these dynamics. For example, bands under the direction of Duke Ellington, Count Basie, Fletcher Henderson, Don Redman, and Jimmie Lunceford all emphasized swing feeling. In his band, Duke Ellington often featured trumpeter Bubber Miley and trombonist Tricky Sam Nanton, who performed using growl techniques.

As big bands continued to prosper through the 1930s, musicians sometimes formed smaller groups to record or perform in small speakeasies, many of which lined 52nd Street in Manhattan. They adapted big band arrangements to fit a smaller group of one or two lead section instruments plus a rhythm section. This format allowed musicians to hone their improvisational skills, which big bands using prewritten arrangements often discouraged. The most notable exponents of this style include clarinetist Benny Goodman and pianist Teddy Wilson.

Formative Trends in the Jazz Continuum

By the 1930s, several important trends had been established in the jazz continuum. These include the small combo format, the use of swing feeling, similar instrumentation, improvisation based on a tune's chord changes, and the division of roles between lead and accompaniment sections in the small combo. These features contribute to seven identifiable substyles in the jazz continuum beginning with early New Orleans jazz and continuing through present-day developments in hard bop (see figure 1), and they are useful for comparing developments in out jazz (see table 1). For instance, the small combo format provides the basis for most substyles of jazz other than big band. Numbering anywhere from three to around seven instruments, the small combo is traditionally divided into lead section instruments, generally consisting of brass and reed instruments, responsible for playing the melody. The piano, drums, and bass form the accompaniment section, whose role is to play the rhythm and harmonic background.[15]

Figure 1. *Historical development of the (mainstream) jazz continuum*

Table 1. *Comparisons between Stylistic Features in the (Mainstream) Jazz Continuum and Out Jazz*

Elements of Musical Style	Mainstream Jazz	Out Jazz
Social organization	Small combo format Division of roles between lead and accompaniment sections	Small combo format Less differentiation between lead and accompaniment sections
Instrumentation	Western military marching band European classical orchestra	Western military marching band European classical orchestra New or unusual (non-Western) instruments
Form	32-measure AABA 12-measure blues	Extended forms Free-form
Harmony and tonality	Chord changes borrowed from preexisting popular songs Blue tonalities	Less emphasis on functional harmony Pitches played outside Western tempered scales
Melody	Theme-improvisation-theme (repeating chorus) Melodic improvisations shaped by chord changes Antiphonal patterns	Melody liberated from chord changes (modal approaches) Less emphasis on functional tonality Antiphonal patterns
Rhythm	Isometric pulse (meter of 4 beats per measure) Swing feeling	Often nonisometric Often lacking swing feeling
Melodic texture	Unison Heterophony-polyphony (early New Orleans and Chicago jazz)	Polyphonic (collective improvisation)

The small combo format has proven itself to be more economically viable than the big band. Whereas the wartime economy of the early 1940s led to the demise of most jazz orchestras, bebop musicians using the small combo format eked out a living performing in small nightclubs. Furthermore, this format is better suited to support the development of solo improvisation, which is an important basis of self-expression and innovation in jazz.

However, in many out styles of musical performance, there is little differentiation between lead and accompaniment roles. For example, drummers may abandon a strict time-keeping role in order to interact more with the lead section performers. Rather than outline the main notes of the chord, bass players may instead improvise melodic lines in order to interact with lead section players.

Except for the occasional appearance of homemade instruments in early styles of jazz, the instrumentation among the different substyles of jazz are mostly similar. All borrow from the Western military marching band and symphonic orchestra. Some out groups, such as the Art Ensemble of Chicago, have added to this repertoire by incorporating a variety of unusual instruments (bike horns, whistles, sirens, and so forth) in their performances.

The melody, harmony, and rhythm of most tunes in the early jazz substyles are distributed over one of two common forms, the thirty-two-measure and twelve-measure cycle. In most cases, each measure contains four evenly sounded or isometric beats. Thus a drummer performing one cycle of a twelve-measure form would be playing a total of forty-eight beats (see figure 2). In a twelve-measure blues form, a I-IV-I-V-IV-I chord sequence may be used. The I-chord is played for four measures before it changes to the IV-chord. In turn, the IV-chord is played for two measures before it changes back to the I-chord. Variations of this particular chord progression are common throughout the blues. A melody or theme is transposed over the first and sometimes second cycle of the tune. A number of remaining cycles are reserved for solo improvisations, which performers construct according to the chords of the tune. To end the piece, the theme is restated during the last one or two cycles. In comparison, out jazz performers may use a number of different forms to structure improvisation. These may include the thirty-two-measure and twelve-measure forms or something entirely different. However, in lieu of a precomposed form, some out performers use a free-form, collectively improvised approach.

Swing feeling remains one of the most salient features throughout the jazz continuum. The fact that it is often lacking in out jazz is reason enough for

I = Measure or bar lines that separate groupings of the beats.

Figure 2. *Twelve-measure blues form*

some to place it on the periphery of the jazz continuum. However, some out performers, like saxophonists David Murray and Charles Tyler, test the boundaries between out jazz and other substyles in the jazz continuum when their performances combine swing feeling with certain features of out jazz. Though saxophonist Archie Shepp was one of the primary figures in the development of out jazz in the 1960s, his groups also used swing feeling and a metrical pulse. He explains, "I like it when people clap their hands and pat their feet to out music. And every once in a while we play in 4/4. Some of the so-called 'avant-garde' guys don't do that. They think it's passé. I don't. It's absurd to throw out everything from the past in order to be 'new.' If things from the past fit, you use them." [16]

Early Precursors of Out Jazz in the 1930s

Surprisingly, innovative approaches that depart from the above trends and that foreshadow developments in out jazz can be traced to unlikely sources (see table 2). For example, Duke Ellington's 1931 extended composition "Creole Rhapsody" is a dramatic alternative to the twelve-measure and thirty-two-measure standard forms. It utilizes five-measure phrases (instead of the standard four-measure phrases) and multiple sections. Its unusual length helps render "Creole Rhapsody" one of the most innovative jazz compositions for the time in which it was written.

Ellington's influence runs deep into the ranks of modern experimentalists.

Table 2. *Partial Listing of the Precursors, Founders, and Succeeding Generations of Out Performers*

Early Precursors (1930s)	Duke Ellington Coleman Hawkins	Lester Young	
Early Precursors (1940s)	Lennie Tristano Jimmie Blanton	Charlie Parker Thelonious Monk	Bud Powell Slam Stewart
Precursors (1950s)	Miles Davis Sonny Rollins	Charlie Mingus John Gilmore	
Founders (1959–1960s)	Ornette Coleman Albert Ayler	Cecil Taylor Eric Dolphy	John Coltrane
First Generation (late 1960s–1970s)	Jimmy Lyons Charlie Haden Dewey Johnson Milford Graves Andrew Cyrille Paul Byron Allen Bobby Bradford Bill Dixon Byard Lancaster Dewey Redman Sun Ra Paul Bley Paul Motian Steve Swallow	Dennis Charles Eddie Blackwell Frank Wright Charles Tyler Earl Cross Donald Ayler Anthony Braxton Julius Hemphill Steve McCall Sam Rivers Henry Threadgill Alan Silva Don Friedman Steve Lacy	Don Cherry Elvin Jones Archie Shepp Ken McIntyre Rashied Ali Lester Bowie Marion Brown Noah Howard Sunny Murray Pharoah Sanders Frank Lowe Joseph Bowie Gary Peacock
Second Generation (1980s)	Jemeel Moondoc Butch Morris Earl Freeman John Zorn Zen Matsuura	William Parker Jeanne Lee Billy Bang James Newton Jason Hwang	Daniel Carter Roy Campbell David Murray Claudine Meyers Michael Keith
Third Generation (late 1980s–1990s)	Bill Frisell Steve Coleman	Hank Roberts Tim Berne	

Marion Brown performing at Soundscape

For example, Charlie Mingus and Cecil Taylor adapted Ellington's orchestral techniques to a small combo performing a collectively improvised approach. Taylor claims, "It's Ellington who influenced my concept of the piano as an orchestra, which meant that the horn players and all of the other players other than the piano were in a sense soloists against the background of the piano."[17]

Butch Morris at his studio in Manhattan

Example 2. *Excerpt of Coleman Hawkins's solo in "Sheik of Araby"*

Another important precursor during this time period is Coleman Hawkins (1904–1969), whose virtuosity on the tenor saxophone helped make this one of the most popular instruments in jazz. Throughout a career as a sideman in some of the big bands of the 1930s and as a leader of several small combos, Hawkins continually demonstrated his talent for improvising memorable and logically constructed solos. In fact, many consider him to be one of the leading soloists in jazz. Hawkins also evolved a manner of shaping the melody line to the chord changes using arpeggiated chords and phrases based on scale patterns. During the first sixteen measures of his solo in the 1940 recording of "Sheik of Araby," Hawkins intersperses three arpeggiated chords (C4m3, C4m4-m5, and C4m7 in music example 2) of the same construction among scale-like melodic figures.

Improvising formulaic responses to changing harmonic contexts in jazz has sometimes been termed "running the changes." Because the chord changes mostly determine the shape of the melodic line, coherence among constituent phrases of the melodic line decreases. Some musicians who favored a high degree of coherence in the melodic line sought alternative approaches.

In the 1930s, while a member of the Count Basie band, tenor saxophonist Lester Young (1909–1959) played "against" the changes. While Coleman Hawkins's melodic line adhered more strictly to the chords of the tune, Young emphasized the internal development of the melody over the chord changes. Young's solos are also noted for their unexpected irregularity of rhythm and phrase shape. Furthermore, he often played phrases that extended beyond the turnarounds and bridges of the tune, foreshadowing developments in bebop.

Early Precursors of Out Jazz in the 1940s

During the 1940s, a stringent wartime economy, entertainment taxes levied against cabarets, and the induction of musicians into the armed services contributed to the disbanding of many popular big bands. In the late 1930s and early 1940s, a handful of jazz musicians met regularly to participate in a series of jam sessions at the now historically significant Minton's Playhouse in Harlem. During these sessions, musicians sought to revitalize and advance the concept of shaping the melodic improvisations according to the chord changes, which in the late 1930s had become stagnant and clichéd. These innovations inspired a separate stylistic label—bebop.

Bebop musicians retained the small combo format, which was popular in small group jazz of the 1930s and early New Orleans jazz of the 1920s. Whereas the tunes performed by big band musicians were composed mostly by outside arrangers, bebop musicians often borrowed the chord changes of popular melodies, upon which they superimposed their own melodic inventions. Charlie Parker's composition "Chasin' the Bird," for example, is based upon the harmonic structure of the popular tune "I Got Rhythm." By adopting more syncopated and faster rhythms, bebop musicians added more complexity to the standard isometric dance rhythms of swing.

Like early New Orleans jazz bands and big bands, bebop musicians frequently arranged their tunes to fit either a twelve-measure or thirty-two-measure form. A thirty-two-measure tune is typically divided into four eight-measure sections labeled accordingly AABA. Played in a meter of 4/4, the melody is stated and repeated in the first two A sections. A key change and new melody or solo fill the B section, or bridge. In the final A section, the melody is repeated. The soloists then take turns improvising against the same harmonic framework repeated over each thirty-two-measure cycle. When every soloist has had a turn, the ensemble repeats the theme and bridge of the initial thirty-two-measure AABA chorus.

Charlie Parker

At the forefront of the revitalization movement was alto saxophonist Charlie Parker (1920–1955). Whereas Hawkins constructed his solos using arpeggiated chords and phrases based on scale patterns, Parker's major advance in solo improvisation is the construction of phrases whose components were drawn from a repertoire of about a hundred brief melodic formulas.[18] Before introducing a specific formula, Parker may alter it by metric displacement, addition and subtraction of notes, transposition, and different methods of phrasing and articulation. Unlike Louis Armstrong, Parker rarely subjected a single formula to extensive development. Depending on the harmonic context, his formulas instead were sometimes linked together in series, whereas others functioned to integrate newly invented material.[19]

In his melodic improvisations, Parker played passing notes, chromatic interpolations, and chord extensions whose pitches were often outside the chord changes of the tune. In this manner he weakened the functional bonds between the improvised line and the harmonic structure of the tune. This tendency foreshadows future developments in which the role of functional harmony in out jazz is severely lessened.

Other Precursors of the 1940s

In the 1940s, two other developments prefigure out jazz. First, instrumentalists in the accompaniment section who had little or no chance to solo as sidemen in big bands were now allowed opportunities.[20] In the context of the small combo, bebop tunes were often arranged to allow each member of the lead section to solo; in some instances, the drummer and bass player also soloed. Second, with increased solo time, more rapid tempos, and the development of complex harmonies, bebop performers raised the standards of proficiency on their respective instruments. Consequently, this had a dramatic effect on drummers, whose traditional time-keeping roles were expanded.[21] For instance, drummer Max Roach evolved complex techniques of shifting accents around the main rhythmic pulse using a variety of kicks, prods, and ornaments on the trap drums. Whereas most drummers in the 1930s explicitly sounded each beat of the pulse, Roach implied their presence. In the 1960s, out drummers Milford Graves and Sonny Murray further advanced this notion by totally eliminating the isometric pulse, that is, a pulse whose accented beats are equally distributed throughout a tune. Sunny Murray adds,

> Most avant-garde horn players and lightweight piano players relate to the beat on the drums, which only brings them to one understanding. But it's about understanding the meaning of acoustics—how not to relate to beats so much because beats is just a hereditary force that has followed us all these years. . . . Like, to get away from beats is to get away from poverty. . . . I don't want to follow the course of any bebop drummers. The best thing I can do for the bebop drummer is liberate him.[22]

In the 1940s, pianists also sought to expand their role in the small combo. Bud Powell was one of the first modern pianists to utilize a technique called comping. Comping refers to the playing of spontaneous chords against the lead player's melodic line for the purpose of complementing it or suggesting a different harmonic direction for it to follow.[23] Powell is also one of the first modern players to advance pianist Earl Hines's right-hand technique that emulates the phrasing styles of the lead instruments.

Pianist and composer Thelonious Monk (1917–1982) was an important figure during this period. He contributed numerous tunes to the bebop repertoire. Monk often placed rhythmic accents in the least expected places, adding to a reputation characterized by some as original and by others as eccentric. His piano style also reflects certain techniques that begin to weaken the bonds of functional tonality in jazz. For example, he sometimes ended phrases on notes that sound dissonant against the chord. Furthermore, he explored combinations of the whole tone scale which allowed him to suspend the work's tonality over several measures.[24]

Prior to the 1940s, the role of bassists in the small combo remained limited to two functions. First, from the late 1920s onward the bassist was expected to sound the main pulse by playing one note per beat. Second, the notes were chosen to outline the chords in the harmonic framework of the tune. This style of bass playing is commonly referred to as walking bass. Exceptions to as well as exponents of the walking bass style include Jimmy Blanton (1918–1942) and Leroy (Slam) Stewart (1914–1987), who was an intermittent member of Art Tatum's trios from 1943 through the early 1950s.[25] When Blanton was a member of Duke Ellington's orchestra from 1939 to 1941, Ellington wrote pieces which featured him as a soloist and which showcased the high degree of proficiency that Blanton achieved on the instrument.

In 1949 pianist Lennie Tristano (1919–1978) became the first jazz musician to explore a free-form, collectively improvised approach. While conducting a recording session for Capitol, he instructed his sidemen to begin playing without any predetermined chord structure, melody, tonal center, or form. For example, on "Intuition" and "Digression" (Affinity AFF149), the piano, bass, guitar, and both saxophonists all play independently improvised lines. They achieve a moderate degree of dialogue in the sense that one performer's line provides the melodic or rhythmic content for another performer to explore and advance, except when Tristano occasionally mimics some of the lines played by saxophonists Lee Konitz and Warne Marsh. Furthermore, the lack of a drummer on these two pieces allows the performers more freedom in shifting the tempo of the implied pulse. Though Tristano's experimentations foreshadow out jazz, they were far too advanced for the time to have any significant impact upon the jazz community (Capitol also refused to release these recordings for several years).

The Precursors

In the 1950s, mainstream jazz performers altered the harmonic frameworks of extant tunes by adding unusually complex chords. This placed an increased demand on the technical abilities and skills of improvisers. Whereas in the preceding decade solo improvisers had to adjust to seven or eight chord changes over a twelve-measure tune, they now had to handle upwards of twelve or more chords. For example, in John Coltrane's 1959 recording of "Giant Steps" (Atlantic SD-1311), almost each note of the opening theme is accompanied by a different chord. Because the tempo of "Giant Steps" is extremely fast, soloists consider it to be one of the more difficult pieces on which to play. When having to adjust their melodic lines to rapidly shifting chords, it becomes more difficult for improvisers to build coherence among the individual phrases with which they construct their solos. That partly explains why the melodic improvisations of hard bop performers often sound jagged and disjunct.[26] Though many fine performers in the 1950s chose to master this demanding style, others perceived these developments as restrictions that limited the freedom of the improviser.

Miles Davis

One such musician who held this view was Miles Davis. In reaction to these developments, Davis evolved a compositional approach that foreshadowed another area of development in out jazz. In order to allow the improviser greater freedom to focus attention upon his or her improvised lines, he drastically reduced the number of chords in the harmonic frameworks of his original tunes. By placing greater emphasis on the melody rather than the chord changes, Davis and his sidemen realized greater coherence among the different phrases of their melodic improvisations. His much analyzed composition "So What" effectively illustrates this achievement. Instead of using several chord changes, Davis employs a relatively static harmonic framework based upon only two changes per thirty-two-measure cycle. A shift

Example 3. *Excerpt of Miles Davis's trumpet solo in "So What" showing variations of the same melodic formula or motive (in brackets)*

from the D Dorian to the E♭ Dorian occurs at the beginning of the B section. At the end of the B section, a second shift back to the D Dorian is observed:

A = 8 measures (D Dorian = D E F G A B C)
A = 8 measures (D Dorian)
B = 8 measures (E♭ Dorian = E♭ F G♭ A♭ B♭ C D♭)
A = 8 measures (D Dorian)

During his solo, Davis's melodic improvisation, except for a few incidental passing tones, remains strictly in the Dorian mode (music example 3). Having more time and "space" to reflect upon the linear development of his melodic improvisations, Davis successfully builds cohesive and lyrical relationships among his phrases.[27]

Davis's so-called modal approach raises certain questions regarding freedom in improvisation. By lessening the number of chord changes, does Davis's approach successfully create more options, hence more freedom, for the improviser? Or is the amount of freedom presumably gained by the elimination of chords offset by a virtually static modal framework, which severely limits the number of pitches available to the improviser? In theory, it seems logical that different kinds of restrictions apply, regardless of whether one uses a chordal (i.e., vertical) or a modal (i.e., horizontal or linear) approach. In practice, however, Davis's compositional approach is loosely interpreted by some of his sidemen, especially Paul Chambers and John Coltrane. On Davis's 1959 recording of "So What," they exploit the added option of playing phrases that freely move outside the prescribed modes. Thus Davis's so-called modal approach does indeed increase freedom in improvisation, since during performance more options to the improviser are available.

Example 4. *Portion of collectively improvised dialogue in real time between bassist Charlie Mingus and alto saxophonist Eric Dolphy from "What Love"*

Charlie Mingus

In the mid-1950s, bassist Charlie Mingus (1922–1979) introduced a number of innovative compositional and improvisational techniques that foreshadow major trends in out jazz. During the 1940s, Mingus acquired a diverse background of experiences while performing with a number of jazz musicians ranging from Louis Armstrong to Charlie Parker. This exemplifies in Mingus, perhaps more than any other musician of his time, an eclecticism and willingness to venture beyond categories.

Charlie Mingus's 1955 free-form, collectively improvised recording of "Percussion Discussion" (re-released on the LP recording *Mingus*) is a kind of highly interactive dialogue between bassist Mingus and drummer Max Roach. In this free-form approach, in which isometric rhythms and a chord progression alike are lacking, musical content determines form. Thus functional tonality is minimal.

Similar features are found in other performances by Mingus, including his 1956 recording of "Pithecanthropus Erectus" and his 1960 recording of "What Love" (*Stormy Weather*). "What Love" is an extended composition in the theme-improvisation-theme format. Approximately eight minutes into the piece, the other instruments drop out and Mingus and bass clarinetist Eric Dolphy begin a collectively improvised dialogue (music example 4). The timbre of each instrument closely approaches the emotional and evocative qualities of impassioned speech. The way in which Mingus mimics Dolphy's melodic line is a far cry from the traditional walking bass technique.

f o u r

the founders of out jazz

and their successors

Between 1959 and 1967, the innovators of out styles of musical performance played major roles in establishing the music as a viable alternative to mainstream jazz. John Coltrane and Cecil Taylor evolved new forms of collective improvisation. Albert Ayler and Eric Dolphy broadened the tonal range of the saxophone, which increased its potential to express a wider range of emotional responses. Ornette Coleman, paralleling Miles Davis's work, furthered the idea of liberating melodic improvisation from restrictive chord structures.[1]

Ornette Coleman

Born in Fort Worth, Texas, in 1930, Ornette Coleman began his professional career playing with local rhythm and blues bands. He experienced limited success in these groups, since his style of playing the saxophone did not always fit the rhythm and blues mold. Eventually, Coleman moved to Los Angeles, where he formed his own group, which worked on adopting and refining Coleman's unorthodox musical ideas. With the help and recommendations of John Lewis of the Modern Jazz Quartet, Coleman landed an Atlantic recording contract and an appearance at New York City's Five Spot Café in 1959. The group's engagement successfully lasted over two months.

Whereas mainstream performers generally conform their solo improvisation to a preset harmonic framework, Coleman's most important contribution was to liberate the melody from preset chord changes. It has been suggested that Miles Davis accomplished this by substituting the high number of chord changes in a tune with a static harmonic movement based on a minimal number of mode shifts. Coleman, however, arrived at the same end by simply telling his sidemen to ignore the chord changes. That is, he wrote out accompanying chords for the composed theme of a tune, though he instructed his accompanists to regard them peripherally to the melody. In his 1959 performance of "Ramblin' " (Atlantic 1327), the melodic material in Coleman's solo improvisations is shaped not by preexisting chords but by melodic formulas that were sometimes borrowed from the opening theme or introduced at different points during the arrangement (music example 5).

On his *Free Jazz* recording (1960) Coleman adapted this approach to a collectively improvised format.[2] The results were startling. In the liner notes to this recording, Coleman explains how random chaos in this approach is avoided and a sense of order and direction maintained. He mentions that the idea

> was for us to play together, all at the same time, without getting in each other's way, and also to have enough room for each player to ad lib alone—and to follow this idea for the duration of the album. When the soloist played something that suggested a musical idea or direction to me, I played that behind him in my style. He continued his own way in his solo, of course.

Trumpet player Freddie Hubbard, who participated as a sideman on Coleman's *Free Jazz*, suggests that "sound," "feeling," and "certain rhythmic

Example 5. *Ornette Coleman's variations of a single formula in "Ramblin'"*

patterns" were the only devices the performers used to organize collective improvisation. He recounts:

> [When Coleman] called me to do the session, I told him "Man, I can't really get into that bag, so I rather you get someone else." "No, man, we need you for the strength," 'cause Don Cherry didn't play that (strong). I didn't want to make it at first, but it was a challenge. We rehearsed twice and the music was really interesting, 'cause that was the first time I had played songs without chord changes. We got it together on sound, it was based on sound and feeling, certain rhythmic patterns we would hit at the same time. I would say that was the most challenging date I ever made in my life. You would have to create ideas that you never created before. . . . If after Eric Dolphy soloed, if I were to come in playing like I was with Art Blakey, I would sound kind of out of context. All of a sudden, I had to come up with some new shit and I had a headache for about two weeks trying to figure this stuff out. It came off pretty good but I still felt I was kind of out of context on that date.[3]

Example 6. *Excerpt from Eric Dolphy's solo (section 1B) in "Free Jazz"*

At approximately four minutes into Coleman's recording of *Free Jazz*, trumpeter Freddie Hubbard and alto saxophonist Coleman play what is basically the same phrase (music example 6). Demonstrating an uncanny "ear," trumpeter Don Cherry anticipates the last three notes of the formula and, in the next measure, extends it with an additional three-note figure that terminates on the Bb. As though predicting when and how Cherry would arrive on the Bb, Dolphy instantaneously spins off a phrase beginning with the Bb. The effect is that Dolphy's line sounds like a continuation of Cherry's phrase, which initially was an outgrowth of Hubbard's and Coleman's formula.[4] Though the interplay is highly spontaneous, the individual musicians respond in an integrated manner. Coleman's efforts to liberate the melody from preset chord changes and to adapt formulaic playing to collectively improvised formats have influenced a number of out performers. Today he is ranked as one of the most important figures in modern jazz.

John Coltrane

John Coltrane's association as a sideman with Miles Davis throughout the latter part of the 1950s earned him the respect of his peers. By the late 1950s, he began to cultivate an unorthodox tenor saxophone technique. By isolating the different frequencies or harmonic overtones of a single tone, he could assimilate the playing of chords on the saxophone. Later, in the mid-1960s, he combined this technique, labeled *multiphonics*, with unconventional-sounding screeches on the tenor sax that gave an added dimension of expressivity to his playing.

Coltrane's 1965 recording of *Ascension* is perhaps the most historically important recording in out jazz. Unlike Cecil Taylor and Ornette Coleman, whose arrival upon the New York City jazz scene was sudden and surprising, Coltrane was well known among his peers. Furthermore, he had accumulated respect for his technical mastery over the demands of hard bop, which he amply demonstrated in Miles Davis's group. Though the dense collective improvisation of *Ascension* was criticized by a number of detractors, no one could argue Coltrane's qualifications or question his motives. He gave out jazz a stamp of legitimacy, which was sorely needed at a time when the music was most vulnerable to the negative evaluation of its critics.

Like Ornette Coleman's "Free Jazz," Coltrane's 1965 recording of *Ascension* sounds chaotic on the surface, due to its very dense and abstract textures. Closer inspection reveals, however, that Coltrane employed several organizational principles for this recording. In table 3 it is noted that the eleven performers alternate between sections of collectively improvised dialogue and sections of solo improvisation with rhythm section accompaniment.[5]

In *Free Jazz*, Coleman uses formulas based on primary and secondary tonal centers to organize collectively improvised material. Though the tonal center acts as an organizing principle, soloists can improvise lines using any combination of notes, regardless of key. However, on *Ascension*, Coltrane uses a quasi-modal approach to organize the soloists.

In Section 1A of *Ascension*, all the lead section improvisers shape their individual lines according to a cycle of four modes, including the B♭ Aeolian, D Phrygian, G♭ Lydian, and F Phrygian (table 4).[6] Trumpeter Freddie Hubbard, who participated as a sideman on the recording, explains:

> The first take we made, I laughed—I mean it was really weird, funny to me. Everybody in there was laughin', 'cause it sounded like a bunch of noise. After we got into it he had four scales he had written. What we would do is play the melody [opening] and that was the end of it. Actually, after we played one note of the scale, everybody hit that note and then you played whatever you felt like off of that particular scale. I had a hell of a time making up stuff, again, you know. Mostly what I did was scream, I think that's what he wanted me to do was scream on top.[7]

Table 3. *The Form of Coltrane's "Ascension" in Real Time*

Real Time	Section	Description
0 secs.	1A	Ensemble statement and development of opening motive in the collectively improvised approached.
3:12	1B	Coltrane's solo tenor sax improvisation.
5:45	2A	Ensemble improvisation.
7:42	2B	Dewey Johnson's solo trumpet improvisation.
9:28	3A	Ensemble improvisation.
11:51	3B	Pharoah Sanders's solo tenor sax improvisation.
14:25	4A	Ensemble improvisation.
15:38	4B	Freddie Hubbard's solo trumpet improvisation.
17:37	5A	Ensemble improvisation.
18:50	5B	Archie Shepp's solo tenor sax improvisation.
20:02	6A	Ensemble improvisation.
21:15	6B	John Tchicai's solo alto sax improvisation.
24:13	7A	Ensemble improvisation.
25:10	7B	Marion Brown's solo alto sax improvisation.
27:15	8A	Ensemble improvisation.
29:48	8B (1)	McCoy Tyner's solo piano improvisation.
33:12	(2)	Duo bassists' improvisation.
35:38	9A	Ensemble improvisation and statement of opening formula in the collectively improvised approach.
40:02		End of piece.

Table 4. *Analysis of Mode Changes in Real Time in Section 1A of "Ascension"*

Real Time	Mode in Which Collective Improvisation Occurs
0 secs.	B♭ Aeolian (B♭ C D♭ E♭ F G♭ A♭ B'♭)
1:45	D Phrygian (D E♭ F G A B♭ C D')
2:10	G♭ Lydian (G♭ A♭ B♭ C D♭ E♭ F G'♭)
2:32	F Phrygian (F G♭ A♭ B♭ C D♭ E♭ F)

Example 7. *Tenor saxophone phrase introducing G♭ Lydian mode in "Ascension"*

During the first minute and forty-five seconds, all the instruments play in the A♭ Aeolian mode. It is not always clear how the musicians are cued when to change to the next mode. Presumably, at the two minute and ten second mark, a brief tenor sax phrase (music example 7) seemingly cues a change to the G♭ Lydian. This change is heavily accented by drummer Elvin Jones, who plays mostly nonisometric rhythms throughout the performance.

This same cycle of modes is also used to organize the polyphonic lines of the improvisers in sections 2A, 3A, and 9A. In the remaining sections of collective improvisation, however, some modes are deleted from the cycle while others become obscured; in this case, clear transitions are negated. Generally, the sections of solo improvisation are rooted in the B♭ Aeolian mode. During some of the solos, however, pianist McCoy Tyner's accompaniment often deviates from this center and even modulates to other modes, such as an E Phrygian (section 4B).

The overall texture in the collectively improvised sections of *Ascension* is extremely dense. As a result, the listener has difficulty separating the individual lines of the seven improvisers. In comparison, the three lead soloists in Coleman's *Free Jazz* remain distinguishable.

During his solo in "Ascension," Coltrane's development of formulas, use of split tones, and sounding of large interval leaps can be accurately portrayed using standard notation; his tonal alterations, growl techniques, squeaks, and squawks, however, cannot. In two different moments of his solo (music examples 8 and 9), Coltrane introduces a primary formula (in vertical brackets) that he develops in subsequent measures. In measure 3 of music example 9, it appears that Coltrane engages in a kind of call-and-response pattern between a phrase played in the extremely high register of the saxophone (measures 3, 5–6, and 8 of music example 9), which is responded to by a descending phrase played in the lower registers (measures 4, 7, and 9 of music example 9). Using an extremely fast tempo (approximately 215 beats per minute), Coltrane's phrases combine several sixteenth notes, which lose their individuality.

Example 8. *Excerpt from Coltrane's solo in "Ascension"*
showing the development of a primary motive

Example 9. *A second excerpt from Coltrane's solo in "Ascension"*
showing the development of another motive

They seem to blend together in a manner that has sometimes been termed streaming.

Eric Dolphy

In the early 1960s, perhaps the first musician to experiment with unusual sounds and timbres on his instrument was the multiple reeds player Eric Dolphy (1928–1964). After leaving Chico Hamilton's group in 1959, Dolphy joined up with Charlie Mingus's ensemble in New York City. Dolphy combines agility on the alto saxophone with an uncanny ability to invent very fresh and creative phrases during his improvisations. Dolphy explored ways in which to connect his musical ideas to his environment. He once mentioned that certain sounds he makes on his instrument came from listening to birds sing: "To me, jazz is like part of living, like walking down the street and reacting to what you see and hear. And whatever I do react to, I can say immediately in my music."[8]

Dolphy played in a multitude of contexts in which traditional concepts of form and improvisation were continually redefined. These included his association with Charlie Mingus, George Russell (who evolved the Lydian Chromatic Concept of Tonal Organization), and John Coltrane. As a leader of his own groups, Dolphy was not hesitant to play standard tunes. His improvisations, however, which included several nonchordal tones and dissonances, posed constant threats to the integrity of the underlying harmonic structure. Dolphy asserts, "Yes, I think of my playing as tonal. I play notes that would not ordinarily be said to be in a given key, but I hear them as proper. I don't think I 'leave the changes,' as the expression goes; every note I play has some reference to the chords of the piece."[9] During the first few measures of Dolphy's alto sax solo in his 1961 recording of Dizzy Gillespie's standard "Woody'n You" (music example 10), several of the passing tones appear to clash with the harmonic accompaniment. On such standards, Dolphy's peculiar improvisational style of "running the changes" resembles Coleman Hawkins's more than the formulaic improvisations of Ornette Coleman. In $Bm7$, $C1m2-m3$, $C1m5$, and $C1m7$ of "Woody'n You," Dolphy plays slight variations (in horizontal brackets) of the same formula. Because they are not developed in any systematic way, they appear instead as formulaic responses embedded in a scalar approach. Except for the large interval leaps and transparent coherence between the melody line and harmonic framework, Dolphy's lines do not radically contrast with some standard bebop phrases. During the last two of his six choruses of improvisation in "Woody'n You," however, the pianist drops out of the accompaniment and Dolphy abandons these beboplike phrase patterns. Instead, he plays phrases whose rapid trilling effects and slides blur distinctions among pitches. Like Coltrane's and Pharoah Sanders's solos in "Ascension," individual notes are perceptible only as a group. The resulting timbre is rough and literally sounds as though the notes are torn apart and formed into a stream of uninterrupted sound. In listening to Dolphy, it is possible that his

Example 10. *Excerpt of Eric Dolphy's alto saxophone solo in "Woody'n You"*

vocallike interpretations of timbre and sound on the saxophone inspired Coltrane to move in this direction as well.

Cecil Taylor

Cecil Taylor was born in New York City on March 15, 1929. His interest in playing piano was stimulated by his mother, who saw to it that her son received formal lessons at the early age of five years. In 1952, Taylor studied music theory and piano technique at the New England Conservatory. Taylor, who was also interested in the music of Dave Brubeck, Lennie Tristano, and Igor Stravinsky, cites Duke Ellington as the most important influence on his style of composing. Ellington's concepts, which include voicing unusual combinations of instruments in contrasting registers to produce colorful textures of sound and sonorities, have been readapted by Taylor to fit settings involving collective improvisation. As the most prolific explorer of new song forms and collective improvisation in the out group, Taylor is an uncompromising artist. Though his music is probably the most complex and challenging for the listener to comprehend, Taylor has remained at the forefront of the out movement since the 1960s.

Like Coleman, Taylor either deemphasizes or altogether abandons the notion of chord changes. The dense clusters of tones that Taylor typically sounds on the piano with the left hand are generally imperceptible as chords. However, Taylor organizes these tone clusters using a highly complex and sophisticated sense of rhythm. Archie Shepp, who was a sideman in Taylor's quartet from 1960 to 1962, describes how he came to understand Taylor's compositional and rhythmic approach. He recalls:

> He'd play these things with a lot of clusters . . . I mean you could interpret these as maybe a C, C-sharp, D, D-sharp, E and F, or C7th,

C-sharp 7th, D7th, D-sharp 7th, E or F . . . it was really up for grabs, and for a while a cat could go crazy wondering, which chord should you play at this point. . . .

Cecil plays lines . . . something like a row or scale . . . that lends itself to the melodic shape of the tune, which is derived from the melody, so that the harmony many times becomes subservient to the body of the tune. And the chords he plays are basically percussive.

But playing with Taylor, I began to be liberated from thinking about chords. . . . It called the whole foundation of what I knew into question. . . . But with Cecil, because there's no steady pulse going, you have to be really conscious of what's going on rhythmically. Cecil plays the piano like a drum, he gets rhythms out of it like a drum.[10]

Taylor's interest in using extended forms in his compositions dates back to his 1957 recording of his composition "Tune 2." Unlike the organization of mainstream tunes into thirty-two-measure AABA forms, "Tune 2" is arranged over eighty-eight measures, which Taylor divides into multiple sections:

A   A' B   C   C' D   B' C'' D' B'' D'' A''
8   8   8   8   8   6   6   4   4   8   8   12 = 88 measures

In Taylor's later recordings, which utilize the free-form, collectively improvised approach, it becomes more difficult for the listener to determine when Taylor moves from one section to another during a performance. For example, the 1962 recording "D Trad, That's What" begins with a brief piano solo, which Taylor constructs using a few melodic formulas. When saxophonist Jimmy Lyons enters the entire complexion of the piece changes. Taylor quickly reverts to playing dense chord clusters and rapid ascending and descending lines on the piano. This sudden change marks a transition into a new section, introduced by a sequence of clustered chords that are different in texture from those of the preceding section.[11] Whereas mainstream performers clearly define individual sections in a piece by a set number of measures, Taylor uses different types of density, sonorities, or kinetic motion to establish transitions from one section to the next. By eliminating the tendency to confine improvisation in this manner, fewer restrictions are imposed on the improviser.

Though Taylor has proven himself one of the most inventive pianists in jazz, his approach to improvisation is partly based on techniques that have an established history in jazz. One such technique is Taylor's use of formulaic development, which lends a certain degree of structure to his playing. During the first few minutes of "2nd Part," from the 1973 recording of *Indent* (QCA 30555), Taylor introduces several formulas that he develops into a number of related permutations. Eventually these lead to the kinds of dense, percussive chord clusters and rapidly played notes for which Taylor is mostly known.

Taylor's 1974 recording of *Silent Tongues* (Al 1005) also uses formulaic development as a structural device. In "Jitney No. 2," Taylor plays a brief formula comprised of only two notes: a perfect fifth based on the interval A to E. During the first sixteen seconds, Taylor plays several permutations of this formula, some of which provide material for longer passages. Over the remainder of the piece, which lasts approximately three minutes and twenty-one seconds, Taylor sporadically refers back on approximately twelve different occasions either to this primary motive or to one of its variations. Each time, the formula is played briefly. Long passages of dense chordal attacks and rapid sequences of tones, which have seemingly little relationship to the formula, then follow. Thus Taylor's permutations of the primary formula are like markers that loosely divide the piece into sections of improvisation.

First-Generation Performers

By laying the foundation for the development of out jazz, the innovators made it possible for other interested musicians to join the ranks. Those who performed as sidemen with the innovators learned many techniques and principles which they eventually adapted to their own styles of musical performance. During the 1970s, these first-generation performers established their careers in the loft scene in New York City. Briefly, the loft scene began when out musicians sought alternatives to performing in nightclubs by converting lofts in abandoned warehouses into performance spaces. Sam Rivers, Jimmy Lyons, Milford Graves, Ken McIntyre, and Charles Tyler were a few of the many prominent first-generation figures performing in this scene.

Though preferring styles of musical performance that often radically differ from hard bop and bebop, many first-generation out musicians cite bebop performers as major influences on their own music. Several developed their musical concepts and instrumental techniques initially through listening to and imitating recorded solos by Charlie Parker, Sonny Stitt, Miles Davis, John Coltrane, and Dizzy Gillespie. When becoming professionals, some performed bebop before making the transition to an out style. Andrew Cyrille (b. 1939), for example, is a drummer whose first influence was Max Roach, one of the principal innovators of bebop drumming. In the mid-1950s, Cyrille played bebop professionally with Duke Jordan, Cecil Payne, Lenny McBrowne, Mary Lou Williams, and others. In the late 1950s, while under the influence of drummers Elvin Jones and Philly Joe Jones, Cyrille began exploring polyrhythmic approaches to drumming. Since then he has molded these influences into a personal and unique style which he terms "sound dialogues" (i.e., multipart rhythms).

Some first-generation performers, like Frank Lowe, Earl Cross, and Charles Tyler, do not perceive a great difference between what they play now and what their predecessors in bebop played before them. By adapting and thus reshaping the compositional and technical devices that were developed in earlier styles, these musicians feel deeply rooted in the tradition of jazz. Frank Lowe may take a standard Thelonious Monk tune, superimpose one or two additional passing chords, and perform this side-by-side with compositions in the out jazz style. He believes, therefore, that ascribing stylistic labels to musicians establishes boundaries which erode the bonds that otherwise unite all jazz musicians within the African-American continuum of music. Instead, Lowe regards the whole development of jazz as a complex of innovators and their innovations that constitutes the wellspring of compositional ideas from which performers today may draw. It cannot be said that Lowe's catholic views, however, are equally shared by his contemporaries.[12]

Many first-generation performers gained exposure to bebop and out jazz through some type of direct contact with leading exponents of both styles. In the late 1940s, Jimmy Lyons (1933–1986) visited the various nightclubs in the Bronx to hear bebop performers such as Charlie Parker, Bud Powell, and Thelonious Monk. After performing bebop professionally with local musicians in the late 1950s, he then attended some of Ornette Coleman's performances. Lyons, however, was not entirely convinced that bebop could be superseded until his first encounter with Cecil Taylor in the early 1960s. By 1961, he was performing with Taylor on a regular basis and discovered

Jimmy Lyons performing on alto saxophone at Soundscape

that the kinds of phrasing he was accustomed to playing in bebop required the support of certain chordal structures that were conspicuously missing in Taylor's music. Determined to remain with Taylor, Lyons was forced to invent new approaches to playing his instrument that fit within the framework of Taylor's innovative ideas and concepts. By the time of his death, he had become a highly respected performer.

Second-Generation Performers

The second generation of out performers, mostly born around 1950, represents a critical stage in the development of out jazz. With few younger musicians presently in the ranks who comprise a third generation, second-generation performers are rightly concerned over the future of out jazz. Most second-generation performers who began their careers in the 1970s played as sidemen in groups led by members of the first generation. Whereas the latter group frequently cites bebop musicians as primary influences, second-generation performers are likely to regard the innovators of out jazz as significant role models.

Since most second-generation performers would have been too young in the early 1960s to participate first-hand in the beginnings of out jazz, their initial exposure to the music came not through direct contact but through listening to the LP recordings of out jazz played by the innovators.[13] While still learning their instruments, many second-generation performers bypassed mastering the techniques and theory of bebop and hard bop while choosing instead to perform out. During an out rehearsal, in which a bebop standard tune was suggested as a warm-up exercise, a participant once commented, "Don't play the preliminaries, let's take it straight up." However, discovering that the basics of mainstream jazz represent an important link in the historical development of the music, many second-generation performers like Billy Bang admit that it was necessary in the 1980s to relearn their instruments and to examine the contributions of their predecessors.

Because out performers and hard bop performers occasionally come into contact with one another, their attitudinal differences in respect to mainstream jazz are sometimes a source of tension between the two groups. One evening, for example, out performers Dewey Johnson and Daniel Carter visited a traditional jam session held at the University of the Streets in the Lower East Side of Manhattan. Johnson, who had played bebop semiprofessionally before coming to New York City in 1963 and had developed an out style since then, was able to play easily in the accepted bebop style; that is, he constructed his phrasing within the given chord progressions of the tunes.[14] In contrast, Daniel Carter has never practiced or performed in the bebop style. When it was his turn to solo, he played phrases which mostly did not fit into the chord structure of the tune and were not constructed in the customary bebop style. A few of the older bebop musicians in attendance exchanged scornful glances among themselves. What had been an "open" session suddenly became closed; although Carter was not asked to leave, musicians argued afterward that he was trying to change the format of the jam session. It was suggested that if he wanted to return in the future he should conform more to the bebop style of performance.

A few older out musicians who played in the New York City jazz scene during the 1960s are concerned that the second-generation musicians have little idea of the kind of out jazz that was being played outside of the recording studios in New York City at this time. The few commercial recordings by Albert Ayler and Don Ayler, for instance, fail to represent what these musicians ordinarily played in performance lofts and at rehearsals.[15] Thus much of their music exists only in the minds of those who were there at the time these events took place.

Jemeel Moondoc

Alto saxophonist Jemeel Moondoc was born in 1951 in Chicago. Although his parents were not musicians, Moondoc's grandfather (his name was Moondoctor) was a minstrel who sold moonshine cure-alls, sang, and danced. Moondoc studied clarinet at an early age and played in rhythm and blues bands. After high school, Moondoc majored in architecture for one year at the Illinois Institute of Technology. Because he discovered that architecture was taught as a rigid discipline, he grew disenchanted with it, and music soon superseded any remaining desire for a college degree. He left college and fell strongly under the influence of Cecil Taylor's music, which he listened to on recordings. He then sought opportunities to play the alto saxophone with Taylor's big band at the University of Wisconsin (Madison) and later at Antioch. His tenure with Taylor lasted for two years and endowed Moondoc with the necessary experience and credentials to attempt a musical career in the New York City jazz scene, a tough, merciless, and competitive atmosphere in which to live and work as a musician.

After arriving in New York City in 1972, Moondoc performed with Ed

Jemeel Moondoc performing on alto saxophone

Example 11. *Excerpts from the theme and solo improvisation in Jemeel Moondoc's composition "Judy's Bounce"*

Blackwell, Dennis Charles, Rashied Ali, Roy Campbell, Jr., William Parker, Fred Hopkins, Dewey Johnson, and others. Though Moondoc knows some of the bebop repertoire of standard tunes and has assimilated many of its stock phrases through listening to Charlie Parker's recordings, he does not believe that he has truly mastered the style. He admits that playing the standard bebop tunes does not satisfy him. Instead, Moondoc feels that he is continually searching for something that is beyond what he is doing when performing and playing an instrument. This he likens to a kind of spiritual drive that originated with John Coltrane and that shaped his desire to explore certain musical directions. On rare occasions when this drive has become particularly intense during a performance, Moondoc claims that he has levitated above the bandstand and observed himself and the other musicians performing.[16]

The primary influences upon Moondoc's style of musical performance and composing derive from Cecil Taylor and Ornette Coleman, though he cites Duke Ellington and Thelonious Monk as secondary influences. In his 1981 recording of "Judy's Bounce" (Soul Note 1051), the influence of Coleman is pervasive. In this piece, Moondoc retains the theme-improvisation-theme format, which characterizes the approaches of most of his predecessors in bebop. Its theme is stated over a conventional thirty-two-bar form, although AABA format divisions are obscured. Moondoc borrows from Coleman the notion of organizing phrases around a main tonal center rather than shaping the melody to fit a prescribed set of chords. Moondoc's accompanists, therefore, like those of Coleman, are required to interact more directly with the soloist by using the melody as a point of departure. Like Coleman, Moondoc borrows formulas from the main theme to construct and build coherence among the phrases of his solo improvisation. In music example 11, note how Moondoc finishes a beboplike phrase (m40–m41)

with an arpeggiated chord (m42) that mimics the motion of another arpeggiated chord in the first measure of the theme. Showing an affinity for Coleman's music, it is perhaps more than coincidence that Moondoc hired drummer Ed Blackwell, a former member of Coleman's group, to perform on
"Judy's Bounce."

Billy Bang

Another second-generation out improviser living in New York City is Billy
Bang, originally named William Walker. Shortly after he was born in Mo-
bile, Alabama, in 1947, he moved to Harlem in New York City with his
mother. Bang acquired his knowledge about music and the violin partly
through the public school system of Harlem but mostly by playing with
local jazz musicians. After high school, Bang was drafted and served in Vietnam for two years. When he returned, he attended college to pursue a music
degree but found it difficult to study music in a classroom. He left college
and began to play more seriously with local musicians. His attraction to
performing out was sparked by his concern over certain political and personal issues that he felt could be expressed through this style:

> It was very natural for me to want to play avant-garde because I was
> very political at the time. It was important for me to maintain my man-
> hood out here. I was shaken up earlier by guys who were taking Mos-
> lem names. It took me awhile to understand this. Then there were the
> titles of the tunes that people like Shepp were doing. It seemed to be
> punching out the system through the music. The music is a strong lan-
> guage. I am able to express certain political attitudes through the mu-
> sic. It can be done literally through the music with poetry.[17]

Billy Bang believes that his music has a didactic function; that is, he hopes
he can awaken people to alternative ways of living and understanding the
world through his music. Bang explains that music can shock or arouse
people, especially if they are accustomed to hearing a certain type of music
or a certain form. If one plays music that radically departs from these expectations, people are forced to come to terms with this incongruity.[18]

Bang had performed with Daniel Carter in the free-form, collectively improvised approach throughout 1973 and part of 1974 in a group called the
Music Ensemble. This group nurtured a deep commitment to the music,
which at the time was linked to certain political ideas:

Billy Bang and Jason Hwang performing on violins at Soundscape.

Musicians had no choice in the 1960s but to get into the political thing. A lot of the musicians did not have to get into the theoretical side of musicianship. . . . But they could pick up an instrument and it was like they were picking up an AK47 [automatic weapon]. A lot of cats who were playing were picking up on the extensions of Coltrane. They did not study what made up a scale or the blues. They just started honking and screaming and the statements sounded like machine gun fire. This happened to me too. So cats like me had to back up and start hearing cats like Leroy Jenkins and Ornette Coleman and even Ray Nance and Michael White.[19]

When Bang's wife gave birth to their first child, his outlook about performing in the free-form, collectively improvised style began to change. The responsibility of supporting a family prompts Bang to explain that one must be independently wealthy to play that freely. When musicians show up intending to play that freely at the gig, furthermore, the audience sometimes

Example 12. *Excerpt from a theme section from Billy Bang's "Outline No. 12"*

feels no obligation to pay an admission fee and may even ask to participate. Wade, a wooden flute player who never rehearsed with the group, would always manage to attend a Music Ensemble performance. He would casually make his way unnoticed to the stage and begin playing with the group before anyone could stop him.

Bang left the Music Ensemble and began a career of his own. Since then, he has often incorporated even-metered rhythms, precomposed melodic lines, and harmonic frameworks in his performances, recorded numerous albums under his own name with popular out musicians such as Don Cherry, and assembled a successful funk rock group on the side.

According to Bang, total freedom exists only if it follows some structure; that is, one must master some form of discipline or structure before one can

be totally free. Bang now cultivates a balance between improvisation and form by writing an introduction, or "head," for almost every piece that he composes. This, he explains, is essential in order to introduce and consequently shape the soloist's improvisation. Bang's compositions for large ensembles sometimes use an ABCBDB form that blends separate themes of a piece (A, C, and D) with sections of improvisation (the B sections). Sections A, C, and D may sometimes be transformations of the main theme which have been progressively altered until they resemble something else. Each of these leads to a B section which may be collectively improvised by any number and combination of instruments for a period of time determined either by the score or by the leader of the group.

This compositional blend of freedom and form is evident in Bang's 1982 recording of his piece "Outline No. 12" (OAO Cell 5004). Music example 12 is a transcription of one of the themes that appears near the end of the piece. It is a short chromatic phrase that is repeated several times by most of the instruments. Its purpose, claims Bang, is to exert a great amount of influence over the following collectively improvised section, involving the same instruments.

In briefly comparing the two approaches above, Moondoc and Bang both use collective improvisation. They differ significantly, however, in the ways in which they manipulate certain compositional devices to control improvisation or to give it free rein during a performance. Billy Bang's approach allows collective improvisation to occur within narrow parameters that are prescribed by preceding notated themes. In contrast, Jemeel Moondoc uses the AABA form of bebop but discovers greater freedom when abandoning the notion of shaping the melodic lines against chord patterns.

Third-Generation Performers

At the Knitting Factory, a small nightclub located on East Houston Street in New York City, there is evidence to suggest the beginning of a third generation of out performers. Musicians such as Tim Berne, Steve Coleman, Hank Roberts, John Zorn, and Bill Frisell have recently appeared there. Some time must pass, however, before their influences upon out jazz can be gauged.

f i v e

the economics of performing

out in new york city

Because of its dense population, New York City provides enough interested people, including listeners and performers, to support an out jazz scene.[1] A number of out performers who depend for their livelihood on the entertainment and music-recording industries often encounter restrictions that seriously threaten the principles on which their music is based. Thus the economic relationship between these two groups has been tumultuous and fraught with considerable tension. To understand more clearly the nature of this tension, it is helpful to consider some of the basic factors in the development of these entertainment industries.

Around the turn of the century, rapid industrialization and a growing population density of a heterogeneous nature radically altered the character of many northern cities.[2] As a result, division of labor and specialization in the work place increased. Thus by the 1920s, New York City jazz musicians began to specialize as full-time professionals performing in nightclubs and cabarets. Furthermore, mass markets and the technological means (e.g., mass media) by which these markets could be reached also grew rapidly. This enabled entrepreneurs to transform music and art into commodities (e.g., sheet music and phonograph recordings) that could be bought and sold on the open market. For this purpose, music-publishing firms and popular song producers multiplied in New York City in the late 1920s.

Jazz and Economics

These economic principles, upon which the entertainment industries in New York City were initially based, have also shaped roles among recording industry producers, nightclub owners, and jazz musicians. To be financially successful, professional jazz musicians living in New York City must negotiate contracts for club dates and recording sessions. Though jazz musicians may consider their music as art, the recording and entertainment industries, with few exceptions, view them and their music as products. In other words, their services can be purchased for the purpose of selling records or luring customers into a bar to buy drinks and food. To insure their economic survival, bar owners and recording producers feel compelled to hire only those artists whose work appeals to the largest section of a particular audience. As a result, out musicians constantly find themselves under pressure to alter their style of musical performance in order to fit more acceptable commercial models. Most, however, continue to develop highly original approaches to performing that resist mass mediation, though they may consequently have few opportunities to perform professionally in public.

Some musicians seek a compromise to this dilemma that allows them to earn money performing more popular kinds of music while continuing to explore styles of performing out at home or in selected contexts. Billy Bang, for example, leads a funk rock group when he is not performing out jazz. Charles Tyler's reputation as an out performer supersedes the fact that he also performs in the hard bop style, depending upon the context and composition of the audience for an engagement. Tyler can recount numerous instances in which club owners have refused to hire him in the belief that his music is too "weird."[3] Tyler explains,

> I don't understand how they consider my music to be so new or hard to understand. . . . I've been doing basically the same thing for twenty years. How long does it have to go before it's considered jazz? [My music] doesn't deviate too much from traditional jazz either. When I broke into the scene, I broke in with people like Ayler. People are influenced by what they heard or read and they think that I'm weird, though they never heard me. When they hear my music, they already have their mind made up.[4]

Today most out performers living in New York City enjoy no more than two or three opportunities each year to perform professionally in public, unless they are well established and have some degree of popularity.

From the time jazz was first performed in the dance halls of New Orleans around the turn of the century, the nightclub or bar has continued to provide the main outlet for the performance of jazz in cities. Because the bar owner pays the musicians' salaries, it is within his or her power to exert certain controls over the leader of the group. The bar owner can instruct a leader to hire a specific number of musicians and even seek to negotiate the names of the sidemen who will perform. The bar owner may also prescribe the lengths and number of performances ("sets") per night, the times of the performances, and sometimes even the tunes that the group will play.

In the 1960s, out musicians continued to practice innovative approaches to performing, and their attitudes diverged more strongly than ever from those of bar patrons and owners. John Coltrane, for instance, spoke out against the policies of bar owners that were often the source of numerous distractions for musicians. The crashing of glasses to the floor, cash registers ringing, or doors opening and closing would have a negative effect on the performers. When Coltrane's compositions written after 1964 lasted well over an hour each, it was apparent to infuriated club owners that customers became intoxicated more by the music than the small number of drinks they purchased. Owners often pleaded with Coltrane to play standard tunes or shorten his pieces to forty minutes so that afterward customers had more opportunities to walk to the bar to order drinks. Since Coltrane was unwilling to compromise, he had difficulty finding employment in some New York

City jazz nightclubs. Buell Neidlinger (b. 1936), who played bass in Cecil Taylor's group from the mid-1950s to the early 1960s, describes Taylor's performances in similar terms. He remarks,

> Trying to make a living playing with Cecil is absolutely unbelievable, because there is no economic advantage to playing music like that. It's completely unsalable in the nightclubs because of the fact that each composition lasts, or could last, an hour and a half. Bar owners aren't interested in this, because if there's one thing they hate to see it's a bunch of people sitting around openmouthed with their brains absolutely paralyzed by the music, unable to call for the waiter. They want to sell drinks. But when Cecil's playing, people are likely to tell the waiter to shut up and be still.[5]

Like bar owners, the survival of record company producers depends upon the marketability of an artist's work. Their priorities often belie the social content in an artist's work or its importance musically to the jazz community. Instead, they are more concerned with whether the artist's work has enough popular appeal to sell records.

The disparate expectations bound up in the roles among jazz performers, record producers, and club owners became perhaps most evident during the incipient stages of growth of out jazz between 1959 and 1965. Record companies shied away from recording the new music since they felt it would not be commercially profitable. Thus between 1959 and 1965, the development of out jazz remains poorly documented at a time in which it was performed most intensively. Similarly, New York City nightclub owners discriminated against out performers and refused to hire them on the grounds that they did not attract enough customers, they alienated bar patrons expecting more traditional styles of jazz performance, and they played tunes that were too long, inhibiting the sale of drinks to customers.

In the early 1960s, a few out musicians who received critical acclaim felt they were being underpaid for performances at nightclubs. Though Coleman drew capacity crowds at New York's Five Spot Café and later in 1962 at the Jazz Gallery, he argues that his earnings were substantially less than what mainstream performers were commanding. By tripling his performing fee, Coleman alienated record companies and club owners, who now refused to hire him.

Similar conflicts presented themselves in the recording studios. ESP-Disc, a record label founded in 1964 by New York lawyer Bernard Stollman, recorded several out performers.[6] Stollman's policy was to pay the recording artist a small amount of money in advance that would later be deducted from royalties once the record began to sell. Expecting that such royalties would quickly appear, many recording artists grew angry when they were not forthcoming.

Some out musicians who did receive recording contracts with large companies altered their styles of performing in order to attract a larger audience. On his earlier LP recordings, such as *Vibrations* (1964), Albert Ayler clearly stands out as one of the most original and innovative tenor saxophonists playing in the New York City jazz scene. In 1968, however, Ayler recorded *New Grass* for ABC's Impulse label. The recording is heavily infused with the more commercially viable influences of rhythm and blues and rock. It is strongly rumored that Ayler was under pressure by his producer, Bob Thiele, to garnish his music with these elements in order to broaden its appeal.

By the mid-1960s, out musicians realized that if they wanted to continue pursuing their innovative approaches to performing, they would have to take the matter of recording, producing, and distributing their music into their own hands. Hence, many out musicians started their own recording labels, often assuming the responsibility of producing and distributing the recordings themselves. Such musician-owned labels include Sun Ra's Saturn label, Cecil Taylor's Unit Core label, and Stanley Cowell and Charles Tolliver's Strata East label. Musician-owned labels were a major source of out recordings, especially during the late 1960s and 1970s.[7] In an effort to further extend their control over the music, some out musicians opened up performance lofts for the purpose of showcasing out jazz.

The Loft Scene of the 1970s

The low rents and ambience of Greenwich Village since the 1920s have continued to attract bohemians, artists, radicals, and intellectuals. During the 1960s, the main jazz clubs in Greenwich Village and the Lower East Side were the Village Vanguard, the Jazz Gallery, the Five Spot Café, the Half-Note, Birdland, and the Village Gate. LeRoi Jones, who was present in the out jazz scene in the early 1960s, reports that these nightclubs maintained a general policy of hiring mostly popular jazz performers and discriminating against the lesser-known out performers.[8] The White Whale, a

Figure 3. *Flyer for an out jazz performance*

coffeehouse on the Lower East Side, was the first such establishment to hire out performers, according to Jones. Other coffeehouses such as the Take 3, the Playhouse Coffee Shop, Café Avital, and Café Metro soon followed suit.

Interested parties leased lofts in business, industrial, and warehouse buildings and transformed them into performance spaces for the growing number of out musicians. Most often it was the musicians themselves who organized the concerts. They took out advertisements in the *Village Voice*, posted flyers containing information about the performance around the immediate vicinity of the loft, and handed out such notices to friends and passersby (see figures 3, 4, and 5). A musician organizing such a performance could call other musicians, pass by their homes on foot, or recruit them during a chance meeting on the street. The musicians might gather for one or two rehearsals or simply perform the gig without a rehearsal and discussion prior to the performance.[9] The audiences that attended loft performances were generally small but sympathetic. People were attracted to these performances by the low admission fee and the prospect of hearing something unusual.

PRESENTS
SKIES OVER AFRICA
INTRODUCING THE FIRST AMERICAN
JAZZ KAMIKAZE
SQUAD
FEATURING:

DEWEY JOHNSON	- TRUMPET
DANIEL CARTER	- TENOR / ALTO SAX
DAVID SUCH	- FLUTES
DENNIS CHARLES	- DRUMS / PERCUSSION
ADE YEME	- CONGA
EARL FREEMAN	- BASS

TEL. 982-0985

★★★

Figure 4. *Flyer for an out jazz performance*

Throughout most of the 1970s, the loft scene in Greenwich Village and the Lower East Side continued. Studio We, the Ladies' Fort, and Studio RivBea were the mainstays of the loft scene where out musicians gathered and interacted. In this scene, the cutting contests, personality cults, and vices that characterized the jazz scene of the 1940s and 1950s were mostly

VORTEX

RALPH BLAUVELT
BRAD GRAVES
STEVE SAMUELS

ALSO APPEARING : MARION BROWN; MARY ANN
DRISCOLL / PAUL MURPHY— KOOL JAZZ FESTIVAL
JUNE 27, 1983 — MONDAY— 8:00 P.M.—TEL.581—7032
SOUNDSCAPE—500 W. 52 ST. CORNER 10TH AVE.
THIS PROGRAM MADE POSSIBLE IN PART WITH
SUPPORT FROM "MEET THE COMPOSER"

Figure 5. *Flyer for an out jazz performance*

missing. Whereas the bebop musician of the 1940s has been stereotyped as a drug addict and social outcast, out performers like Daniel Carter, Jeanne Lee, and William Parker do not use drugs.

Throughout the 1970s, lofts provided an open and unrestrictive environment for out performers. However, performers often found themselves too overburdened with the responsibilities of overseeing all the business aspects of performing as well as directing the music. Some musicians look back upon the loft scene as a struggle, especially since it rarely provided enough opportunities for all musicians to perform.

The Collectives

The civil rights movement of the 1960s prompted government agencies in the 1970s to lend support to African-American artists. This support helped a few musicians to open lofts, though it was too meager to sustain the entire community of out performers. To address the remaining economic problems and artistic needs of out musicians, performers engaged in collective enterprise. During the 1960s and 1970s, most of these collectives operated under the belief that out musicians were frequently exploited by record producers and that economic and political power in the music industry would come only if they organized. Such collectives enabled out musicians to exert considerable control over the different phases of recording and distributing their own music.[10] In some cases, the notion of collectivity among out musicians living in New York City stemmed from many of the social philosophies that emerged in the 1960s. For example, out musicians who were avid supporters of civil rights viewed it as an opportunity for African-Americans to take charge of their own culture and destiny.

Some of the earliest collectives among jazz musicians in New York City were formed by Charlie Mingus and Max Roach. In 1960 the two musicians organized the Alternative Newport Festival, a series of out performances staged as a protest against George Wein, the promoter and organizer of the annual Newport Jazz Festival. It was argued that Wein's hiring policy for the festival conspicuously discriminated against out performers, though the real reason may stem from Wein's decision not to hire them that particular year. That same year, the Jazz Artists' Guild was formed as an extension of the Alternative Newport Festival. Though it was able to produce a series of concerts in a small Manhattan theater, deficient business skills caused the guild to disband a short time later.[11]

Collectivity also became a focal issue surrounding the "October Revolution in Jazz," a series of artist-organized out performances held October 1–4, 1964, at the Cellar Café in Manhattan. More than twenty performing groups participated and demonstrated that, with some initiative, musicians from isolated pockets in Manhattan could perform together and attract large and supportive audiences. Soon afterward, the Jazz Composers Guild was organized by Sun Ra, Bill Dixon, Cecil Taylor, Paul and Carla Bley, Archie Shepp, and others. Their doctrine was to "establish the music in its rightful place in society; to awaken the musical conscience of the masses of people to that music which is essential to their lives; to protect the musicians and composers from the existing forces of exploitation; to provide facilities for the proper creation, rehearsal, performance, and dissemination of the music."[12]

To assure that collectivity would succeed among out performers living in

New York City, a long history of competitiveness among musicians, strong individual personalities, tight-knit musicians' cliques, and the lack of managerial and business experience among musicians had to be overcome. However, because of personality conflicts among members of the Jazz Composers Guild and because musicians often accepted performing jobs without consulting the guild, it was forced to disband.

Collectives were initiated among experimental musicians living in other cities as well. The most notable of these is the Association for the Advancement of Creative Musicians (AACM), which had formed in Chicago in 1965. Begun as a collective "self-help society," the AACM provided its members with rehearsal space, opportunities to perform, and recording facilities. Due much to the administrative skills of its long-reigning president, Muhal Richard Abrams, the AACM has proved to be the most durable and successful collective. Other collectives include the Underground Musician's Association, which Horace Tapscott began in the Watts area of Los Angeles in 1964. In 1968, musicians living in St. Louis formed the Black Artists Group. Also in 1968, a number of out performers originated the Detroit Creative Musicians Association.[13]

In recent times, out musicians have renewed their interest in forming arts cooperatives. In 1985, for example, trumpeter Lester Bowie, multireed player Oliver Lake, and pianist Cecil Taylor originated the Musicians of Brooklyn Initiative (MOBI). MOBI hopes to achieve its goals of providing employment for its members by "increasing the public's awareness of America's indigenous music and developing greater appreciation for regional musicians by presenting the works of known and unknown artists alike."[14] Requiring members to pay regular dues, the organization produces concerts for its members. It hopes eventually to provide rehearsal space and serve as a clearinghouse for musician- and community-related services.

Performance Outlets in the 1980s

Milford Graves, a leading innovator of out drumming styles since the 1960s, commented that the loft sessions in the 1970s amounted to a "cooling off" period. He explains, "The 1960s was a move toward civil rights and social issues. But the 1970s were like a cooling out stage. Programs started happening, and money was given out to the community. [The 1960s] was a period when everyone was up and the music was hot and burning. But the

1970s is like when everyone went to sleep. Everyone got split up."[15] Thus musicians who were involved in the intense atmosphere of the out scene of the 1960s retreated to reflect on their experiences. To some extent, this accounts for the comparatively smaller number of attempts to form collectives in the 1970s. Also in the 1970s, some key figures of the out scene in the 1960s altered their styles to appear as though they were catering to a wider audience that might include listeners who usually favored rock and disco styles.

In the mid- and late 1970s, the loft scene declined when the major lofts such as Studio We, the Ladies' Fort, and Studio RivBea closed their doors. Sam Rivers closed Studio RivBea as the result of losing his lease. He also adds that it was difficult for him to serve both as an administrator and a musician; when he would go on tour, no one was available to handle the business. Having met with too many economic hardships, the other lofts also discontinued business. By the end of the 1970s, out musicians were facing fewer performance opportunities than ever before. Whereas some sought employment as college instructors if they were qualified, others resorted to performing more conventional styles of jazz or pop.

Soundscape

In recent years, however, Verna Gillis has organized the opening of Soundscape, a performance loft located on West 52nd Street. Soundscape receives partial funding from the city of New York as well as the federal government and arranges performances of out jazz sporadically throughout the winter months. On some occasions, musicians are paid a fee and also receive part of the proceeds of admission. On other occasions, performers might receive these proceeds in lieu of a fixed fee. Since attendance depends on the popularity of the musicians, the extent of the publicity, and the night of the week on which the performance is scheduled, musicians generally agree to perform under such terms with mixed feelings. For example, Commitment is a group of four musicians (William Parker, bass; Jason Hwang, violin; Takeshi Zen Matsuura, drums; and Will Connell, Jr., flute, sax, clarinet) who have cultivated a strong group philosophy and who have remained together, despite few opportunities to perform. When they perform at Soundscape perhaps no more than ten or fifteen people are present in the audience at a time. Thus if the group is paid only from admission, each musician receives little more than his traveling expenses.

Since it requires less time to record a live performance than to record the same tunes in a studio, it is cheaper for out musicians to produce an album by hiring the services of an engineer for the recording of live performances. During the series of concerts at Soundscape, about four groups had their performances recorded in such a manner.

The size of the audiences for the out performances of the Kool Festival at Soundscape varied mostly according to the popularity of the performer. Jimmy Lyons, Marion Brown, and Charles Tyler, for example, are more established performers and attracted larger audiences for their performances (i.e., about sixty to eighty people). Less established musicians, such as Steve Colson and Jemeel Moondoc, drew only about twelve to twenty-five people for each of their performances.

Some out performers enjoy the type of concert setting that Soundscape provides, whereas others do not respond well to its ambience. Others claim that the hiring policies of Soundscape favor a few musicians at the exclusion of others. Despite these grievances, Soundscape continues to support out jazz in New York City.

Aside from Soundscape, the hiring policies of the major jazz clubs in New York City have changed little in regard to out performers. Such clubs continue to operate under the profit motive and hire musicians who have proven that they can draw an acceptably large enough audience. For out musicians to build such a following, they must usually perform for several years in New York City and have at least a few LP records credited to their names.

Sweet Basil

Sweet Basil, a large jazz club located in the Lower West Side of Manhattan, has made some effort in recent times to support a small number of popular out performers. The owners produced a minifestival that spanned the months of January, February, and March 1984 entitled "Music Is an Open Sky." During this period, Sunday and Monday of each week were set aside for a different out jazz performer. Jemeel Moondoc, who had been negotiating with the management for three years to perform at Sweet Basil, was finally given a night toward the end of January.

8BC

Some out performers who are unable to secure opportunities to perform at any of the outlets mentioned above, for whatever reasons, have to seek alternatives. Daniel Carter, for example, performed on different occasions at a club called 8BC. This establishment, which opened around 1983 and closed roughly a few years later, was located amidst the abandoned and gutted apartment buildings on 8th Street between B and C Avenues in the Lower East Side. 8BC's rising ceiling, eight-foot-high stage, dim lighting, poor heating, peeling walls, and scuffed floors, as well as the bizarre art objects scattered about, lent an eerie ambience to this setting for the performance of music.

The hiring policy at 8BC was to use a wide range of performers from diverse backgrounds. Performances in the past at 8BC, for example, ranged from Chinese opera to punk rock. The audiences at 8BC considerably varied from those one might find at Soundscape or Sweet Basil. The adventurous tastes of the management and the club's bizarre ambience were perhaps more responsible than the specific performing groups for attracting a majority of the audience, composed mostly of young white males and females between the ages of fifteen and twenty-three who dressed either in punk or new wave fashions. The reaction of this cross section of the audience was favorable, if not enthusiastic, toward Carter's performance. They could relate to the conscious avoidance of conventions in Carter's style of musical performance; however, they lacked awareness of the significance of the music in the overall development of jazz. The remaining part of the audience was made up of friends of the performing group or other musicians curious to hear new music groups.

Customers at 8BC sat either at the bar or at a group of crooked and worn tables on the west wall. Soft drinks and wine were available for purchase. Two or three groups performed each night through the weekend and earned half the admission fees for the time-slot in which they performed or a little more if a very small audience was in attendance. Management at 8BC imposed few restrictions upon the musicians except that they start on time and not exceed the limit of forty-five minutes for their performance. Within that time, musicians were free to play whatever they chose. The management employed acts after listening to a tape of the group's music and judging that it would be interesting to their patrons. The revenues from the club were enough to allow the club owners to break even and perhaps reinvest in the building's upkeep.

Jazz Cultural Center

If out musicians are able to set aside money from their meager earnings, it is possible for them to rent a performance space in a loft or small theater for one night for fees beginning at $100 minimum. Much like the loft scene a decade earlier, musicians must handle their own advertising. Even with a conscientious advertising campaign and a meager admission fee, audiences may be small. Funded by Baroness Pannonica de Koenigswarter, the Jazz Cultural Center, under the direction of Barry Harris, sometimes allowed out musicians to rent its theater for a nominal fee and helped with the publicity.

Kwami Shaw

Since 1982 Kwami Shaw has been one of the first successful producers to promote out jazz in New York City. When living in the Caribbean Islands, he became interested in producing jazz concerts locally for musicians such as Jimmy Hamilton, who played clarinet and saxophone in Duke Ellington's band. When Shaw felt he needed a change, he moved to New York City, where it seemed odd to him that none of the other jazz producers took a genuine interest in out performers. He then set out to create an alternative venue for listeners who rejected the atmosphere of nightclubs or bars and who preferred music that was not shaped by the economic value system of bars.

Consequently, Shaw rented performance space at the Healing Arts Center on Broadway Avenue and formed Jazztrack, which featured performances by out musicians. Unafraid to compete with the mainstream jazz nightclubs, Shaw scheduled two Saturday-night concerts per month. He provided an intimate and friendly atmosphere for each concert, and since then he has had nearly all well-known out musicians perform for him.

Because Shaw's policy in dealing with musicians is based on honesty and fairness, he has gained the hard-earned trust of the out group. Shaw, for example, never pays a sideman less than $100 for a performance, and musicians are paid either in advance or immediately after a performance. Shaw also provides complimentary beverages such as beer for the musicians and a comfortable dressing room prior to the performance. As a producer, Shaw makes a modest income. If he did not like the music and was interested in making more money, he claims he would be producing Michael Jackson or Prince.

The Knitting Factory

In 1987, Michael Dorf, Bob Appel, and Louis Spitzer opened the Knitting Factory on Houston Street, a low-rent area of Manhattan. Like 8BC, it began as an experimental nightclub that booked alternative kinds of music.

The Knitting Factory currently features a variety of rock groups and out musicians, including regular appearances by the Lounge Lizards, Cecil Taylor, and John Zorn. Many performers play at the Knitting Factory in different combinations with other musicians.

Recently, the media have given inordinate attention to the Knitting Factory, elevating its status as one of the trendiest clubs in the downtown scene. Thus it attracts larger audiences who are not necessarily knowledgeable about jazz.[16] Instead, many members of the audience attend because of the club's reputation as a fun place where unusual things happen. In other words, the sizes of audiences attending out performances at other nightclubs have not increased dramatically due to any widespread surge in the popularity of out jazz. The audiences for most out performances at the Knitting Factory consist of a mixture of musicians, writers, and young rock fans wanting to hear something different. Audience members are mostly white; whereas the small number of black listeners who attend are generally musicians who know the performers.

The reputation of the Knitting Factory also has an effect upon performers. That is, some are motivated to adapt their music to the expectations of the audience and management instead of their own aesthetic preferences. For example, one young drummer commented, "I am going to put together a band that is so far out it will blow everyone's mind at that club."[17] In a sense, all he is saying is that he wants to be accepted at the Knitting Factory.

In response to the image of the Knitting Factory and its impact upon out jazz, Bob Rusch, editor of *Cadence Magazine*, refers to out performances at the Knitting Factory as the "popular avant-garde." He adds, "Once the music becomes popular and musicians adapt their styles to continue that way, it is no longer the true avant-garde."[18] Indeed, the intentions and motivations of some performers at the Knitting Factory are not in keeping with those that first spawned out jazz back in the 1960s.

In all fairness, the Knitting Factory benefits out jazz by giving it exposure to a wider audience and by providing much-needed opportunities for out musicians to perform. Though the owners of the Knitting Factory claim only a small profit from running the club, it appears successful enough to justify further attempts in the commercial marketing of out jazz. However, time will tell how long out jazz will continue to be economically viable as a trendy commodity.

Additional outlets for the performance of out jazz include Life Café, which is a small bohemian-style coffeehouse located in the Lower East Side. Out musicians may also find opportunities to perform at college theaters or at festivals in which several out groups are represented.

On Tiny Tim, the Monkees, and the "Pet Rock" Hypothesis in Out Jazz

In the 1960s, both independent and major recording companies chose to promote rock and roll, which had quickly proven itself to be more than just a passing fad. Though out jazz will probably never become "popular" music, some musicians believe that it has potential to be profitable and to attract a wider audience if it were promoted to the same extent as rock. Tenor saxophonist Frank Lowe offers the following comments:

> Those who use the term avant-garde sometimes assume that you have to be poor to play it. This attitude keeps work away. We have to clear a lot of these misconceptions up. Avant-garde people don't have as much money as the other people. We are in a capitalistic world and that isn't right. [Musicians] have given a lot of thought and creativity to the music. I don't believe that they should be poor. If you can sell Tiny Tim records or pet rocks you can sell avant-garde music.[19]

Lowe's "pet rock" hypothesis in out jazz, however, is challenged by the axiom in the economics of capitalism that if the demand is lacking then the supply will not sell. Thus large recording companies are reluctant to risk spending enormous sums of money promoting out jazz without any guarantee of increased sales and profits. Like early bebop, which the general public rejected, out jazz is too abstract and complex.

If out jazz is to reach a wider audience through promotion and media exposure, listeners will need to be educated on how to appreciate and listen to the music. Presently, recording companies are reluctant to assume this responsibility. George Butler, vice-president and executive producer for CBS Records, addresses this problem as it pertains to jazz in general; however, it is equally applicable to out jazz. He contends:

Frank Lowe playing tenor saxophone at his apartment in Manhattan

Jazz today is caught in a vicious cycle in which radio and recordings have programmed a simple-minded music to appeal to a mass market—the lowest common denominator. In so doing, they have cultivated an audience that is prejudiced against and largely incapable of comprehending anything more substantial than that which is regularly programmed for it. Commercial radio won't play jazz because their audience doesn't like it; the audience doesn't like it because it hasn't been exposed to it enough to begin to understand it.[20]

This raises the issue of who dictates taste in a capitalistic free society. It is easy for large recording companies to claim that they do not shape the tastes of popular culture; instead they are simply trying to satisfy demands that already exist. Thus they are absolved of any moral responsibility. Even if it can be proven that large recording companies do indeed influence popular taste, how does one judge which types of music are too simplistic for public consumption? By attempting to make such judgments, the same freedom that allows out musicians to play what they choose is not extended to include record companies, who decide which artists to record and market.

The solution is for out musicians, writers, and jazz organizations to pressure the major recording companies as well as radio and television networks to give wider public exposure to out jazz and the other substyles of jazz. If these companies begin to promote out jazz in an educational manner, the general public will eventually develop the necessary tools for appreciating it. Such a venture will initially involve some risk and an investment of capital. However, if television saturation can catapult groups like the Monkees to stardom, the promotion of out jazz seems less risky.

s i x

perceiving out music

through metaphor

The specialized language of out musicians provides an important key for understanding how they perceive and act toward their music. For example, out musicians use certain verbal metaphors to reason about particular stylistic features in their music or to draw distinctions between themselves as out performers and mainstream (hard bop) jazz musicians. These metaphors also enable them to organize aesthetic responses toward music. Broadly speaking, metaphors are tools that members of a group use to broaden understanding and build meaningful relationships among different phenomena. More specifically, they are ideas about an event, performance, or experience that are communicated in terms of other ideas.

Origins of Specialized Speech among Out Musicians

Linguistically, except for the use of jargon and metaphoric terms, out musicians use a dialect that does not substantially differ from standard English. Since they are mostly African-American, however, and some have grown up in predominantly urban, African-American, lower-class neighborhoods, their speech betrays these environmental and social influences.[1] In such neighborhoods, it is common to hear culturally based modes of linguistic forms, termed by their users as "rapping," "jive," "shucking," "running it down," "gripping," "copping a plea," "signifying," and "sounding." It is not unusual to hear out musicians, especially those that currently live in such a neighborhood, insert in their speech elements borrowed from these forms to enhance their meaning or to infuse their speech with added color and dynamics. The expression "drop a dime" or "I'm going to drop a dime on my lady," for example, is occasionally used by an out musician who means that he intends to telephone his girlfriend.

Out violinist Billy Bang grew up in Harlem, where he recalls having heard many of these expressions before they filtered into other segments of the dominant society and mass media. About twenty years ago, Bang heard expressions such as "on the case," "out to lunch," and "deep." Eventually, jazz musicians borrowed and adapted these expressions to a variety of new contexts. Today they are even occasionally heard on the radio or television and sometimes are used by other groups including businesspersons or college students.

"Ghettoized" African-Americans prefer to communicate via the aural-oral modes and place a higher value upon these than upon written forms of communication. For instance, gifted with colorful and convincing lines of rhetoric, hustlers become emulated models in urban black ghettoes. Furthermore, African-American ghetto youths commonly engage in storytelling or verbal contests ("playing the dozens"). By doing so, they develop their verbal skills, transmit cultural values, and compete for status.[2]

Some of the expressions of out musicians have filtered down from previous generations of jazz musicians. Initially, jazz musicians borrowed these from a variety of occupational groups with which they came into contact in the urban environment. During Prohibition, for example, jazz musicians often performed in New York City cabarets, which were owned and operated by gangsters, who contributed many such terms. Tenor saxophonist Lester Young gained initial exposure to such expressions when working as a young musician in minstrel shows and carnivals.[3] Subsequently, he borrowed and introduced these terms into the jazz community.

During the 1940s, a large number of establishments on 52nd Street in New York City featured live jazz entertainment. Taking advantage of the large crowds seeking entertainment, pimps, hustlers, and prostitutes found work in the neighborhood. Though their contact with jazz musicians may have been minimal, some interaction and the exchange of new expressions were likely to occur.

The use of metaphors also accompanies a mode of speech in the out group that addresses values and competing claims for status. Its origins may lie in a form of urban African-American speech called rapping. Styles of rapping are individualistic, and the composition of one's audience largely determines the manner and content of delivery. When discussing their music, many out musicians are forthright in instructing listeners of its import or connections to a view of the world. The style of their delivery is emphatic as well as authoritative. Especially in situations where this mode of speech is expected, to do otherwise would betray weakness or the possibility that one's music has little redeeming social value. This verbal approach educates listeners how to perceive and interpret the highly personalized styles of out musicians. Since some degrees of factionalism exist in the out group, a few musicians occasionally use this mode when leveling criticisms against other musicians or to justify the validity of their music. In so doing, they may imbue their speech with verbal metaphors, jargon, and other descriptive terms to strengthen or add color to their argument.

Verbal Expressions among Out Performers

The repertoire of unconventional verbal expressions among out musicians falls into three general categories. The first category includes jargon or a specialized set of technical terms related to performing music or to the lifestyle of jazz musicians. Under this category, one finds terms such as "axe" (musical instrument), "cat" (musician), and "box" (guitar and sometimes piano). Most of these are now shared by the general public and by several jazz groups from different stylistic periods. I will limit my discussion, however, to the remaining two categories. The second category contains expressions used to communicate evaluative or aesthetic responses about music or something or someone in a nonmusical context. The third category consists of out metaphors or metaphoric expressions that contain the word "out"; these have spatial orientations frequently tending upward or outward.

Expressions for Evaluative and Aesthetic Responses

During interviews and conversations with musicians, I have noted the usage of approximately twenty-five expressions whose function enables musicians to offer a critical or aesthetic comment upon a performer or musical performance (see table 5). For any single expression, there is a multitude of different contexts in which it can be used. Many of these expressions are also shared by other groups of jazz musicians, and some are now common among the general public.

Expressions such as "crazy," "terrible," "bad," "cold," "weird," "shit," and "cold-blooded" can be employed as either positive or negative referents to a musical performance or musician, depending upon the context in which they are used and the tone of voice of the user. For example, during a conversation about John Coltrane, alto saxophonist Daniel Carter remarked, "I laughed when I heard Coltrane because he was so *far out* it was beautiful. . . . I mean this *cat* was *crazy*." Using the term in a more conventional manner, one out musician, referring to another performer, commented, "He is too *crazy* to deal with. . . . I'd rather work with musicians who have it together more." The terms "cold" and "cold-blooded" can be used to describe someone's music in a positive manner. For instance, trombonist Michael Keith posits, "Cecil Taylor's piano playing is *cold-blooded* . . . no one else is doing anything like him. He's *out there* in his own world." The trope "shit" may be used broadly as a noun to refer to a musician's style of musical performance. When reflecting upon a recording session in which he participated with Steve Lacy, drummer Dennis Charles remarked, "During one take, Lacy never stopped, he just kept going. He played some *heavy shit*."

Certain expressions such as "on point," "dig," "deep," and "out there" suggest a spatial orientation or direction. For example, having a downward orientation, the terms "dig" and "deep" refer to the act of penetrating the essence of something. Trumpeter Roy Campbell mentions, "If the musicians

Table 5. *Examples of Evaluative or Aesthetic Responses among Out Jazz Musicians (Musical Contexts Only)*

Term	Mode		
	Positive or Negative Connotation	Spatial Orientation	Limited Usage
Crazy (adj)	x		
Terrible (adj)	x		x
Bad (adj)	x		
Cold (adj)	x		
Weird (adj)	x		
Shit (n)	x		
Cold-blooded (adj)	x		
On point (adj)		x	x
Dig (v)			
Deep (adj)		x	
Out there (adj)		x	
Kill (v)			x
Dynamite (n)			x
Daf (adj)			x
Drug (v)			x
Wig me out (v)			x
Out to lunch (adj)			
On the case (v)			x
Happening (adj)			
Smoking (v)			
Hip (adj)			
Doing it (v)			
Tore up (adj)			
Solid (adj)			

are into it and they are bringing the music up to a certain level, I get inspired and say, 'Yeah, I *dig* this.'" Referring to one of John Coltrane's performances, Frank Lowe stated, "When I saw Coltrane play, he was always into some *deep shit*, like some spiritual thing."

"On point" is relatively uncommon among out musicians. I traced the origins of the expression to a single musician, Michael Keith. He likely borrowed it from one of the navigational professions, which use it to indicate that one is correctly following a prescribed course. For Keith, it suggests that during a performance a performer skillfully executes proper technique and succeeds in realizing his or her intent. When talking about the mechanics of a particular performance, bassist Earl Freeman remarked, "It was precise. They played no slobs or slipups. It was *right on point.*"

Other examples of aesthetic and evaluative responses which have limited occurrence among out performers include "kill," "dynamite," "daf," "drug," and "wig me out." For various reasons, some of these terms may be considered dated and inappropriate; others are favored only by a few and have yet to gain wider usage. Many of these terms probably originated first in urban African-American neighborhoods and were eventually picked up by musicians. These terms are all used as positive referents to a musician or musical performance. For example, Milford Graves commented, "Cecil [Taylor] *killed* the other night. I mean he played more *shit* than he could ever play." When reflecting upon the first out performance he ever attended, another musician remarked, "They were playing this music, screaming and ranting and raving; and Lord—I was so *drugged.* I said, 'What? Is that jazz?' "

Two other terms, "out to lunch" and "on the case" (see also "on point" above), are common business terms which out musicians have borrowed. "Out to lunch" usually has a negative connotation, and it is used by out musicians to refer to a musician who is not taking care of business or who is unable to fulfill his or her responsibilities as a musician. One out musician commented, "I tried to get this drummer I liked to do the gig with us, but he went *out to lunch* on me." In contrast, "on the case" (a legal term) has positive connotations. It refers to a musician who is taking care of business or addressing important matters in his or her music without deviation or distraction from set goals. When attempting to make all the preliminary arrangements and necessary contacts for one of his upcoming performances, Michael Keith stated, "I've been *on the case* lately, trying to get this performance I'm doing happening."

Other frequently used terms that convey a positive response to a musical performance or musician include "happening," "smoking," "hip," "doing it," "tore up," and "solid." For example, "solid" has connotations of firmness and substance. Out musicians often use it as an affirmative reply to a question or offer that has been posed. During a conversation between two out performers, one suggested to the other that they do a concert together in the near future. The latter musician replied, "*Solid*." In referring to an especially good performance, musicians might comment that it was "smoking" or it was "hip." They might also suggest that the performers "tore up" or were "doing it."

Orientational Metaphors among Out Jazz Musicians

Orientational metaphors among out performers include out metaphors which have spatial references. "Out of this world" is the root phrase from which variations of out metaphors evolve. Since its origin around 1925, musicians have either shortened, altered, or completely transformed the expression and broadened the parameters of its usage to include many different contexts.[4] Some of the variants of "out of this world" include "far out," "way out," "out of sight," "out," "outside," and "out there." Robert S. Gold posits that these are "escapist terms" that reflect the depressing realities under which African-Americans live.[5] On the contrary, these terms and their relationship to music are important tools for confronting and addressing important social issues. Based upon interviews and conversations with musicians and my observations of numerous contexts in which these phrases were used, the terms "out" and "out there" are relatively recent alterations that seem to be favored more by out musicians than by any other jazz group. In more radically changed versions of "out of this world," the component "out" is dropped and substituted with a related word: "send" (as in "the music *sends* me out of this world"), "gone," "go off," "beyond," and "something else." Related to these (i.e., in the sense that a different spatial orientation is suggested) are the expressions "straight up," "deep," "on," "straight ahead," "shook me down," "on point," "straight down," and "up here."

In the development of jazz, stylistic change is often accompanied by changes in the metaphoric or descriptive terms that musicians use to refer to the most salient qualities of the new style. In other words, when conventional terms fail, metaphors are readily adapted as instinctual and expressive tools for perceiving these aspects of their music. The inspiration for the term "swing" jazz (ca. 1930s) is the peculiar rhythmic treatment (i.e., swing rhythm) that seemed to propel the beat forward and arouse ecstatic emotions among listeners and dancers.[6] The metaphoric referents to this heightened state of arousal were the expressions "send" and "out of this world." Robert S. Gold posits, "The power of musicians of skill to transport is verbalized in *send me*. . . . It is little wonder that swing devotees . . . on the general observations of music as 'heavenly' and 'melody of the spheres,' proclaimed they were sent—propelled by the centrifugal force *out of the world*." [7]

In bebop, the fanciful flights of alto saxophonist Charlie Parker among the extended intervals of the chords in the tunes he performed defy commonplace descriptions. The rhythms of his drummers, furthermore, grew more complex and began to mimic and interact with the rhythmic contours of the lead instruments. Since the term "send" had run its course with swing musicians and lost its novelty as the big band period seriously declined in the 1940s, new aesthetic responses were adopted. These functioned to accentuate innovations and to channel a listener's excitement into a speech mode.

For bebop musicians, the terms "crazy" and "weird" were used. Detractors first used these terms to refer to bebop's fast tempos and jagged melodic lines, which were too abstract for average listeners to comprehend. Parker and his colleagues, reacting to their critics, transformed these expressions into positive aesthetic responses. For example, they might term a laudable solo improvisation by Thelonious Monk as "weird" or "crazy." [8]

In the 1960s, though the terms "crazy" and "weird" survived among out performers, the term "out of this world" resurfaced but in a shortened form. Whereas in the swing period "out of this world" referred to the tension (i.e., swing feeling) between the steady rhythmic pulse and the melody line, "out" and "out there" were developed among out jazz musicians to focus upon features in their music such as the abandonment of a steady, discernible pulse and, in some cases, functional tonality.

Another reason why some expressions such as the swing expression "out of this world" did not survive in their original forms but were shortened to "out of sight" or "way out" in later times was that they were too cumbersome. Jazz musicians favor individuals who communicate meaning "out front," or in a quick and concise manner. They prefer the same concept to be preserved in a shortened form of the expression. Thus "out there" or simply "out" replaced the phrase "out of this world." In purely musical terms these phrases refer to the out style of performing which lies outside the norms of bebop style.

A term that addresses the opposite end of this spatial continuum is "inside." Over the last twenty to thirty years, the term "inside" has been used by both out and bebop musicians to refer mostly to the harmonic approaches to playing chord changes in conventional bebop and to musicians who are proponents of that style. In contrast, the alternative approaches devised by Ornette Coleman, Miles Davis, and Sonny Rollins circumvent the tendencies of chord changes to restrict melodic coherence. By extension, inside also implies the isometric rhythms of bebop. In the early 1960s, drummer Sunny Murray performed with Cecil Taylor in the free-form, collectively improvised approach and evolved a style of playing highly interactive, nonisometric rhythms. Hence, they played "far out" or "out there" (i.e., beyond the chord changes and conventional rhythms).

New linguistic expressions not only signal musical change but also demonstrate among jazz groups the deep bonds between music and speech about music. Furthermore, for many musicians the out metaphors indicate a coherent system of musical, conceptual, and philosophical relationships. They reflect the group's perceptions of the world and music that contrast significantly with those of other jazz groups.

Metaphors as the Building Blocks of Meaning

Two basic premises generally underlie the cognitive functions of metaphors. First, the use of metaphors helps one to perceive something in terms of something else; and thus, second, it creates a new idea for the hearer. Metaphoric expressions often have two separate domains that the listener brings into an interactive relationship.[9] The hearer of the expression "Jones is a tiger on the football field" abstracts a coherent system of concepts from the vehicle "tiger" and superimposes this upon the topic "Jones."[10] The hearer may associate such concepts as ferocity, agility, and strength with the vehicle "tiger" and use these to infer the qualities of the topic "Jones." As a result of this synthesis, a third domain is created to include the new meanings and concepts arrived at by the hearer.[11]

Several functional and grammatical distinctions can be made among different types of metaphors.[12] "Out" metaphors and other orientational metaphors of the out group are organized according to broad polarities, including up-down, in-out, deep-shallow, and so forth. How one feels, for example, is a concept that can be organized in terms of either an "up" or "down" orientation. The expressions "I am feeling up today" and "I feel on top of the world" are derived in part from a general tendency among many groups in the West to view happiness in terms of an upward orientation. Conversely, the expression "I am feeling down today" is consistent with tendencies to associate sadness with a downward orientation.

Orientational metaphors have cultural as well as physical and emotional bases. In the out group, certain culturally defined concepts have both an upward and downward orientation. A kind of spiritual awareness with a downward orientation, for instance, is suggested in the expression "he played some deep shit." This is also consistent in meaning with the term "dig" and the expression "get down," which mean in part to penetrate the essence of a situation or event. Hence, in this usage, spirituality has a downward association. In the out group, the concept of spiritualism also has a more conventional upward orientation as indicated by John Coltrane's LP recording entitled *Ascension* (Impulse A-95).

It is interesting to note that the dominant society and blues musicians associate sadness with a downward orientation, whereas out musicians do not. The blues, for instance, often portrays feelings of futility and hurt due to loneliness, departed lovers, or the wrongdoings of mates. Perhaps because of its secular nature, these feelings are expressed in metaphors which entail a downward orientation. Documented by Paul Oliver (1972), Robert Johnson's lyrics from his blues song "Hell Hound on My Trail" (Vocalian 03623) metaphorically cast the blues as particles that descend from the sky:

I got to keep movinnnn', I got to keep movinnnn',
Blues fallin' down like hail, blues fallin' down like hail,
Mmmmm-mm-mm-mm, blues fallin' down like hail, blues fallin' down
    like hail,
And the days keep on worryin' me, for a hell-hound on my trail,
Hell-hound on my trail, hell-hound on my trail.

In the out group, sadness or unhappiness, however, may be expressed in metaphors whose orientation is outward as opposed to the tendency of the dominant culture and blues singers to organize these downward. An out musician may identify a personally unstable situation and feelings of depression through the expression "everything is *out there*."

In the out group the same metaphor is sometimes used to mean different things in different contexts.[13] The metaphorical expression "out there," for example, can be employed differently in any number of contexts to comment upon an equally indefinite number of things (e.g., a bad or good musical performance, style of dress, an unusual situation). Because of its flexibility, the term's meaning is constantly reshaped from one usage to another in the out group and cannot be considered, in a strict sense, to have a stable or traditional past.[14] It is possible, however, to discern patterns from the various ways in which out musicians use this expression. Over time, out musicians develop a mode of awareness based on how the expression is used by their colleagues. In this manner, they acquire skill and confidence in using the term themselves.

The success of a metaphor in communicating meaning depends on the cognitive abilities of both the user and the hearer. This communicative process involves observation, selection, and interpretation. This point is illustrated by the following actual experience. An experienced out musician A decides to bring a second musician B to participate in a rehearsal that was organized by musician C. Musician A argues that musician B belongs at the rehearsal because he is perfectly suited spiritually, emotionally, and musically to the concepts musicians C and A are working toward. Musician A, furthermore, claims that these notions of collectivism must supersede the formal procedures for organizing rehearsals. To validate his claim, he redefines the purpose of the performance in terms of certain spiritual goals. On the other hand, musician C argues that since he organized the rehearsal, it is his decision whether musician B will participate. Musicians A and C continue to argue heatedly for twenty minutes in the studio. Musician D, a sideman, turns to musician E, another sideman, and says, "This is getting *out there*." Musician E smiles approvingly.

Thus musician D observed a situation that did not fit any of the conventional modes of behavior one sees every day or, for that matter, at rehearsal. He organizes this experience with the selection of an appropriate term "out there" to indicate the incongruity or distance that the logic of the argument has with normal events and expectations. The listener must interpret the expression in relation to the event and to his or her knowledge of the expression from past usages. If the listener achieves a coherence between the two and the use of the expression fits the mode of awareness of the listener, the term is successfully applied to the context and accomplishes its purpose.

Orientational Metaphors in the Out Group

The mode of awareness that enables out musicians to use metaphors in a variety of contexts can be inductively drawn by looking at a number of such examples and the meanings that are communicated. I have observed the usage of the term "out there," for example, in several conversations among musicians that were held in both musical and nonmusical contexts. Table 6 lists examples of the usage of "out there" in musical contexts which fit under

Table 6. *Usages of the Expression "Out There" in Musical Contexts among Out Jazz Musicians*

Reference Domains	Musical Contexts
Suggests certain norms related to a distinct style of musical performance.	"Musicians can't start where Coltrane stopped. Coltrane knew what was happening when he got *out there*. The people who play the *out* music really got to have their thing together." "I have two sets of playing chops. One is for playing inside [bebop] and one is for playing *out*." "Paul Murphy's a drummer who fills a lot of space. He's an action drummer. He stays on it all the time. He keeps the other musicians *out there*."
Refers to certain musicians who perform the *out* style.	"How many trumpet players are *out there* who can last that long and can still play?" "Some musicians like Cecil Taylor and myself are *out there* all the time." "Daniel Carter knows how to take the music *out there*." "I heard Pharoah play *out there*. He played two or three hours nonstop. When the music reached a certain level, you'd feel high."
Refers to a personal feeling, awareness, approach, or ideology about performing.	"When I'm *out there*, my trumpet is like an echo. It sounds magical." "If the music is *out there*, it's like space trying to grasp all the sounds you can possibly make and pass them through your system." "When me and Daniel Carter play, we're free but still connected. Everything is connected. Nothing's just *out there*. There is a reason for all existence."
Refers to a particular performance or the formal elements of music.	"I allow soloists in some of my compositions to go *out*. There is enough structure in the piece for the soloists to work with." "I use a tonal center in many of my compositions. Soloists can take the tonal center *out* and recreate it."

Table 7. *Usages of the Expression "Out There" in Nonmusical Contexts among Out Jazz Musicians*

Reference Domains	Nonmusical Contexts
Refers to an individual, event, or phenomenon in either positive or negative terms.	"Carl Lombard was *out there*. He was in his own world. He used to set up his office in Nathan's Delicatessen on Broadway Avenue." "My old lady tells me I should get a job. The rent is due, and I lost my gig. My *shit* is really *out there*."
Refers to the public domain.	"I don't like the term black music. It's racist. It jumped *out there* in the 1960s. I do not know if it was the musicians or writers who did it." "It's important to get the music *out there*. Then people will know what you are doing." "Avant-garde musicians today are getting their materials and ideas second-hand. There were only a few innovative horn players really got their shit *out there*."

four general reference domains.[15] For example, "out there" can refer to unique aspects of a musical performance, certain musicians, attitudes about performing, and certain formal elements of music. Table 7 lists examples of the usage of "out there" in nonmusical contexts which fall under two reference domains. These are individuals or events and everything and everyone outside the out group.

Since the meaning of orientational metaphors is dependent upon their relationships with other orientational metaphors, "out there" needs to be considered alongside its antonym "inside," another commonly used metaphor among jazz musicians. Table 8 lists three reference domains for its usage, including norms related to a distinct style of performance (i.e., one in which solos and themes are shaped according to an accompanying chord progression), certain musicians who perform the inside (i.e., hard bop) style, and a particular performance event. In many instances, the term "inside" was used to differentiate the out group from the hard bop group who either resented the newcomers or simply wanted to reinforce feelings of ingroup solidarity. As with the expression "out there," "inside" is both an orientational and container metaphor. Container metaphors lend a bounded physical space to a style of musical performance that has certain prescribed ele-

Table 8. *Usages of the Expression "Inside" among Out Jazz Musicians*

Reference Domains	Contexts
Suggests certain norms related to a distinct style of musical performance (e.g., hard bop).	"*Inside* refers to music that has changes whereas *outside* is the music that goes beyond." "Somebody's tone or whatever can go *outside* the *shit* and still be *inside.*"
Refers to certain musicians who perform the *inside* style.	"A lot of players have come *inside*, back to the tradition. They feel that the tradition is more valid." "Dewey Johnson played *inside* at the jam session." "Cecil Taylor and Ornette Coleman did their thing *outside* the tradition from the start, whereas John Coltrane started *inside* and then went *out.*"
Refers to a particular performance event.	"The *shit* they are doing on the street is mostly *inside.*"

ments of form, rhythm, harmony, meter, and melody. A key figure in the out jazz scene during the 1960s, tenor saxophonist Pharoah Sanders characterizes the distinction between "inside" and "outside":

> When I play, I try to adjust myself to the group, and I don't think much about whether the music is conventional or not. If the others go "outside," play "free," I go out there, too. If I tried to play too differently from the rest of the group, it seems to me I would be taking the other musician's [*sic*] energy away from them. I still want to play my own way. But I wouldn't want to play with anybody that I couldn't please with the way I play. . . .
>
> Naturally, you have elements of music and musical skills to work with, but once you've got those down, I think you should go after feelings. If you try to be too intellectual about it, the music becomes too mechanical. It seems that for me, the more I play "inside," inside the chords and the tune, the more I want to play "outside," and free. But also, the more I play "outside" the more I want to play "inside," too. I'm trying to get a balance in my music. A lot of cats play "out" to start with. But if I, myself, start off playing "inside" and then let the spirit take over, wherever it goes, it seems better to me.[16]

Both out and bebop musicians are able to distinguish other musicians according to this dichotomy. Musicians who consistently incorporate many of the conventional elements of hard bop (i.e., chord changes, isometric rhythms, theme-variation-theme format, and twelve-bar and thirty-two-bar forms) in their performance are said to be "inside." Sometimes a musician who normally plays inside may occasionally deviate from these conventions and temporarily journey "out there." During a live performance, Charles Tyler, for example, might play three or four precomposed tunes with chord changes and then introduce a piece based mostly on collective improvisation without a preconceived harmonic framework. Conversely, Frank Lowe, who has made a name by performing the "out" style, may occasionally utilize the conventions of bebop and momentarily play "inside."

Whereas many out musicians may on occasion play inside, Cecil Taylor is one of the few out musicians who play strictly out; that is, he never reverts to using conventional elements of hard bop in his performances. For nearly thirty years, Taylor has performed in this manner, and he has evolved an unusual personality that is both unpredictable and coherent with his music. Thus some of his peers consider him so far out there that he is "in," no matter what he plays or how he plays it (see the small circle in figure 6). In this sense, he is the consummate out performer. Multiple instrumentalist Ken McIntyre, who has worked with Taylor, describes him as one whose "persona is an extension of his music."[17] Since Taylor is an uncompromising artist, his music always stems from his deepest motivations.

Figure 6 graphically illustrates the spatial relationships among "inside," "outside," and other related terms. It also delineates stylistic boundaries that separate out concepts from those of mainstream jazz. The "inside" styles are distinguished from those that are "out there" by the larger circle, which contains terms whose verbal referents are related to the inside styles, such as bebop. A forward-moving horizontal orientation, for example, is suggested by the term "straight ahead." In one sense, this expression emphasizes the observance of the stylistic devices of hard bop. In a different sense, however, it can also mean moving ahead undeviatingly, regardless of whether one is playing hard bop or out.

"Straight ahead" is derived from the association of "nondeviation" with a straight orientation. "Straight up," however, is derived from the association of "nondeviation" with an upward-moving orientation. This orientation is based upon out styles of performing and attitudes. According to an out musician who chooses to remain anonymous, "straight up" is used to

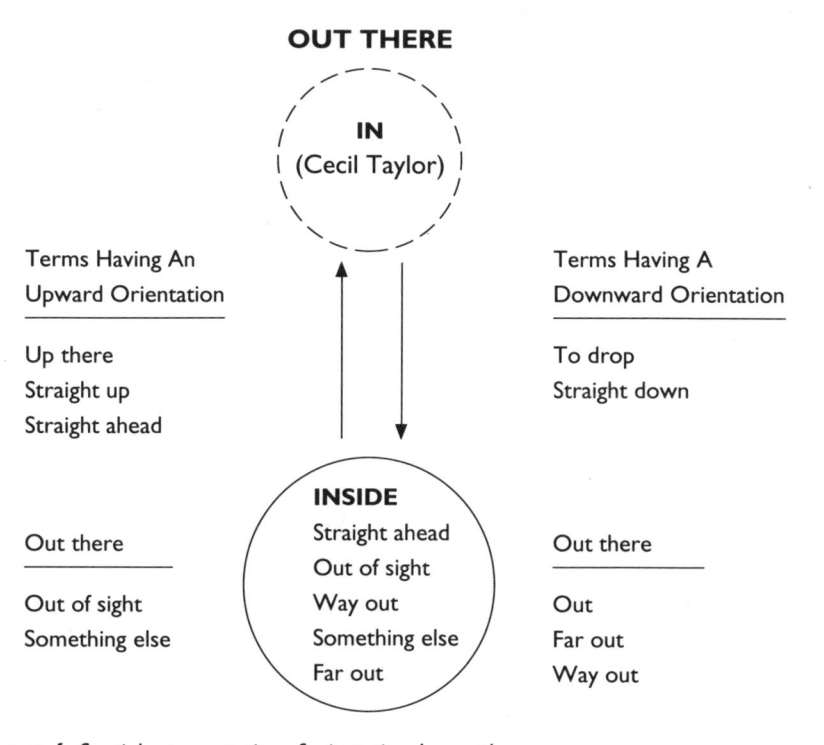

OUT THERE

IN
(Cecil Taylor)

Terms Having An
Upward Orientation

Up there
Straight up
Straight ahead

Terms Having A
Downward Orientation

To drop
Straight down

Out there

Out of sight
Something else

INSIDE
Straight ahead
Out of sight
Way out
Something else
Far out

Out there

Out
Far out
Way out

Figure 6. *Spatial representation of orientational metaphors among the hard bop and out jazz groups*

distinguish among out musicians who adapt more commercially marketable musical styles, on the one hand, and those who remain unaffected by the lure of success and continue to perform pure out music, on the other: "Oliver Lake is an important musician, but now he is making a lot of money with [his funk group] Jump Up. I see Ornette [Coleman] into this thing and Blood Ulmer as well. I don't want nothing to do with that thing. I want to go straight up, one way." [18]

An up-down continuum is suggested in figure 6. Whereas out musicians' terms such as "up there" and "straight up" have an upward orientation, expressions like "to drop" and "straight down" imply a downward orientation. To "drop" on someone refers to a situation when features in the performance style of a highly respected innovator are emulated by or passed along to other performers in the ranks. When describing the development of out music in the early 1960s, drummer Milford Graves remarked that several innovators, including Albert Ayler, Archie Shepp, Pharoah Sanders, McCoy Tyner, and Ornette Coleman, all "dropped" on musicians. [19] In other words, those musicians who were "dropped" on learned from the innovators.

Additional evidence of a vertical design is rooted in the more conventional performance practices (e.g., the vertical stacking of chord tones) of the inside styles and how out musicians may approach these. Though most out performers can play in a variety of different styles, trumpeter Earl Cross remarks that they prefer to play melodic lines based "on top of the changes" instead of using notes from the lower degrees (e.g., the first, second, and third degrees of the chord).[20] Playing on top of the changes increases a musician's options for selecting tonal material to compose his or her melodic lines and the potential for dissonances to emerge. It was Charlie Parker's exploration of the upper or extended range of tones of a chord that partly revitalized jazz in the 1940s. Perhaps Cross would agree that Parker is out even in today's sense of the expression.

Venturing "straight up," however, is not without risks. Alto saxophonist Daniel Carter considers: "Some of them, like Frank Lowe, connect with the earlier traditions of jazz. I sometimes just go straight up and find I have no solid footing."[21] These comments are echoed by Frank Lowe, who believes that when a performance goes completely "out" it loses purpose. One who performs without at least some structure risks the onset of monotony. Lowe also observes that those who play out successfully have a strong background in harmonic theory, regardless if they choose to use it or not.[22]

Upward Orientation and Performing Out

It has been noted that certain orientational metaphors suggest ways in which some out performers observe and draw stylistic (musical), linguistic, and ideological boundaries in regard to out jazz groups and the dominant society. To the observer, these boundaries lay mostly dormant and unnoticed in the day-to-day affairs of the musicians. On occasion, however, when intergroup conflict or tension arises, they are reinforced as strategies for coping and thus become more perceptible.

I observed the occurrence of this situation during a performance by Coldlight, a group of out performers. The center of controversy was the drummer, who shall remain anonymous. During the performance, he was unable to provide the correct kind of rhythmic accompaniment for the other instrumentalists, who later said they felt stifled and were unable to attain their desired goals. During the performance, listeners could sense conflict and the fact that little was "happening" in the music. Following the performance, the musicians discussed possible reasons why the music never attained satisfactory levels of interaction. In their speech, they frequently inserted orientational phrases to address abstract musically related events that took place in the performance.

The performance occurred in January 1984 at the nightclub 8BC and featured Daniel Carter, alto saxophone; Dewey Johnson, trumpet; a bass player (name unknown); and the drummer. A few days prior to the performance, I attended the group's rehearsal. The performers did not use any precomposed materials; from the short time in which they removed instruments from their cases, the musicians seemed to ease naturally into playing them in the free-form, collectively improvised approach. They played in this manner for about forty-five minutes. Afterward, discussions concentrated upon the numerous moments when some unpredictable or spontaneous "flash" occurred in the music. Carter, who organized the rehearsal, seemed satisfied with the performances of the musicians and was confident all would go well for the performance.

During the night of the performance, the musicians followed virtually the same format. Carter emerged from stage right playing the alto saxophone, as though he had been playing it en route to the nightclub. The other musicians soon followed. Together, the group performed in the free-form, collectively improvised style for approximately fifty minutes. But the drummer, who had used a nonisometric rhythm and a more implicit mode of stating the beats during rehearsal, reverted to isometric meters of four beats to the measure during the performance. In effect, the drummer awkwardly introduced a standard rock and roll rhythm that contrasted negatively with the other performers.

A few days after the performance, I invited everyone, except the drummer, up to my apartment to listen to a recording of the performance and attempt to weed out the problems:

> [Carter:] There is much more tension in the horns than what is being dealt with by the drums. There is no call-and-response. You are not getting any energy from the cat. [Johnson:] There is no "bottom" to it . . . the drummer is "gone." He is playing the stuff too even.
> . . . [Carter:] The music that night was the result of the struggle with this drummer. [Johnson:] It makes you play stuff you don't want to do

but you do it with 100 percent conviction. It seems like we overpow-
ered the rhythm section. That is hard to do. It is like I'm looking high
off from a window and saying when you all going to come "up here."

. . . [Carter:] I was screaming [on my instrument] and there was no
bottom; the drummer let it fall. [Johnson:] You need a background to
get the sound "up there."[23]

The musicians used several orientational metaphors, including "up here,"
"up there," and "bottom," to describe the problems encountered by the lead
instruments when playing against the rock and roll rhythms of the drummer. They felt that the drummer was unable to lend adequate support to the
high degrees of interaction and emotion that the horn players attempted to
exhibit. Mostly inexperienced in performing in out contexts, he perhaps
became nervous during the performance and fell back upon more familiar
approaches. This inhibited the other players from blending their approaches
into the desired textures.

According to the perceived spatialization chart in figure 6, a successful
performance in the free-form, collectively improvised approach has an "upward" or "outside" orientation (e.g., "the musicians were *up there*" or "the
music got *out there*"). During the performance, Johnson claimed that the
drummer failed in his responsibility to generate enough interaction. As a
result, the "bottom," or foundation, of the music collapsed. Musicians
struggled and the system momentarily failed.

This analysis draws attention to certain roles and stylistic expectations
for the drummer in out jazz settings. A drummer should play in a more fluid,
implied style and rely less on isometric rhythmic patterns. Introducing isometric beats into this performance suggested to the lead instruments no alternative directions to explore other than those conventionally associated
with music based on these rhythmic patterns. The predicament remained
unresolved throughout the performance.[24]

seven

communicating out worldviews

through music

One of the most revealing aspects of out jazz is its capacity to communicate certain meanings to listeners. For example, many listeners to John Coltrane's music during the mid-1960s interpreted both social and spiritual messages. Furthermore, a small number of out jazz musicians who consider New York City to be a hostile environment engage music as a tool for building meaningful relationships among the disparate phenomena they encounter in urban living.

Because such claims are difficult to prove, they magnify the issue of where meaning in out jazz resides. Is meaning in out jazz referential in the sense that it communicates or symbolizes something other than itself? Or is the meaning of out jazz strictly intrinsic and thus limited only to the ways in which the musicians organize its component parts?[1] If the latter is true, how do performances of out jazz in the free-form, collectively improvised approach render any meaning to the listener, especially since they often lack discernible rhythmic, harmonic, or melodic patterns?

Most Western scholars and listeners tend to agree that all types of music have at least some degree of referential value, especially when considering their effect upon emotions. For instance, listeners in the West commonly select music based on its "soothing" or "happy" character. This raises the issue of whether the music contains "soothingness" or "happiness," which transfers to the listener as a physical response, or if listeners simply perceive these qualities on the cognitive level.

Either case is difficult to prove, since responses to the same musical passage may likely differ from one listener to another. Hence, the referential meaning of music is highly subjective and resistant to most empirical methods of testing. Consequently, Western music theorists generally downplay its importance in favor of the intrinsic domain, which is more rationally based.[2]

Intrinsic Meaning in Music

Concerned mostly with the intrinsic aspects of music, Western music theorists have sought to link the origins of certain components of music to natural law. As early as the fifth century B.C.E., Pythagoras and the Pythagoreans proposed that certain consonant pitch intervals are products of natural law, which they attempted to reveal systematically and mathematically. Thus the Pythagoreans, who equated truth with number, perceived pitch intervals as physical manifestations of numerical order.[3]

Fascination over the components of music and their natural origins continued into the eighteenth century, when theorist Jean Philippe Rameau posited that the laws of harmony mimic the laws of nature and the physics of sound. Rameau concluded that certain chords function well harmonically because they respond to natural law. As proof, he demonstrated that the individual pitches of a major triad also appear as partials of a vibrating string.[4]

However, because these approaches tend to isolate the rudimentary components of music, they neglect the context in which composers combine them into larger and more complex structures, constituting complete musical works.[5] In recent times, theorists have addressed this problem, and they have devised suitable methods for analyzing the form of a musical work and how the composer develops major and minor themes.[6] For instance, in the early twentieth century, Austrian theorist Heinrich Schenker evolved a sophisticated model for revealing tonal patterns that appear in a variety of altered forms throughout a given work. However, the more grand and sophisticated these models become, the more likely they are to yield different interpretations in the hands of different users. Furthermore, such models fail to reflect how the average listener, who lacks such specialized training, perceives the same musical work.[7]

Musical Expectations and the Intrinsic Value of Music

In the West, identifying form and function in music constitutes one's musical expectations. These expectations develop through repeated exposure formally and informally to various sound patterns and functional relationships among different tones.[8] However, the expectations of the average listener, who as a child likely had few if any years of formal music training, are generally insufficient to handle complex forms of music.

Suppose that music can be reduced to a continuum where it is said to be simple or redundant on one end and complex or difficult on the other. An example of complex music is the free-form, collectively improvised approach to playing out, in which form often becomes an unstable variable. Hence, the dense, random sound patterns that this approach produces confront the listener's expectations, which are based upon the principles of Western functional tonality. Thus for the listener, the music reaches a high level of complexity or unpredictability.

In contrast, consider the level of predictability in a nursery song such as "Mary Had a Little Lamb." Because of its limited number of tones, this song is noncomplex and mostly predictable to the average Western listener, especially since the role of the tonic is very discernible within the melody. Though the two examples considered above are extreme, the listener's reaction to each is the same. High levels of redundancy as well as unpredictability predispose the listener to boredom. Because out jazz exceeds certain boundaries or expectations, the listener fails to grasp any rational underlying stylistic norms.[9]

However, a few listeners may be compelled to utilize the cognitive processes of reflection and learning in order to understand how their expectations may have been disturbed by the free-form, collectively improvised approach.[10] In turn, this engenders the possibility for listeners to imagine meanings for out jazz on the referential level. For example, some may view the music as a symbolic alternative to Western modes of rational thinking and expression.

Referential Meaning in Music

The communication of referential meaning in out jazz involves the musician or composer (encoder), the listener (decoder), and the message. All three interact in specific contexts that can range from listening to a live performance to listening to an LP recording. When musicians transform messages into sound patterns, it is called encoding, whereas the task of interpreting or decoding messages is subsumed by the listener.[11]

This model of communication is especially helpful in gauging certain types of referential meaning in programmatic music, written to depict nonmusical ideas, images, or emotions. For instance, Haydn's *The Creation* utilizes unpredictable modulations in the harmony to communicate the notion of primeval chaos to the listener. As is often the case with programmatic music, the composer usually indicates the mood or image of the work with a suggestive title or preface. Thus communication is facilitated when listeners are aware beforehand of the composer's intent to encode his or her music with certain messages.

However, what happens when the listener is unaware of the intent of the composer? For instance, few out jazz performers announce beforehand to their audience what specific emotions they intend to communicate through their music. Can an out performer encode music with anger, perform it, and cause the listener to experience this emotion, even though the performer's intent is unknown?[12]

Music philosopher Peter Kivy argues that music is not like a drug that a composer can inject into the listener in order to produce a desired physiological or emotional response.[13] Though music cannot stimulate a prescribed physiological response in the listener, music can represent certain emotions that listeners identify with and respond to on the cognitive level.

This explains why a group of listeners to music that is supposedly represen-
tative of anger do not grow angry or engage in fistfights among themselves.

This argument does not preclude the possibility that in certain well-
defined contexts listeners to out jazz can react emotionally based upon how
they perceive the music symbolically. Consider a listener who believes out
jazz to be an expression of protest. He attends a performance by a musician
who in a recently published interview expressed anger over the poor working conditions under which out musicians continually perform. By reading
the interview prior to attending the performer's concert, the listener is perhaps predisposed to associate the music with sociopolitical ideas or even
personal experiences in which racism had figured. During the performance,
these associations may become so vivid in the listener's mind that they trigger anger. However, the associations the listener makes between the music
and his personal experiences are a cognitive response leading to an emotional one, in which case the music remains an indirect factor.

This illustrates that the listening experience cannot be limited only to the
intrinsic domain. It is a multifaceted experience, involving both the perception of form and function as well as the symbolic transformation of human
feelings. In the case of out jazz, the listening experience further incorporates
the interaction of one's musical expectations with one's beliefs about the
world.

Worldview

The belief that music has the capacity to communicate and to perform other
meaningful functions (e.g., healing) is not exclusive to out jazz musicians.
In fact, it is common among a number of non-Western groups. For example,
in Indian music theory, certain *ragas* are classified according to specific
moods they may evoke.[14] Furthermore, the Pacific Northwest Indians accept
the notion that supernatural power resides in humans and nature, and music
mediates significant links between the two.[15] In the 1920s, some Americans
attributed the cause of a suicide to an evil power which they believed to be
inherent in jazz.[16]

Referential beliefs about the power of music and one's musical expectations form part of a coherent system of beliefs and attitudes often termed
worldview. One's worldview includes notions of time, the relationship of
the self to the universe, and causal relationships involving human beings,

society, nature, and the supernatural. Worldviews express our universal need to impose order and meaning upon an otherwise chaotic world. Clifford Geertz comments,

> Between the approved style of life [ethos] and the assumed structure of reality [worldview], there is conceived to be a simple and fundamental congruence such that they complete one another and lend one another meaning.
>
> . . . For the Navaho, an ethic prizing calm deliberateness, untiring persistence, and dignified caution complements an image of nature as tremendously powerful, and mechanically regular, and highly dangerous.[17]

Worldviews are individually specific. Even when members of a particular group are exposed to the same worldview through learning and observation, each will likely develop a slightly different outlook toward it that reflects their cultural experience.

Though out jazz musicians have grown up in a culture that supports a rational and empirical worldview, some have evolved intricate and coherent worldviews in which the power and communicative function of music are central themes. In the styles of musical performance among the following out performers, the high levels of unpredictability and de-emphasis on form play key symbolic roles in conveying certain aspects of the performer's worldview to listeners.

Spirituality and the "Universe View" of Sun Ra

In May 1914, Sun Ra was born as Herman ("Sonny") Blount in Birmingham, Alabama. He grew up near Birmingham, where he led his own band in high school. After graduating, Sun Ra attended Alabama A & M University and majored in music education. After moving to Chicago, Sun Ra began to work as an arranger and pianist in Fletcher Henderson's band. In the mid-1950s, Sun Ra formed his own band called the Myth-Science (or Solar) Arkestra. In the early 1960s, Sun Ra moved the Arkestra to New York. The band gained notoriety after performing in Cecil Taylor's and Bill Dixon's "October Revolution in Jazz" concert. Since then, Sun Ra and his Arkestra have continued to record and tour the world, performing in Egypt, Europe, and other countries.

Sun Ra is the first out musician to fuse a spiritual awareness with his worldview and style of musical performance, which he says he began to do around 1949 or 1950. The underlying theme in Sun Ra's metaphysics is the exploration of the cosmos through the mediums of music, the imagination, or other means; for instance, Sun Ra claims to practice astral projection.

Sun Ra's perspective of the cosmos does not center around the Earth. Instead, Sun Ra claims Saturn as his birthplace, and he envisions the Earth as one planet among several that he has visited in the universe. Thus it is perhaps more fitting to refer to Sun Ra's worldview as a "universe view."

Sun Ra sees himself as a liminal figure. As a child, Sun Ra's experiences differed from those that influenced the growth and development of most other children, and he did not internalize the same values. Sun Ra has evolved a unique wisdom and perspective on society which he links to a vision of the cosmos. He explains,

> I never been part of the planet, I've been isolated from a child away from it. Right in the midst of everything and not being a part of it. Them troubles people got, prejudices and all that, I didn't know a thing about it, till I got to be about 14 years old. . . . That's the kind of mind or spirit I have, it's not programmed—from the family, from the church, from the schools, from the government. I don't have a programmed mind. . . . I started to put in the music what I know is going to be the future of humanity. I've always played about space.[18]

Sun Ra is like other figures whose roles in society are never fully integrated. For example, medieval court jesters and shamans remain immune to the values and norms that shape the perceptions of others and may perceive social realities much differently. Because they are not fully integrated into society, they are free to apply nontraditional courses of thinking to a variety of issues. Hence, kings sometimes sought the advice of court jesters on political and social matters.

As a visitor from other planets, Sun Ra offers constructive criticism and advice for those living on Earth. He suggests that we are too caught up in mundane worldly matters (e.g., politics and drugs) which have little meaning when viewed in relation to events in the universe. According to Sun Ra, we should strive more to explore our spiritual side through music, which effectively builds happiness and meaning. Sun Ra professes:

> I belong to the Angel race. . . . You got terrestrials, people who only deal on the earthly plane, thinking earthly and doin' things earthly and

nothin' else. But the Angel race, the celestial beings, can conceive of
Earth beings and also directly communicate with other types of beings.
Earth people are just here, that's all. They need to be enlightened on
certain things. They're just concerned with eatin' and sleepin' and sex
and dope and politics and religion and philosophy. . . . Angels like their
minds and spirits to take wings. They're always movin' forward. . . .
The point is, dealin' with things that does keep people alive and one of
the things that keeps people alive is happiness and music is happiness.[19]

While performing live, Sun Ra communicates his metaphysics through
music using a multimedia approach. Depending on where Sun Ra claims to
be during his space and time travels, the musicians don the appropriate
attire. For instance, they may dress in garb resembling a cast of space ex-
plorers in a futuristic science fiction film. Sun Ra may also use a film projec-
tor to show images of space on a screen near the stage. Sun Ra adds,

Some of the things I have spoken concerning it may sound impossible,
and I realize that, so at some performances I use lights and props and
film projections, so that the people can see as well as hear the sound-
image-impression of everything. . . . This music is of the realm of the
alter-destiny. In order to develop it, I had to separate myself from the
world. Such a state of being has its untold splendors. It is something no
one can ever take away from one.[20]

The titles that Sun Ra gives to his compositions also refer to aspects of
his travels through the universe. For instance, his LP recording *Live at Montreux* (Inncr City IC-1039) includes titles such as "For the Sunrise," "On
Sound Infinity Spheres," and "Gods of the Thunder Realm." Sun Ra's music
is programmatic in the sense that listeners likely connect aspects of the music to images of space. Many of the compositions on *Live at Montreux* are
performed using the free-form, collectively improvised approach. The dense
and atonal sound clusters that often result can easily suggest images to the
listener, including asteroid showers or the type of music one might hear on
Mars (assuming Martians exist and have an affinity for music).

During live performances, Sun Ra might perform a piece in the free-form,
collectively improvised approach and follow this with a standard tune arranged for a big band, such as Billy Strayhorn's "Take the 'A' Train." The
performance of standard tunes might seem inconsistent with designing music that is coherent with the theme of space travel. Sun Ra resolves this

inconsistency when he explains his transition from playing space music to playing intergalactic music.

> Intergalactic music concerns the music of the galaxies. It concerns intergalactic thought and intergalactic travel, so it is of the realm of the impossible. That is where I found myself, and that is why earlier I called the ensemble "Myth-Science Arkestra." . . . The intergalactic music is of the precision-discipline order of things. It includes free-form, but that is because it includes everything in its proper place, or improper place, if there is a need for it.[21]

Spirituality and the Music of John Coltrane

John Coltrane (1926–1967) was born in Hamlet, North Carolina. He grew up in High Point, North Carolina, where he began to play the alto saxophone around the age of fifteen. While performing with Eddie ("Cleanhead") Vinson from 1947 to 1948, Coltrane switched to the tenor sax. After leaving Vinson's band, Coltrane performed in a variety of bands with Dizzy Gillespie, Earl Bostic, and Johnny Hodges. From 1955 to 1957, he gained much notoriety as a sideman in Miles Davis's quintet, which included Red Garland, Paul Chambers, and Philly Joe Jones. In the late 1950s, Coltrane performed in Thelonious Monk's quartet, and he rejoined Miles Davis in various quintet and sextet settings.

By 1960 Coltrane had established himself as the premier tenor saxophonist in jazz. About this time, he formed his own quartet, which included pianist McCoy Tyner, drummer Elvin Jones, and bassist Jimmie Garrison, who joined in 1961. During the early and mid-1960s, other seminal musicians, including Pharoah Sanders, Eric Dolphy, Roy Haynes, and Rashied Ali, intermittently played in the band.

Throughout the 1950s, Coltrane struggled with his addictions to alcohol and drugs. However, shortly after leaving Miles Davis's group in 1960, he overcame these problems. To fill the void that drugs had left in his life, Coltrane vigorously sought to develop himself spiritually. Multi-instrumentalist John Gilmore, a member of Sun Ra's Arkestra, claims that Sun Ra was the main impetus behind Coltrane's spiritual transformation. Sometime in the late 1950s, Sun Ra and Coltrane met. Gilmore recalls:

> Now Pat Patrick introduced Trane to Sun Ra and to Sun Ra's material—his poetry, philosophy—and to his records. That's how Trane

managed to kick his habit. He heard our records and was given this philosophy which Sun Ra was printing on pamphlets . . . and Trane got these and got these records and three months later he quit Miles and that's when his sound started booming through.[22]

In listening to John Coltrane's music of the mid-1960s, many of Coltrane's colleagues began to interpret notions of spirituality and transcendence of social and musical norms.[23] Drummer Billy Hart comments, "John was deeply religious, he always had a religious attitude. I think this affected his playing . . . that kind of inspiration is so rewarding, so satisfying. That's what I get from him."[24] Drummer Freddie Waits also remarks, "Bennie Maupin took me to hear John. . . . after hearing the band, it was just incredible. It completely turned me around, musically and spiritually. I walked out almost crying."[25]

During this period in his career, Coltrane explored free-form, collective improvisation. Because of its dense sound textures and lack of predictability, this approach commanded considerable impact upon listeners' visual and auditory senses as well as their perceptual orientations. Charles Ellison observes: "When Coltrane's message reaches a person, he is obviously affected. He begins to reject actions and thoughts detrimental to mankind and starts to direct his energies toward the betterment of human conditions. When a whole mass of individual people thinks this way, the social strength of music is very obvious."[26]

To understand how Coltrane's music was heavily coded with symbolic information, it is useful to pry a little deeper into Coltrane's motivations that may have inspired his view of the world and music. One line of thought to consider is Coltrane's social philosophy. In the context of the civil rights movement of the 1960s, Coltrane's beliefs about racial issues, American social democracy, and the social and cultural development of African-Americans are organized around the central attitude of brotherhood. Coltrane studied the teachings of civil rights leaders such as Martin Luther King, Jr., who in the 1960s professed the notion of brotherhood among all people, regardless of race, as the new African-American social philosophy. Underlying this nonmilitant philosophy is the need for each person to develop enough inner strength and spirituality to rise above prejudicial boundaries.[27]

For Coltrane, these beliefs were translated to action in the musical domain. Along with his need to transcend racial boundaries, Coltrane sought avenues of performing music that extend beyond the stylistic limits of conventional jazz. For example, in the mid-1960s he experimented with a style of performing on the tenor saxophone that streamed together rapidly played notes. Coltrane embellished this approach with devices such as sudden shifts to the extreme registers of the instrument, split tones or multiphonics, growls, squeaks, and squawks.[28]

Coltrane's worldview also incorporated spiritual and religious concerns. These are attributable not only to the influence of Martin Luther King, Jr., but also to his maternal grandfather, who was a preacher. Furthermore, it is likely that Coltrane sought religion and meditation as sources of strength in order to abandon the vices (alcohol and drugs) that plagued his life in the 1950s.

If Coltrane did in fact encode his music with the notions of brotherhood, transcendence of musical and social norms, and spirituality, how were listeners able to decode these messages on the cognitive level? Perhaps for some listeners, the decoding process for music works much like the way in which humans interpret verbal or literary metaphors. One who hears the remark, for instance, that "life is a bed of roses" begins to superimpose the physical characteristics of a bed of roses upon certain features of life to produce an inferred meaning. Since the hearer may envisage a colorful, well-kept garden of blossoming rosebuds, the new meaning that is created is the idea that life is basically beautiful and problem-free.[29] In like manner, listeners who reflect upon Coltrane's music may superimpose on it bits of information which they may gather from written sources (e.g., interviews with musicians in periodicals, titles of compositions, and so forth) in order to infer a causal relationship between the social and musical.

For example, consider the titles of some of Coltrane's recordings, like "India," *Meditations*, and *Om*. Though these suggest an Eastern spiritual or religious theme, the recordings do not reflect any attempt on Coltrane's part to incorporate specific features of Eastern religious music to which the titles allude. *Meditations* (Impulse AS-9110) and "India" (MCA 5887), for instance, are predominantly performed using Western instruments. Coltrane's collectively improvised approach, furthermore, is dissimilar to any of the religious, folk, or classical music of India's various ethnic and religious groups. Perhaps the only viable reference to these musics is Coltrane's broadly applied modal approach, though traditional observances of modes in the different regions of the Near East and India differ considerably from Coltrane's adaptation of these as highly flexible compositional devices. In addition, other compositions that Coltrane performed during his "spiritual" period such as "Naima" or "My Favorite Things" (Impulse A-9124), a Rodgers and Hammerstein show tune, suggest little connection with spiritual matters.

Though it may appear that some of the titles of Coltrane's compositions may simply refer superficially to those cultures which cultivate spiritual awareness, there is one referent in the music whose potential to communicate information can be isolated. This is the manner in which Coltrane applies collective improvisation. For example, in his recording of *Ascension*, performers are not bound to traditional expectations that accompany the distinction in most styles of jazz between lead and accompaniment roles. In fact, the roles among performers in *Ascension* are minimally differentiated. Musicians are required only to play in the prescribed modes while occasionally observing either ascending or descending melodic contours. Chord changes and discernible melodies are lacking. During a performance, this approach enables improvisers to blend collectively tones and phrases to a degree in which dense textures of sound result. Such a highly interactive approach enables soloists and improvisers to fuse their emotions and personalities more effectively; hence, egos become undifferentiated.[30]

Pharoah Sanders, who played tenor saxophone on *Ascension*, recalls that Coltrane's approach to organizing collective improvisation did in fact lead to feelings of spirituality and communality among the performers.[31] Like Coltrane, Sanders is deeply religious (he is a follower of the Islamic faith) and employs musical performance as a means of achieving spiritual awareness. Thus Sanders was ideally suited to help carry out Coltrane's intentions on *Ascension*.

In the case of Coltrane, it remains to be seen just how much of the aural components of the music alone can convey to listeners the abstract notions of spirituality. Not all listeners superimpose the social upon the musical in order to arrive at a message. Those who do are likely to be familiar with Coltrane's personal and social philosophy, which they may have read about in a variety of printed sources. To these listeners, therefore, Coltrane's approaches to energy playing, collective improvisation, and the nondifferentiation of performers' roles during performance are coherent with his view of transcending social and musical boundaries. In addition, first-hand observers describe the powerful physical energy with which Coltrane infused his performances. This visual cue is congruent with his personal interest in developing inner strength.

Other listeners to *Ascension* who are less knowledgeable of Coltrane's background or whose expectations are ill suited to gauge the levels of integration among the performers, especially without the aid of visual cues, will predictably be confused. I recently conducted a series of tests with a large number of college students who were taking one of my introductory courses on jazz. The majority of them had little formal musical training and were majoring in areas other than music. The purpose was to measure students' abilities to perceive significant changes in texture in a free-form, collectively improvised jazz performance. Preliminary results indicate that students were unable to recognize moments in the performance which the musicians, having afterward seen and listened to a videotape of the performance, claimed were climactic, that is, in the sense that peak levels of excitement and interaction were attained.[32]

On the contextual level, the problem of communication is compounded by the fact that musicians are often hired to perform over several consecutive nights. As is the case with most performers, off nights occur, and musicians may wish only to end the performance early. Thus it is hardly reasonable to assume that Coltrane encoded the same tunes with the same symbolic information each time they were performed.

Out Worldviews and the Didactic Function of Music

The attitude that music contains the power to influence the perceptions and views of the world among its listeners is cultivated by bassist William Parker, trumpeter Dewey Johnson, and alto saxophonist Daniel Carter. They represent only a small cross section of the out group who share similar worldviews and whose styles of musical performance are closely related.

In the worldviews of these performers, music is the primary ingredient that transfers meaning across several nonmusical domains of day-to-day living. It links together such things as family, perceptions of the local urban environment, relationships with other people, and sociopolitical attitudes. Like African societies, which tend to be communal and highly integrated, out musicians strive to connect the disparate parts of day-to-day experience through music. In this manner, an effective buffer is raised against feelings of anomie and alienation that commonly accompany urban living.

The three musicians attribute music ultimately to a supernatural source which affects the way in which their ethical beliefs are organized. For these out musicians, financial gain is not a primary motivation for performing. In fact, they would be content to avoid completely the business of music if they did not have to worry about earning a living. Because of a long history of conflicting interests, bound up in the roles of performers and representatives of the entertainment industries, the musicians are often forced to become shrewd and suspicious in their negotiations. When the context shifts to musical performance, however, more idealistic perceptions of reality are incorporated. The performance event, therefore, allows these musicians to transcend the mundane and permits their ideal perceptions of reality to fuse with their ethos and attitudes.

All three musicians share a uniform conceptual approach to musical performance and have played together on different occasions over a fifteen-year period. Around 1973 they had formed a group with other out musicians, including Roger Baird, Malik Baraka, Earl Freeman, and Billy Bang, called the Music Ensemble. Like the mid-1960s performances of John Coltrane, the Music Ensemble rehearsed in the free-form, collectively improvised approach three or four times a week for over a year. The ideas and concepts developed in the group's distinctive style of musical performance were thus refined and given opportunities for expression. Written charts were rarely brought to or used at a rehearsal. To begin a performance, one musician might play a phrase and then be joined by the remainder of the ensemble. On other occasions, the musicians simply start together at the nod of a head and play continually without a break for three or four hours. In a concert situation, sometimes management imposes a restriction upon the musicians to keep the duration of their performance within an allotted time.

In their style of free-form, collectively improvised playing, time relationships are not structured according to a regular rhythmic pulse, which, as some musicians claim, narrows the options for responding musically. By altogether abandoning or radically altering the conventions of functional harmony, the musicians can achieve heightened states of community feeling and generate high levels of interaction. As a result, both preperformance roles and the roles generally ascribed to lead and rhythm section instruments among the musicians during a performance become undifferentiated.

Sometimes performance is likened to a spiritual or religious experience, whereby the music emanates from a greater source than human beings in the universe and through which their music first passes. Whether this source is called the Creator, Nature, or God, musicians recognize the need to be constantly open to it.

As mentioned above, Parker, Johnson, and Carter regard music in terms of a catalyst for social change. They believe that the aural and visual components of their music disrupt the conventional expectations of listeners. When this happens, listeners sometimes sense the need to alter routine modes of perception in order to interpret meanings in the music. Like the way in which metaphors structure a new idea, music should generate a novel and strikingly positive awareness that will perhaps transfer to the listener's view of life; thus it may prompt him or her to improve upon its quality.

These performers believe, furthermore, that mass marketing has increased concern over money and materialism in society while overshadowing the needs and perceptions of people as thinking, creative, and individual beings. Listeners readily discover, for example, that the music does not fit the usual commercial categories of the music industry. It is not a commercial commodity, since compositions are not named, nor do they have a prescribed beginning or end. These musicians are also aware of other numerous social and political factors that have emerged in recent times and that often affect our lives in negative ways. Rapid social change, brought on by the increasing rate of technology, can inflict instability upon people's lives and wear down vital traditions. Because American mainstream society allows its artists in some cases to starve or live in poverty, musicians are outspoken against dominant capitalist and materialist values.

If we are to continue to survive under the current conditions that we have imposed on this planet, Parker, Johnson, and Carter agree that the world needs to be recreated and its conventional meanings altered. Certain old values must be abandoned or revised and new modes of perception be made responsive to current needs. The musicians manage their inward experience and emotions to match, as best they can, these notions of a new world. They live in one world and envision another. The former is the tragic, everyday reality of violence, injustice, and decadence; the latter is a vision of life striving toward peace and the elimination of confined imagination, prejudice, and greed.

Though the worldviews of Parker, Carter, and Johnson are compatible in many respects, it remains to be shown how each performer encodes his own style of musical performance with these views.

William Parker

William Parker was born January 10, 1952, in the Bronx, New York. His mother worked as a school aide, and his father was a furniture polisher. Before his family moved to the North, Parker's grandfather lived as a share-cropper in South Carolina. Though his parents were not musicians, his father was an avid listener who especially enjoyed the music of Duke Ellington. He bought William his first trumpet and trombone. Parker believes that his father, who had ambitions to be a musician, gained vicarious satisfaction by encouraging his son to play music. After Parker completed high school, he attempted on several occasions to begin college. Dissatisfied with college, however, he left to take a variety of jobs with the post office and the New York City housing authority. He was also employed as a cook and mail clerk.

Parker is quiet, unassuming, studious, and sincere in his manner. He does not imbibe alcohol or often eat meat, though he is careful not to impose these views on others. He is serious about his role as a musician and is solicitous in the choice of words he uses to describe it. Parker presently lives with his wife, Patsy, in a small one-bedroom apartment in the Lower East Side of Manhattan. He is unemployed except when he works as a musician. If Parker needs the money, he sometimes accepts gigs playing the bass as a sideman in conventional bebop jazz groups. Whenever they are available, however, he prefers to play in settings that favor more innovative approaches to performing.

In the early 1970s, Parker began his performing career and also studied bass with Richard Davis and Milt Hinton. Several years later, he performed regularly at Studio We, one of the loft studios in the Lower East Side, with Sunny Murray, Charles Brackeen, Frank Lowe, Charles Tyler, Rashied Ali, Gato Barbieri, and others. Since 1981, he has performed with both Cecil Taylor's small band and big band and in groups with Daniel Carter, Dewey Johnson, Bill Dixon, Milford Graves, and Billy Bang.

In his early performing career, Parker did not devote a lot of time listening to bebop performers like Charlie Parker or Thelonious Monk. He was influenced, instead, by John Coltrane, who was a model for many of Parker's spiritual and social concepts. Parker calls Coltrane a "visionary," or one who masters a "vision of the world that works."[33] Because visionaries perceive logic and meaning in the world and express these beliefs with firm

William Parker at his apartment in New York City

conviction through their music and speech, they can influence and sometimes change other people's lives and ways of thinking.

In the external world, Parker believes that a mode of awareness or state of consciousness superior to the mundane exists and emanates from God or the Creator. Early in his performing career, Parker evolved methods to tap this source through meditation or prayer prior to a performance. By emptying himself of extraneous and mundane thoughts, he could evoke the "spirit" of this awareness. Parker discovered he could achieve similar effects when playing certain tones on the bass which he believes are like agents that enable him to fuse his inner emotions and values with a vision of an ideal world.[34] Influenced in part by his familiarity with some of the meditative techniques and religious philosophies of India, Parker may associate names and functions with many of these tones.

Because they essentially clear the mind of all the unnecessary debris that collects during the day, the inducement of trancelike states is important in Parker's music. By using a variety of unconventional bowing techniques, Parker can produce certain tones that have a hypnotic effect on performers and listeners. The "Dance of the Tremolos," for example, is one of Parker's compositions which he begins by bowing on the D string and humming with the tone until he achieves the desired state. On a few occasions, he reports that the bass had risen a few inches by itself off the stage.[35] Other trancelike states can be attained by playing certain melodies or phrases and, at the same time, envisioning a picture of heaven or an image of the world that is at peace. The appearance of these images is occasionally so vivid that Parker pictures himself there. He describes this image as a powerful force generated through the music which must be presented with firm conviction if it is to have an effect on listeners as well. For Parker, many of these techniques over the years have evolved into an intuitive process rather than a conscious one.

From the point of view of the listener, Parker posits two functions that are served by his music. First, it must "uplift" the listener in a way that results in feelings of happiness. Second, the listener must contrast the awareness of joy with the lack of such experiences in everyday living. This leads to the realization that one's spiritual and creative needs in a technologized society are not being met. If one becomes outraged by this injustice, one is perhaps predisposed to act in a political arena in order to adjust the situation.

Before a performance, however, Parker does not consider engaging the audience directly in this kind of response, nor can he predict how an audience will react to the music. In order for positive reactions to be evoked in the listener, Parker instructs that the music must be "happening"; that is, the musicians must achieve certain levels of interaction. For this purpose, Parker writes compositions containing a number of interchangeable sections which can be ordered in any way for an evening's performance. Parker's composition "Vega," for example, is loosely written in sixteen sections. Immediately before a performance, Parker may prescribe the order in which the sections will be played, or sometimes the musicians may agree to delete certain ones or perform only one section for the entire concert. A consensus may be reached, depending upon which sections Parker and his sidemen feel will enable the group to generate high levels of interaction so that the music will "happen." Through composition, Parker can control some of the intangible variables that especially affect collectively improvised performances in unpredictable ways. If during a performance Parker senses that the audience might respond better to a different section of the composition, he will use an aural cue to signal a transition among the sidemen.

Like "Vega," Parker's composition "Vision Peace and Battle Cries" is also written in several sections that loosely prescribe melodic material in the absence of a prescribed rhythmic framework. Music example 13 is an excerpt of two sections from the original score. Though melodic material and the order of the sections of "Vega" and "Vision Peace and Battle Cries" can be predetermined, Parker allows his sidemen to impose anything they desire (e.g., chord changes, isometric and nonisometric rhythms, and so forth) upon the music. Parker's method of composing brings into play all available options, including both freedom and form, in a collectively improvised setting. On the composition "Vega" itself Parker writes, "The musicians are given scores and each phrase is sounded and shaped at rehearsals. I will play the phrase on the piano, each musician will repeat the phrase until it is learned and fits into the piece. Musicians can develop repeated phrases to enhance them."

On rare occasions, a bad performance may occur, and Parker regards it as one that does not "happen" or fails to produce desirable degrees of "vibration" or "intensity"; that is, it lacks the necessary power to achieve a physiological and emotional impact upon listeners. Though this happens only occasionally in his own performances, it is a constant source of frustration when he performs casuals (weddings, parties, bar mitzvahs, etc.). Parker is required to read charts that "don't take you where you want to go." Often, the music does not "happen," and the level of interaction remains low among the performers. A creative musician such as Parker can take the

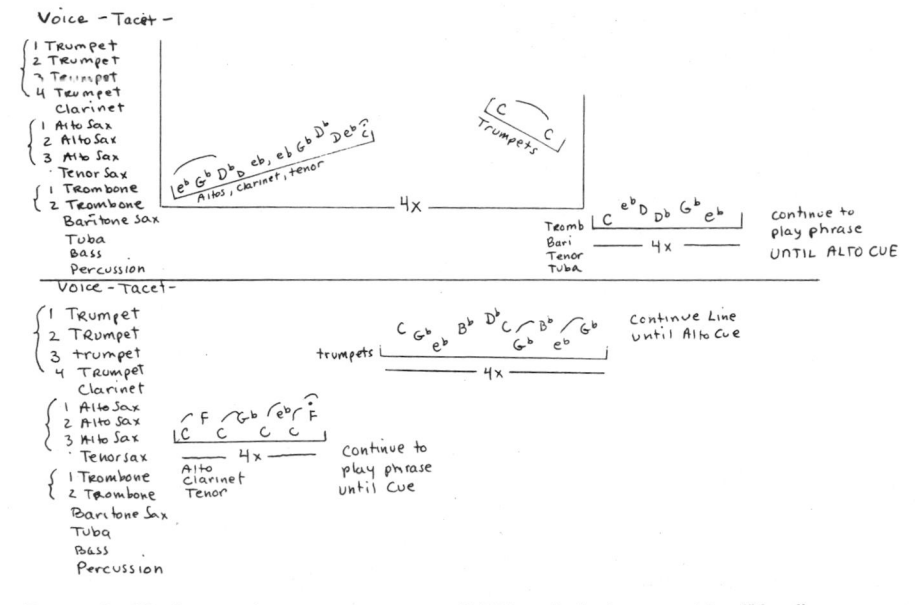

Example 13. *Excerpt showing two sections of William Parker's composition "Vega"*

leader's ideas and transform them. Depending upon the leader's temperament, however, he runs the risk of being fired from the job.

Although he is a professional musician, Parker's approach to music is based on the perspective of being human and addressing the issues concerned with understanding the essence of life. Music in the free-form, collectively improvised style is his vehicle for attaining this knowledge since it allows him to discover the greater sources of inspiration and life:

> Free music can be a musical form that is playing without pre-worked structure, without written music or chord changes. However, for free music to succeed, it must grow into free spiritual music which is not . . . a musical form; it should be based off of a life form. It is not about just picking up an instrument and playing guided by math principles or emotion. It is emptying oneself and being, [playing] without [placing] a label on the music. . . .
>
> . . . There is a music which is not based on technique, but on being a messenger of the Lord.
>
> . . . we are not the creators [of music], we are vehicles through which the Creator sends vibrations. . . . Music has little to do with notes; it has to do with life.[36]

Inspired by these ideas, a successful performance, according to Parker, cannot be evaluated by conventional aesthetic criteria. Notes that are "out of tune," for example, apply to the principles of functional harmony in most forms of Western music and mainstream jazz. In his music, Parker gives these a completely different role in evoking spiritual awareness.

Dewey Johnson

Dewey Johnson was born November 6, 1939, to parents of African-American descent in Philadelphia. He became interested in music and the trumpet through his brothers, who were performers. Johnson dropped out of high school in order to play professionally with one of his brothers and to take music lessons. Like William Parker, he has worked at various odd jobs, including employment as a clerk in a record store, mopping floors, washing dishes, and unloading boxcars. Currently, he is working full-time as a maintenance employee at a large factory. He would prefer to work full-time as a musician if there were enough opportunities to perform professionally.

Johnson's technical concepts about performing on the trumpet came from listening to LP recordings and live performances of Miles Davis, Clifford Brown, Lee Morgan, and Donald Byrd. Like William Parker, Johnson did not spend a lot of time attempting to master the bebop style, though he enjoys listening to many bebop trumpet players and sometimes participates in jam sessions. Like William Parker, Johnson's spiritual attitude toward music and life was influenced by John Coltrane.

Johnson first visited New York City in 1960. After spending brief periods back in Philadelphia and on the West Coast, he returned to New York City in 1963 to record with Byron Paul Allen. He met John Coltrane, who immediately took a liking to him and the way he played trumpet. In 1965, Coltrane asked Johnson, along with Freddie Hubbard, Frank Wright, Pharoah Sanders, John Tchicai, and Marion Brown, to take part in the recording of his next album, *Ascension*. Though *Ascension* would mark a crucial development in Coltrane's career and was soon to become a landmark recording, bebop performers questioned Johnson's and Frank Wright's qualifications and lack of experience. Today, Johnson has nearly mended the rift between his detractors and himself. Since the recording of *Ascension*, Johnson continues to align his views of the world with performing out. For younger out performers, Johnson's stamina and conviction are sources of inspiration.

Dewey Johnson at Columbia University, New York City

Neither talkative nor shy, Johnson is very warm and friendly around those whom he knows and trusts. During a conversation, he may weave many keen insights about life and people around the topic of discussion. Johnson's openmindedness and sincerity allow him to interact with numerous kinds of individuals, whether or not they happen to be musicians. He sees himself metaphorically as a warrior who continues to survive countless battles, though he is unlikely ever to become a household name. Johnson claims to wage such battles against any force that inhibits him from playing his music and his listeners from understanding it.

Like William Parker, Johnson is sensitive to the problems of the outside world. He is concerned that society places an inordinate value upon material things, superseding a desire to fulfill life with a higher regard for humanity and a certain spiritual awareness. Johnson envisions a world in which life and other phenomena are bound together by "connections." For example, musical performances in the free-form, collectively improvised approach work to establish essential connections among musical-acoustical phenomena, life, and nature. These interrelationships may be illustrated by the way in which Johnson applies the compositional process to a given source of inspiration. When he stops to listen to a bird singing or to the voices of children engaged in intense play, Johnson interprets these stimuli as musical tones that can be fitted into conventional major and minor chords or rhythmic frameworks. These become the ingredients of a composition or the catalyst to ease the performer into the free-form style. By connecting the sounds of birds singing with tones on the trumpet, he has brought together two otherwise disparate domains in the world. Johnson claims that he does not create but only discovers these relationships, which he believes some supernatural force has already established.

Johnson's compositional approach evolved in part from the fact that he could not afford enough money to take lessons as a classical trumpeter and become steeped in the formal principles of music composition. He explains that if one is committed to music but does not have enough financial resources to take lessons, one goes out and plays wherever and whatever one can. In his case, the inspiration for ideas to play on the trumpet must often come from direct physical contact with his environment rather than from a theoretical and systematic model for formulating musical passages. Johnson explains, "I didn't have funds to take lessons. I just went out and played. If you didn't have $3.50 for lessons, you went out and played. I developed a spiritual understanding with the instrument by not studying it in the classic way. It's natural that you pull more from inside for your inspiration than from a piece of paper."[37]

Johnson prefers to perform in the free-form style because it allows him to express whatever he is feeling while playing. Because the musical-acoustical phenomena are direct responses to immediate emotions of the performers, the music is vital. If one writes out a tune and performs it at a later date, it is likely that the same sensations or feelings that initially inspired the tune cannot be duplicated. Johnson believes that because we live in a time when change occurs not only from day to day but from minute to minute as well, written tunes can sometimes become outmoded as references to these dated feelings. In other words, they become like "extra baggage" which musicians accumulate.

Johnson's attitude toward the world as a system of interrelated phenomena with music at its center is closely tied to the ethical belief that he must first feel "good" about himself and the world around him. He remarks, "If you were playing chord changes and commercial music, if you didn't feel good no one would notice. But if you are playing free, there might be a chance that someone might hear that you aren't playing free—not that you are playing bad notes but the mood or rhythm might indicate this."[38] When he is feeling good, Johnson is free to develop coherent relationships between the world and his music. Thus he places a high value on little things that most people perhaps take for granted. If one opens up to them, they will make one feel good. Johnson feels good, for example, when he is truthful, successful when fulfilling a small endeavor, taking time out from a private practice session to eat some fruit or drink some water. When feeling negative about the world, Johnson has found that this carries over into his trumpet playing and creates imbalances and distortions among the relationships of his music to nature. At moments like this, he has to leave his music temporarily. Johnson's goal is to approach the trumpet purposefully and not as an outlet for confused thoughts or aggressive emotions.[39]

Johnson also uses the expression "connected" to refer to certain situations that might occur during a performance. For example, on one occasion when playing with another horn player, both performers suddenly became engaged in an improvised call-and-response exchange of brief but rapidly played passages. After the performance, Johnson said to the horn player that they had "connected" at that moment.

One means of attaining connections which Johnson utilizes in his approach to playing the trumpet is to evolve musical phrases or patterns that serve as transitional material into the free-form style. He practices, for example, cycles of arpeggiated major, minor, and diminished chords. In a free-form, collectively improvised performance with pianist Mary Anne Driscoll and drummer Paul Murphy at Soundscape during the summer of 1983, Johnson began to play a cycle of major chords on the C scale as a prelude to free-form improvisation. After playing through the cycle for a short time, he began to add inflections such as minor thirds (e.g., C, E♭, G) and diminished fifths (e.g., C, E♭, G♭) to each sequence of chords until the patterns were no longer discernible as a cycle. At this point, he abandoned the notion of playing chords in a particular key and turned his attention toward establishing more abstract relationships among various tones and phrases.

Daniel Carter

Alto saxophonist Daniel Carter was born in 1945 in Wilkinsburg, Pennsylvania, to parents who possessed a musical background. After graduating from high school, he began to study physics at Wesleyan University. While studying, he also worked at a variety of odd jobs. Though he always envi-

Daniel Carter at a park on the Lower East Side of Manhattan

sioned physics as a magical and wonderful field of study, he grew disenchanted when it was taught as a rigorous discipline. Two years later, Carter joined the army and was stationed in Italy. He married there and, after his term was served, moved his family to New York City in the hope of starting a new life.

Carter grew to appreciate out jazz through musicians like Albert Ayler, J. C. Moses, Noah Howard, Archie Shepp, and Pharoah Sanders, who performed at the different lofts in the Lower East Side of Manhattan. Western contemporary composers such as Arnold Schoenberg, Karlheinz Stockhausen, and Pierre Boulez have also influenced Carter. Eventually, Carter took up the tenor sax and joined groups led by local out musicians. Since then, he has performed with Cecil Taylor, Sam Rivers, Ted Daniels, Dewey Johnson, Earl Freeman, and many others.

Carter's belief system is based on the primary notion that order and meaning in the external world are attributable to a supernatural force far greater than human beings. Like Dewey Johnson, Carter insists that the ritual of performance in the free-form, collectively improvised style helps him to gain limited access to this source and to expand knowledge of the meanings and relationships of music, life, and the universe. It is the collective purpose of the musicians in the group, who regard themselves more like agents than creators of music, to connect with this source.

This central belief, in which music and the supernatural are linked, engenders additional beliefs. Carter, like Dewey Johnson, metaphorically pictures himself and others like him as warriors marching off to combat the forces of darkness that keep people locked in conventional ways of perceiving life and the world. Sometimes he may greet other musicians by asking how they are doing with the "march." Carter is aware of this struggle daily, though he occasionally takes breaks from it.

Some of Carter's beliefs lead to certain kinds of prescribed behavior. For example, he views the use of notated music during a musical performance as an obstacle which inhibits the musicians from attaining higher states of communal feeling and closeness to supernatural sources. In other words, a chart can exert too many boundaries on the music. When performing with musicians who use notated materials, Carter may ask to be excused from reading any musical charts. Instead, he prefers to improvise around the written parts. In extreme cases, he may refuse to participate in the performance.

The fact that notated music suggests a composer and ownership opposes Carter's belief in the supernatural source of music. Music that is composed and notated by a person becomes a commodity that can be bought, sold, or recorded for commercial purposes. Carter, however, prefers not to give titles to the music that he performs, since he believes it emanates ultimately from a supernatural source.

I was once involved in a performance with Carter and bassist Earl Freeman. In using the free-form, collectively improvised approach, we decided that no one individual would become the composer, director, or producer. Discussions that preceded the performance pointed out that the music must retain its independence from the pressures of mass marketing, which would entail ascribing ownership to something that we felt we did not own. Indirectly, our intention was not to alter the form of expression in the music to commercial models. We did not refer to the music by a given title, since this would connote a prearranged idea that is reenacted or recreated on stage. We did arbitrarily choose a name for the group simply for the benefit of the club owner, whose responsibility was to advertise the groups that were performing that evening. Though Carter is mostly flexible, he sometimes must turn down opportunities to perform with the more popular and leading out figures in New York City because they require him to restrict his playing too much to a written score. Carter, like Dewey Johnson, believes the performance of music should fit the moment and be a vital extension of life. For this purpose, Carter allows all the events leading up to a free-form, collectively improvised performance (e.g., the exchange of ideas among musicians at rehearsals, political events, the mood he happens to be in) to have a free hand in influencing the shape of the performance. When written materials are used, this release of dynamism into the performance is impeded. Carter is zealous to insure that his role during performance is not restricted either by the leader or composer. Otherwise, the development of communal feeling is inhibited.

When Carter finds himself in a setting with musicians who oppose his views, he regards the actual performance as an arena in which the issues are debated, and the resulting tension, or its release, is expressed through the music. Even if tensions cannot be resolved during the actual performance, Carter is satisfied that the importance of the issues at stake justifies the attempt. Carter, who has practiced this approach for more than ten years, no longer draws significant differences among concert performances, group rehearsals, or private practice sessions. They are part of the same cycle of life and, like the source from which they emanate, have no real beginning or end; they are continuous. Thus it is not unusual for Carter to begin a concert by warming up backstage on his instrument and walking onto the stage while continuing to play

For Carter, it is crucial to cultivate states of "openness" to sources of inspiration, including the "supernatural" or "spiritual." This involves a transition from the musician's preperformance roles to undifferentiated states during performance. Preperformance roles are those roles (e.g., parent, record store salesperson, band leader, and so forth) that musicians assume in their day-to-day social interactions. Through musical performances in which preperformance roles are dissolved, Carter explains that the musicians strive for a mystical state of awareness referred to by many names, including undifferentiated unity, oneness, or selflessness.

Because we are imperfect beings, Carter points out that the complete attainment of truly undifferentiated states is impossible. In the past, he remarks, only a few people have approached such states and have related their newly gained wisdom to the rest of humanity. Relating this experience, Martin Luther King, Jr., once stated, "I have been upon the mountain, and I saw the light." Carter further draws an analogy of Jesus, who descended to earth as a vehicle for the teachings of God. In a sense, he is the embodiment of his Father.

The realization of undifferentiated states is essential in order to trigger a "flash," comments Carter. This is a brief moment of insight into some aspect of being or way in which the universe operates. In order for Carter to reflect upon this flash, however, he must return from the state of undifferentiated awareness to the mundane.

Music example 14 combines conventional and graphic notation to illustrate the events leading up to what Carter identified as a flash during one of his performances in the free-form, collectively improvised approach.[40] In instances when the performers are playing simultaneous, rapid, or slurred passages that are too difficult to transcribe note for note, I use jagged or straight lines to represent the melodic contour. These lines refer to approximate pitch values, whereas the notes are in absolute pitch. Since the performers do not observe the isometric meters of the drummer, I use real time or two-second intervals rather than bar lines to indicate the relative time relationships of the notes.

For the first fourteen seconds of this performance, which features a bassist, a drummer, and Dewey Johnson on trumpet, some stylistic parameters are apparent. First, the players seem to observe both parallel and opposite melodic contours. Johnson, for example, leads with a fast ascending and

Example 14. *Excerpt from Daniel Carter's performance (February 1984)*

chromatic phrase which the trumpet imitates by playing a short phrase in parallel motion that intersects the same register as Carter. At about the eight-second interval, however, Carter continues to ascend chromatically while Johnson plays a rapid flurry of notes in a descending direction. At the twelve-second interval, the different phrases played by Carter and Johnson suddenly terminate simultaneously on the B♭. This "flash," which was later identified by Carter when hearing a tape of the performance, was an exciting moment. Carter claims that such moments are not left to chance but are predetermined as if they were included in the genetic codes or DNA of the performers.[41]

Carter has developed a style of improvisation on the saxophone that is instantly responsive to cues from other musicians or to the flashes of inspiration emanating from nonhuman sources. He describes these principles in the following terms:

This is a process of dismantling old connections and building new ones, . . . It is trusting the flush. It is trying to trust the positions of the fingers on the horn that you may not know what key or note will come out. Rather than wondering about it, I play it. That is the quickest way to know if your guess was right. I don't always know what is going to be important. Sometimes an expression or a note comes at that moment and, boom, it is there. There might be some other intelligence that works through you that might know if it's important. Ornette Coleman talked about how, at times, he never knew what was going to come out of his group when performing. He has conditioned himself to react to or to receive the signal or flash of inspiration at a moment's notice.[42]

According to Carter, the mind must be properly attuned to respond quickly to signals from various sources. Whether he is practicing at home or performing a concert, this is done through a process of playing a phrase and "connecting" it to another phrase. The established relationship of the two phrases is not necessarily based on musical elements, such as harmony or scale relationships, but rather upon the intuitive awareness that informs him what to play and how to play it. Carter's approach to performing requires a moral emphasis on clean living and a life-style which does not clutter and create negative influences on his mind. He abstains from drinking and smoking. He does not work at other jobs. Instead, Carter remains at home most of the time, except when attending rehearsals or performances, and he rarely socializes outside the contexts in which he performs.

Another means by which Carter conditions his mind to receive and respond quickly to signals from various sources is through a special use of language. When walking along the street, he observes certain signs or advertisements and instantly alters some of their syllables to create a dramatically different meaning. The sign South Building, for example, can be altered to "mouth budding." Mouth budding is imagined by Carter to mean a person who has something important to say. Carter then imagines that such a person has experienced personal growth and fulfillment as a result of his or her connection with the institution that is housed in the building.

Carter points out that meanings are flexible and could change the next day. This tendency is less like a conscious act than a spontaneous apprehension of the union of the object with the intuition. The associations that are generated, according to Carter, are not randomly or freely selected by the mind. He believes that these responses, like his music, are conditioned in part by other supernatural sources. His ability to use language in this manner thus becomes an extension of the way in which he approaches improvisation on his instrument.

Other examples that Carter keeps in a small notebook include the lexical transformation of New York into "new stork." New York City is metaphorically symbolized as the stork whose role in children's stories is to deliver babies. Thus New York City, according to Carter's interpretation, gives birth daily to new ideas and meanings. Mode of income becomes "moan for income" for people who are not satisfied with their present income. Members of the press becomes "members of d'press" to symbolize the news media, which Carter claims are responsible for exploiting news for commercial profit.

The inspiration for Carter's use of language in this manner comes from people he often observes "hanging out" on the streets and who use language in creative ways. He is also influenced by the work *Finnegan's Wake*, in which James Joyce portrays in writing the operations of the verbal parts of the brain. Based upon his pursuit of wisdom from spiritual or nonhuman sources, Carter's purpose is to "remake the world with the words that it has." He believes that people need to evaluate and reconsider more closely many of the conventional meanings of life and other phenomena.

As in the case of John Coltrane's music, the didactic functions of William Parker's, Dewey Johnson's, and Daniel Carter's music can have effect only if listeners have acquired a certain amount of information regarding the attitudes and worldviews of the performers and the basic ways in which the music is organized. If these conditions are met, listeners are better able to ascertain some of the meanings with which performers encode their music.

Rationalism, Postindustrialization, and Egoism

The above musicians communicate and acquire knowledge of the world through musical performances, which are largely sensory experiences. This contrasts dramatically with Western science and the methods it uses. For instance, in order to verify assumptions about the operations of the physical universe, it relies upon rationalism and empirical testing.

In the West, rationalism extends back to the Greek philosopher Aristotle, who established the existence of reality independent of human consciousness. Thus we attain knowledge through secular reason rather than with our senses. In the seventeenth century, developments in Newtonian physics helped to further advance the tenets of rationalism by providing the impetus for the scientific investigation of nature. When America was founded in the same century, it adopted rationalism as the core of its social philosophy and worldview.[43]

Whereas Western rationalistic worldviews are based upon objective investigations of nature, the above musicians pursue knowledge through a mystical state of awareness, which they achieve when performing in the free-form, collectively improvised approach. However, this knowledge rests upon the foundations of faith and intuition rather than on objective reasoning.[44]

The above out performers and their music also oppose postindustrialization, an additional byproduct of modernization in the West. A postindustrial society incorporates a service economy, that is, an economy in which information is both produced and consumed in a cyclic manner. To perpetuate this economy requires the expansion of information and information services. Proponents of worldwide postindustrialization such as Marshall McLuhan envision a communal world bound closer together by the need for interdependency. As people's actions become more interdependent, however, less possibility for autonomous action is generated.[45] Therefore, people grow alienated in such a complicated, information-generating system.

Out jazz, however, symbolizes autonomous action, which is a necessary alternative to our growing dependence upon a wealth of complex information systems. For example, Daniel Carter and William Parker, who attribute supernatural origins to their music, believe that their music cannot be owned and marketed as a commercial commodity. Thus it has not been altered to conform to any of the entertainment industry's mass-marketing models.

In regard to egoism, the above performers assign it a low priority, especially in musical performances involving the free-form, collectively improvised approach. Not only is it counterproductive for musicians to assert aggressively their egos during such performances, it also opposes the belief that musicians are agents for the music.

In contrast, egoism in the West is highly valued. For example, the perpetuation of the capitalistic economic system is dependent upon the principle that one's own actions should provide for one's own welfare and profit. The imposition of our ego on the ecosystem, however, presents one of the most pressing problems we face today not only as a nation but as an entire planet. For example, in the West, we associate feelings of self-worth and security with our ability to control the natural environment by conquering it. Eventually, if this pattern continues unchecked, we will deplete our natural resources. Sensitive to this crisis, contemporary Western composer John Cage has devised methods of composing music that use chance operations to negate imposing human will, ego, personal taste, or memory upon a piece of music. The potential for a multiplicity of events arises whereby heterogeneity increases. It is a system of composing that requires low energy but yields high information.

Though the means differ, the goal to reduce egoism remains essentially the same in some of the compositional approaches by both out musicians and John Cage. In out jazz increased information is produced as the result of collective improvisation rather than by means of a chance medium. Because improvisation in out jazz is a human phenomenon, however, it is bound to the human variables of emotion and the needs of the ego. Thus the role of the ego in out performances can often become a source of tension. Of those performances in the free-form, collectively improvised approach which I have attended, the most successful ones, in my opinion, seem to achieve egoless states, whereby the resulting music is a dramatic or symbolic enactment of undifferentiated unity.[46]

eight

the implications of fusing

out jazz and culture

This study on out jazz is more than just a description of the backgrounds of out musicians and their styles of musical performance. It is concerned with why musicians choose to perform out jazz and how listeners perceive its meaning. This work also considers the symbolic value that out jazz engenders when viewed in connection with aspects of culture, including worldviews, sociohistorical factors, and social context.

Music and Culture

One of the important functions that music serves in culture is to help maintain the social system. For example, among African groups music is a central activity in rituals, ceremonies, and most communal events. By organizing the participation of group members, it strengthens communal bonds.[1]

Though this explains why music exists in African culture, it does little to suggest its symbolic role and the meanings people ascribe to it. To discover this meaning, one must look at how music interacts with other aspects of culture. For instance, the Shona of Zimbabwe maintain a worldview in which spirits of dead ancestors continue to affect the lives of their progeny. The Shona believe it is important to contact these spirits when attempting to solve certain disputes among members of the group. For this purpose, the Shona hold a *bira*, or spirit possession ceremony. In order to induce spirits to take possession of human mediums, Shona musicians play the *mbira*, a musical instrument constructed of five to thirty or more metal tongues attached to a box resonator.[2] *Mbira* players are successful in attracting spirits if they can perform numerous songs over many hours with great intensity.[3] In this context, the meaning, function, and aesthetics involved in the performance of the *mbira* can only be determined by examining the Shona worldview.

This suggests that culture is a body of diverse knowledge that is largely connected and understood through the interpretation of symbols. It provides information that people need in order to communicate among themselves and to comprehend their role in the universe.[4] Thus everyday experience—whether it involves the performance of music or shopping for groceries—is based upon recognizing and decoding these symbols.

This definition of culture is especially applicable to situations involving face-to-face interaction. For example, during a conversation, listeners respond to what a speaker says as well as the manner in which it is said. A slight smile here, a frown there, and the raising of an eyebrow at the mention of a crucial detail are nonverbal symbols that may convey the speaker's attitude toward the topic of discourse.

Out musicians are also sensitive to the symbolic components of their environment which might bear an influence upon their music. For instance, William Parker is especially attentive when he first enters a club or theater in which he will perform. He comments, "One of the things we have to do, aside from the music, is to transform the room and the audience. At first, it might just be a room that feels cold, and we got to change that to make it a place where things can happen for us and the listeners."[5] He might notice some of the following things: Is there an admission charge to enter? If so, how much is it? Is it a bar that profits from the sale of liquor and attracts a particular clientele? Or is it a trendy coffeehouse decorated with colorful designs and modern paintings that bohemians and businesspeople both like to patronize? What are the size and acoustics of the room? What is the relationship of the stage to where the audience sits? These factors might carry symbolic significance for some musicians more than others. For instance, the composition of the audience might cause some musicians to slightly alter their approach to performing or to select only certain pieces to perform. Others might consider it less important and choose to perform whatever they feel.

The Symbolic Interaction of Out Jazz and Culture

Though symbols are pervasive in one's day-to-day encounters with people and situations, they are meaningful only if one recognizes them as such and if one has the proper knowledge to interpret them. It is possible to determine the meanings of out jazz by looking at points where it overlaps with other domains of culture.

Table 9 outlines many levels of interaction between out music and culture.[6] The first level is out jazz itself, that is, the physical components of sound that performers produce during a performance. On this level, the intrinsic value of out jazz is emphasized over its referential meaning. However, as one's analysis proceeds upward, one begins to view the relationships between out jazz and culture in more abstract terms. Thus the potential increases for out performers and listeners to generate symbolic or referential meanings for the music.[7]

For example, during a live performance in the West, a listener is preoccupied mostly with processing sensory stimuli that musical sounds trigger. However, when the same listener at a later date recalls the performance from memory, he or she can reflect upon it. This cognitive process allows the listener to compare it to other performances or to superimpose abstract meanings (e.g., political or spiritual connotations) upon it.

The potential for out jazz to symbolize or communicate various meanings

Table 9. *A Model for the Symbolic Interaction of Out Jazz and Culture*

Modes of Symbolic Meaning	Levels of Symbolic Capacity	Domains of Meaning in Culture	⟷	Out Jazz
Referential	High	Worldview	⟷	Out jazz as knowledge, communication, and metalanguage
		Sociohistorical	⟷	Stylistic change in out jazz
		Social context	⟷	Musically related behavior
Intrinsic	Low	Out jazz itself	⟷	Aural components of out jazz

raises key issues and questions. For example, what out jazz means to one individual may contrast with what it might symbolize to others. This degree of subjectivity makes it extremely difficult to verify what messages out jazz actually communicates on the symbolic level. Furthermore, the meanings of out jazz are never static in the minds of the performers. They evolve as performers continually redefine their music and the social situations in which it is performed. Another problem lies in deciding which components of an out performance to isolate. In other words, is it a musical phrase, an entire piece, an improvisational approach, or the social organization of an out musical performance that has the capacity to communicate messages?[8]

Out Jazz Itself

In out musical performances, or in any kind of musical performance for that matter, the main referent is sound. As a purely physical phenomenon, sound is a pulsation of air that may emanate from a live performance or an LP recording. It then travels over distances and through time. When the sound is monitored by the listener's auditory sense organs, it becomes a *percept*. The response then travels to the brain as a neural impulse. The brain, which handles and stores these impulses, deduces a general *concept*, and it may attach a meaning to the sensation. It is at this stage that sound becomes a so-called tone, a pleasant melody, or lively rhythm; hence, music.

Michael Keith rehearsing at a studio on the Lower East Side of Manhattan

Out performers, however, may not generally work with precomposed patterns of sound, such as a discernible melody or harmonic framework, during a performance. Thus the cognitive processes that operate among out performers during a live performance are different from those that require musicians to render faithfully precomposed parts. In free-form, collectively improvised out performances, performers must constantly monitor a potentially unlimited number of sound combinations that arise instantaneously. At the precise moments that these occur, performers must gauge their relationship to preceding sound combinations and to the prevailing emotion or "flow" of the performance.

Western forms of notation are generally awkward in handling most features of an out performance, since the music is highly complex and especially sensitive to the context in which the performance occurs. If many instruments are collectively improvising at the same time, for instance, the texture may become so dense that it is impossible to separate aurally one instrument from another; thus they cannot be notated. Nor is it possible, using Western notation, to illustrate adequately dramatic changes that occur in the overall texture, especially when certain instruments are added. Trombonist Michael Keith, for example, often carries with him a Pakistani bugle that he sometimes plays during a free-form, collectively improvised performance. Its piercing and brilliant timbre rarely fails to arouse the other performers and to generate increased levels of interaction. He posits, "I carry the Pakistani bugle around with me a lot. Sometimes the music gets so dense and layered, it's hard to penetrate with most instruments. Then I pull out the bugle and I get it to cut right through, then it changes things in the music for a minute." [9]

Other things like squeaks or squawks that are commonly played by out performers present similar difficulties. Furthermore, notes that are played so rapidly in tempo that they blend together into a long, undifferentiated stream of tones also cannot be notated conventionally. Despite its many drawbacks and for lack of a better system, Western notation does serve a limited role in representing some aspects of out performances, such as descending melodic contours, tonal centers, or instrumental dialogues among performers.

Social Context

Certain norms or patterns of behavior commonly associated with musical events help guide the performer's behavior. Since one's actions can either conform to or deviate from the accepted norms, norms are not static phenomena, nor are they frozen in the minds of actors. More realistically, they are recast each time they are brought into play by the actor. In this sense, because individuals become role makers rather than role players, social norms and actual behavior are recursive; that is, they presuppose each other. [10] In her study of Kpelle music events, Ruth Stone postulates that "music both reflects and restructures culture, and can only be understood as we learn to interpret nuance, subtlety, and ambiguity in the processual creation of music performances." The idea that norms of behavior are redefined by actors on a daily basis anticipates that the self has a large degree of autonomy which propels the actor's own creative and emotional personality into the foreground of the issue.[11]

Though norms of behavior are guidelines for one's actions in a social setting, culture tells the participants what the setting means. Consider the way in which the setting for musical performances in the West is structured. The West regards musical performers as highly specialized and skilled professionals who master their trade only after undergoing years of intense study and refinement. Consequently, listeners are not deemed qualified to participate in such musical performances. To accentuate these differences, rigid boundaries are often erected between performers and listeners. For example, in a concert situation, musicians perform on an elevated stage that physically separates them from the audience. Before a performance, a large curtain may be drawn across the stage in order to enhance further this separation. Lastly, while preparing for a performance, performers use private dressing rooms located backstage.

Some out performers, like pianist Claudine Meyers, view boundaries between the performer and audience as inhibiting factors in the listeners' abilities to relate to the music. In order to engage listeners as participants, Meyers sometimes presents multimedia presentations whereby audience members become involved in aspects of drama, poetry, dance, or music.

One performance which I attended focused on the theme of rural, southern, African-American culture. During the two periods immediately following World War I and World War II, numerous African-American families migrated from the rural South to northern industrial cities. While adapting to urban living, successive generations of these families increasingly lost touch with the traditions of their rural homeland. Meyers used drama, song, and narration to recreate these traditions on stage. For example, she ended the performance with a culinary exhibition of Creole cooking; audience members lined up to taste the individual dishes. By becoming integrated into the performance, listeners were able to close cognitive as well as physical gaps that normally separate them from the music.

Some out musicians may even go a step farther by attempting to dissolve boundaries that traditionally separate the performance of music from the various domains of everyday living. I once observed a group of out musicians arriving at a rehearsal studio. Some casual conversation ensued while musicians removed instruments from their cases. Without need for instructions from the leader of the group, some members began playing their instruments or made tuning adjustments. Others continued to talk. After everyone eventually joined in, some time passed before everyone grew accustomed to performing with one another. Over the next few minutes, the levels of interaction and integration among the performers increased, decreased, then increased again. This pattern continued for about an hour or more. During this rehearsal, musicians did not formally recognize any transition point from the mundane to the musical. While the leader of a group performing mainstream jazz will instruct the musicians what tunes to play, the keys and tempos to play them in, and when to begin, these were lacking in this out rehearsal.

How out musicians act toward their music is also influenced by personal and psychological components. For example, when the personality of an individual, from one situation to another, is affected by moods and other variables, the outcome of behavior is also affected.[12] This was especially noted in Dewey Johnson's statement concerning his need to feel "good" in order to play music that he considers meaningful. Cecil Taylor once began a solo piano performance by first acting out a series of animal-like movements and gestures. He then segued into playing the piano, thereafter becoming completely absorbed in his music. It would appear that this preperformance ritual enabled Taylor to draw upon deep-seated sources of energy that are necessary in order to sustain long durations of solo improvisation. Since I know of no other musician in the out group who engages in this kind of preperformance ritual, it is indicative of Taylor's uniqueness as an artist.

Out performers who feel that their music carries an important social message may imbue their roles as performers with added symbolic significance. While one musician stops playing, allowing another member of the group to take a solo improvisation, the former may listen intently with bowed head or closed eyes to the new soloist. Though the implied seriousness of these types of gestures is not exclusive to out performers, one finds that humor is more common in substyles of jazz other than performing out. For example, out musician Michael Keith treats musical performances with utmost seriousness. Keith projects this awareness as a boundary that establishes his membership as an out musician and excludes outsiders. He expects friends and other people with whom he is in direct contact to recognize and appreciate his demeanor, since its source is linked to his music as a personal expression.

Other variables which may lie outside the immediate control of the performer can impact directly on the performer's ability to function during a musical performance. This includes innate or biological abilities, such as perfect pitch or well-developed eye-hand coordination, that musicians use to master easily the mechanics of a musical instrument. Conversely, an individual's limitations can also affect a performer in a variety of ways. After a particular performance, for instance, cornetist-composer Butch Morris expressed concern over the fact that some of his sidemen got lost reading the charts. As a result, the music suffered.

It is helpful even to look back upon a musician's home environment and the influence it had upon his or her decision to become a musician. The parents or siblings of most out performers had some formal musical training or at least developed knowledge and enthusiasm for jazz or other kinds of music. In part, this explains the aspirations for becoming professional performers that many out musicians had as youngsters or teenagers.

The Sociohistorical Aspects of Out Jazz

To state that the development of out jazz symbolically reflects the influence of broad social movements requires that out jazz and culture be handled as very general or even abstract terms.[13] I alluded to this earlier by suggesting that civil rights, having shaped in some cases African-American preferences for out jazz, wielded a limited impact upon out performers and listeners in the 1960s. When one generalizes the influence of civil rights not only on the individual but also upon the out group as a whole, implications follow. Since most out performers are African-American, positing a causal relationship between the social and musical raises the need to define what constitutes African-American culture as well as dominant culture.

The values of the dominant society refer to the values that are observed by the majority of white middle-class Americans, values that are rooted in the economic system of capitalism and the work ethic. The dominant society wields the greatest power and controls the avenues of mass media through which these values are transmitted and exposed to other segments of society. In contrast, the experiences of slavery, emancipation, poverty, mother-led families, and so forth have no doubt left an indelible imprint upon the collective consciousness of African-Americans. Thus many African-Americans find themselves torn between their own customs, values, and ethics and those which they encounter daily in their interactions with the dominant society.

The impact of broad sociohistorical pressures often engenders change in a style of musical performance.[14] Generally speaking, change in a musical style can occur as a minor innovation that is easily accommodated by a musical system or as a major innovation that significantly alters the system to the extent that it is said that a new style is introduced.[15] Urbanization and Europe's political and economic impact on West Africa, for example, were largely responsible for the creation of Ghanaian highlife music, a syncretic form that fuses the traditional African approach to rhythm with melodic concepts borrowed from Western popular music.[16] In the early 1940s, one of the main reasons for the decline of the big bands and the development of small combo bebop was a stringent wartime economy.

It is possible, however, that the social may reflect itself upon the musical as a stabilizing agent. For example, the invention of the phonograph enables a listener to rehear an indefinite number of times an exact duplication of a musical event. Thus in a sense the event becomes timeless, and the act of playing the recording becomes ritual.

Because recordings enable aspiring jazz musicians to rehear solo passages of innovators they may want to emulate, a musical style can spread and eventually take hold within the jazz community. In the 1940s, one of the reasons that bebop acquired a following outside the Manhattan area, in which it initially developed, was because of the availability in later years of recordings by bebop's premier co-innovator, Charlie Parker. Thus musicians did not have to travel to New York City in order to access the latest developments in bebop.

In other situations, the musical may be counteracting social trends.[17] Because out jazz on the symbolic level represents autonomous action, it opposes the policies of postindustrialization, which require individuals to grow increasingly dependent upon others for services and goods. In still other cases, it is possible that developments in the musical domain simply parallel, rather than counteract, those in another. The notion of "modernism" in the arts, for example, is a trend whereby the emphasis is shifted from the product to the means of production. It is difficult, however, to prove this as the reason why form in out jazz is secondary to the various applications of collective improvisation.

Statements regarding the causal relationship between the social and musical are difficult to prove. Though social phenomena can influence change in a style of musical performance, one also has to consider the individual, whose decision-making capacity is crucial to the outcome of any musical performance. If one ignores this, broad constructs, such as technology or the social domain of culture, remain isolated and abstract phenomena.

Worldview

This level focuses on how out performers integrate music with a coherent worldview. In this worldview, music is not only a source of knowledge but helps performers build meaningful relationships among the disparate experiences they encounter in urban living. Thus out music arises as patterned responses to the events that one encounters in one's urban surroundings and which form the basis of self-identity.[18]

The potential for music to be imbued with symbolic content is greatest on this level, since often the cognitive mode of reflection is brought to bear on what music communicates. Reflection involves thinking about music as an abstract notion of a past event or as typified behavior. Typified behavior refers to the sum total of acts drawn from past and present experiences and observations related to musical performance.[19] Since they are well removed from the here and now and the actual performance contexts involving face-to-face interactions, they are more anonymous. Out musicians, in this case, express the meaning of music in terms of its impact upon life or the world in general rather than its significance for a particular performance on a certain day.

Relatively speaking, it has been easy to outline some of the symbolic relationships that out musicians hold in regard to their music and worldviews. This is because most out musicians who do cultivate a highly symbolic design for music and worldview do so consciously. As they reflect upon these relationships, they are willing to discuss them openly. In contrast, many non-Western groups do not consciously or fully analyze, at any one time, the entire spectrum involving symbolic relationships among their music, behavior, and culture. This would account for why in Tiv society, for instance, the activity of producing patterns of sounds has no equivalent to what we in the West call music.[20]

Likewise, many non-Western cultures do not consciously ponder a worldview or the way in which it affects musical performance. This has not discouraged Western anthropologists from attempting to infer relationships between music and worldview based upon the group's own terms for classifying these phenomena.[21] For example, a group may use metaphors to link perceptions of the world to perceptions of music.[22] Among the Kaluli of Africa, writer Steven Feld discovered that in Kaluli myths the metaphor *halaido* (hard) is also an aesthetic referent to their music:

Myth has it that the world was once mushy and soft; *alin* the goura pigeon and *ode:n* the scrib turkey together stamped on the ground, "making it hard," so life could flourish. The model for social life recapitulates the model for the world. Infants are "soft"; their bodies and bones must "harden." A "hard" person is one who is strong [and] assertive. . . . When a song "hardens," coalescing poetic and performative structures, people are moved to tears.

"Hard" (*halaido*) then means social competence, physical maturity, verbal competence, sound competence; control of energies, ability to perform, influence outcomes, take control over one's life, invoke proper social strategies.[23]

Similarly, among out musicians, "out there" is a metaphor that links perceptions of musical performance with perceptions of spirituality and transcendence of certain norms of behavior. For Daniel Carter, the music has to get out there in order to attain the flash.

To some, it may seem that out jazz worldviews are misplaced in a Western city, which favors secular modes of living; nor are they very coherent with the Western emphasis on rational and empirical thinking.[24] Western secular worldviews, however, are drawn from a long history of identifying specific problems, collecting data through observation, and testing and formulating hypotheses. So-called superstitious beliefs involving the supernatural, furthermore, tend to be dismissed as poor logic and bad science. How is it possible for a group, some of whose members are even college educated, to believe in the efficacy of the supernatural or to maintain the proposition that music can alter the world? Because beliefs establish a mental condition in the individual which may serve as the basis for voluntary action, people will act just as determinedly and energetically upon the basis of so-called false beliefs as of true beliefs. When out performers discuss the didactic function of their music, they are expressing a belief in its potential to communicate meaning or to alter the listener's perceptions.

Some Implications for the Listener

This model, which is designed to look at the symbolic relationships of out jazz and culture and which is based on ethnographic analysis, addresses the meanings that are coded in different aspects of out musical behavior. The question of there being a right or wrong interpretation of a message in out jazz is nearly irrelevant, since modes of listening in the West are largely dependent upon one's subjective and personal use of imagination.[25] Thus it is proper to speak of a repertoire of responses or multiple interpretations that range from the spiritual, to the sociopolitical, to the personal.[26] Listeners approaching out jazz for the first time may do well to recall that not all out performers cultivate a coherent worldview or belief system; hence, they may perform in this style for the simple reason that they like it and enjoy being a musician.

This factor of flexible meanings in jazz can be forwarded as a possible explanation for its appeal across political and cultural boundaries. Albert Ayler alluded to this in the title of one of his recordings, *Music Is the Healing Force of the Universe*. Whereas a speaker of English may not be able to understand someone who uses a Russian dialect, it is possible that both may enjoy the works of Tchaikovsky. In the former Soviet Union after the revolution, the symbolic component of jazz had numerous connotations, depending mostly on the ruling party's stance toward the West and its tolerance toward popular tastes among citizens. It was viewed either as "decadent" culture of the West, as a significant proletarian art form, or as something in between.[27] In turn, these attitudes determined the kinds of restrictions that the government imposed upon record sales and performances.

Different listeners respond to out jazz by applying different meanings. Kwami Shaw and Irving Stone, whose opinions as listeners to out jazz are respected among performers, have become bored with the high level of predictability in many forms of mainstream jazz. For them the free-form, collectively improvised approach in out jazz is a refreshing change strictly on a musical level. For others who imbue it with more symbolic value, out jazz represents autonomous action. To specify what minimal unit of out jazz triggers a particular response in a particular individual is a difficult challenge. This is especially true for out jazz, whose musicians practice highly original and flexible styles of musical performance. Hence, the possibility of predicting a listener's responses diminishes severely. Commenting upon how audience members react to his music, multi-instrumentalist Ken McIntyre posits,

They are able to see things and experience different things through listening to the music. They get different images. . . . If a person has a brain, he has within that brain some faculties, like imagination. There are some people you can say a sentence to, and it has only one meaning, and for some maybe no meaning, for others there may be many ramifications in that one sentence.[28]

Saxophonist and composer John Zorn adds,

After a performance, some people come up and say it's very visual and then describe these images they were seeing. Some people say that they didn't know what was going on and they were confused by all the signs and the communication among the musicians. . . . I don't think I'm capable of doing any kind of objective music where everybody feels the same way when I play it. I'm really not interested in that. The plurality is more important to me. Everybody gets something different and everybody experiences it in a different way. As far as the audience is concerned, I have nothing to do with them whatsoever when we're performing. . . . I'm concerned with the music itself.[29]

Implications for the Writer

When referring to the high degree of spontaneity in his music, multi-instrumentalist Eric Dolphy states, "After it's over [a musical performance], it's gone, into the air. You can never capture it again."[30] Dolphy's statement races to the core of the problem which befalls writers who undertake the task of describing music through a form of communication entirely different from the one in which it was initially conveyed. For this purpose, writers engage a metalanguage or language used to communicate properties of another language, which in this case is a different mode of symbolic behavior, that is, music. Ideas in music, however, are not always transferable in meaning to a language about music.[31] How does a writer illustrate for a reader the subtle changes in the levels of interaction among out performers during a live performance? Likewise, how does one convey the kinds of emotions expressed by the same performers?

Even if the writer was to evolve a metalanguage that could suitably communicate to readers the subtleties of a live out performance, other problems arise. Consider what happens from the time patterns of sound are perceived by the senses, conceptualized by the brain, and finally set down on paper at a later date. In this process, one's initial experience of a performance undergoes radical permutations over time before it is ever expressed in writing.

The reader of ethnographies or reviews of concerts is often removed both in space and in time from the dimensions of what, where, when, and how something actually happened.

This reiterates the axiom that an out performance is heavily dependent upon its context for the effect that it produces upon its listeners. Thus recordings are a poor substitute for a live performance, since they lack the full impact derived from observing the musicians' interaction on stage. These visual interactions enable the listener to interpret, or perhaps misinterpret, emotional cues and signals that the musicians are responding to during the performance. Without these, the listener lacks the complete set of tools necessary to comprehend the music fully.

I have been told more than once by out performers that the nature of their music transcends even the most discriminating kinds of scholarly and analytical description. The reason for this seems to arise in part from the contrasting values between the aural-oral mode of communication that characterizes many African-American groups and the Western scholarly approach, which is more abstract and tends to intellectualize in ways that are detached from emotion and physicality.[32]

In comparison to performances based on complex, precomposed materials, out jazz incorporates highly flexible, noncomplex rules governing performance. This approach leaves open a direct channel between the inner mechanisms of creativity and physicality and the formative elements of music. Successful out performances seem to be vitally alive, as though the musicians and the music interact as a living organism that responds to a collective reservoir of psychobiological impulses. It is problematic for the writer to channel description of these processes into a nonaural or literate form without sacrificing to some degree the essence of the music as it unfolds moment by moment in a performance.

Some Implications for Living in the West

Understanding how meaning is conveyed through the use of symbols is a timely tool for Westerners, who struggle with existential questions regarding the nature of being. By imposing an objective view upon phenomena, the West has evolved strategies for survival that largely depend upon the ability to detach oneself from nature. Subsequently, nature is viewed in terms of categories and objects which Westerners feel the need to control and manipulate. In gauging the value and meaning of existence, the West chooses scales, such as the manifestation of physical energy and accumulation of material goods. Driving a new car, for example, triggers an emotional response of self-worth.

In contrast to the low regard commonly held for the arts in the West, Mihaly Csikszentmihalyi envisions the arts as an effective key to the survival of our society.[33] Because we draw heavily upon our natural and material resources to provide those material goods that we feel are necessary for our survival and self-worth, we should devise means that require low energy and yield high information. One such means is to select symbolic information about existence through the discourse of the arts. Csikszentmihalyi remarks, "Art is a source of constructive knowledge that is very low on energy, yet practically limitless in the amount of information it can provide. By acting within the various symbolic media of art, a person can find out who he or she is at very little expense to the environment."[34]

In this light, out jazz, like other art forms, can be appreciated as a vehicle for building meaning across different domains of experience which do not further deplete the planet's natural resources. By conveying nonmaterialistic values and autonomous action, out jazz speaks to many social issues that affect us in important ways. Above all, it provides an alternative view of the world based on the elimination of those human qualities such as greed that someday perhaps will be discarded as meaningless pursuits.

A Music Deserving of Wider Recognition

Out music renders successful attempts to blend freedom in form with collective improvisation. However, due to the flexible frameworks in which out jazz is performed and the chaotic surface textures that result, much unjustified criticism has plagued the music for years. Thus its importance in the development of jazz as well as in the social domain has been overshadowed or rarely given serious treatment.

For some out performers, the free-form, collectively improvised approach is fused with a coherent, complex system of beliefs and worldviews. With utmost seriousness, out jazz performers view their music as a didactic tool through which listeners can envision alternative modes of living creatively. In performances of out jazz, these values are given musical expression in aspects such as the attainment of high degrees of communal feelings. This not only suggests the efficacy of music but teaches that our differences on the moral level are insignificant when weighed against the things that bind us together as human beings. Because out music connects the mundane and the physical with the emotional and spiritual, life achieves purposefulness. According to the musicians, this view is an important preliminary step toward solving at least a portion of the problems and misunderstandings in the world.

notes

1. Introduction

1. Such, "'Out There,'" pp. 83–95.

2. Further examples of Western music which are based on the principles of functional tonality include rock, muzak, most forms of Western classical music, country and western music, and Anglo-American folk music.

3. Salzman, *Twentieth-Century Music*, p. 4.

4. The influence of classical music on jazz dates back to the 1920s, when it was common for jazz musicians to quote snatches from compositions written by Western classical composers. For example, in his rendition of "The Man I Love," Paul Whiteman quotes an extract from *Tristan und Isolde*. See Harrison, "Traditions and Acculturation," p. 185.

5. In general, third stream jazz is characterized by experiments with counterpoint, form, and arranging. George Russell's "Concerto for Billy the Kid" (1956), for instance, is based on the concerto form. By raising the importance of compositional technique above improvisation, these approaches were sometimes criticized for their lack of drive, spontaneity, swing feeling, and collective interaction, which are normally key features of jazz.

6. Many of Ornette Coleman's and Cecil Taylor's early recordings did incorporate swing feeling in the traditional sense. However, other aspects in the music, such as the liberation of the melody from preset chord changes or the extensive use of dissonant clusters of tones, are considered outside the normal boundaries of the other substyles of jazz.

7. A few of the leaders of such camps include Frank Lowe, Butch Morris, Billy Bang, Jemeel Moondoc, Frank Wright, David Murray, and others.

8. Earl Freeman, interview held December 30, 1983, at his friend's apartment in New York City.

9. See also Andrew White's comments in his article "The Coltrane Legacy," pp. 63, 61, 48.

10. Milford Graves, interview held January 25, 1984, at his home in Jamaica, New York.

11. Tynan, "Take 5," p. 30.

12. DeMicheal, "John Coltrane and Eric Dolphy," p. 52.

13. Feather, *The Encyclopedia of Jazz*, p. 22.

14. Oliver, Harrison, and Bolcom, *The New Grove Gospel, Blues and Jazz*, p. 340.

15. McDonough, Haden, and Litweiler, "30 Years of Free," pp. 30–31.

16. Jost, *Free Jazz*, pp. 142–143.

17. Wilmer, *As Serious as Your Life*, pp. 9–16.

18. Litweiler, *The Freedom Principle*, p. 50.
19. Such, "Music, Metaphor and Values," p. 121.

2. Labels and Out Jazz

1. See Tamony, "Jazz, the Word," pp. 33–39; and Merriam and Garner, "Jazz—the Word," pp. 373–396.
2. Litweiler, "Shepp," p. 15.
3. Gillespie, *To Be*, p. 492.
4. Dennis Charles, interview held June 24, 1983, at his apartment in New York City.
5. Earl Freeman, interview held December 30, 1983, at his friend's apartment in New York City.
6. Whitehead, "Steve Lacy," p. 26.
7. Some contemporary classical composers apply aleatory approaches in order to eliminate these factors from the music.
8. Whitehead, "Steve Lacy," p. 26.
9. Frank Lowe, interview held June 29, 1983, at his apartment in New York City.
10. Charles Tyler, interview held July 11, 1983, at his home in Brooklyn, New York.
11. Earl Cross, interview held January 3, 1984, at his apartment in New York City.
12. For additional discussion of the debate over the origins of spirituals, refer to Wilgus, *Anglo-American Folksong Scholarship*, pp. 349–350. See also Epstein, *Sinful Tunes*, pp. 191–192.
13. See Wallaschek, *Primitive Music*, p. 60, and Krehbiel, *Afro-American Folk Songs*, pp. 22–23, 83.
14. Jackson, *White Spirituals*, pp. 242–302.
15. See Herskovitts, *The Myth of the Negro Past*, p. 267, and Tallmadge, "The Black in Jackson's White Spirituals," pp. 139–160.
16. Refer to Marshall Stearns's discussion of Africanisms in jazz in his book *The Story of Jazz*, pp. 3–15. Stearns draws upon the findings of Richard Waterman which appear in Waterman, "African Influence," pp. 207–218.
17. Tallmadge, "Blue Notes," pp. 161–162.
18. The term *fire music* is the title of Archie Shepp's 1965 recording *Fire Music* (Impulse 86). It is also the title of John Gray's bibliographical work *Fire Music: A Bibliography of the New Jazz, 1959–1990*. The term also serves as the title for Rob Backus's work *Fire Music: A Political History of Jazz*.
19. The distinctiveness of African-American culture is based on the effects that slavery, emancipation, racism, ecstatic religion, and mother-led families have had on how African-Americans define their past and perceive themselves today. This perspective must also be balanced against the fact that African-American culture shares many ties with the dominant society. Thus their cultural expressions not only influ-

ence the larger body of American culture but they in turn are influenced by those of the dominant culture. Some African-Americans, especially among the middle class, may find themselves bound to the values of their own group and those of the dominant society. See Ellison, *Shadow and Act*, pp. 262–263.

20. In his work *The Ominous Parallels*, pp. 138–139, Peikoff projects that the nonrational modes of thinking that form the basis of the counterculture revolution can be traced to the views of Immanuel Kant. Kant downplayed our ability to reason, suggesting that our minds are unable to acquire any knowledge of reality. Thus he believed that reality can only be defined by faith. Because Kant's philosophy held sway over American social thought since the late nineteenth century, Peikoff claims that it eventually spawned the existential movement of the 1950s and 1960s. Existentialism holds that because reality is absurd, irrational passion is the only means of knowledge. When reason seemed to fail in the 1960s, intellectuals in the West sought recourse in the religions of the East. Subsequently, they explored selflessness while rejecting physical reality in favor of LSD, parapsychology, UFOs, or witchcraft.

21. Baker, Belt, and Hudson, *The Black Composer Speaks*, p. 300.

22. Rivelli and Levin, *Giants*, p. 119.

23. Shepp, "A View," pp. 39–42, 44.

24. Milford Graves, interview held January 25, 1984, at his home in Jamaica, New York.

25. Jones, *Blues People*, pp. ix–xii.

26. Ibid., pp. 181ff.

27. Kofsky, *Black Nationalism*, p. 131.

28. In ibid., pp. 9–67, Kofsky claims that racial discrimination and an economic structure that ignored the plight of impoverished blacks led to the development of bebop in the 1940s. Some writers have responded to the claim that bebop symbolizes a black separationist movement by mentioning the fact that most of the bebop musicians in the 1940s were motivated to play bebop in order to compete economically with whites in the entertainment market. For instance, see Ellison, *Shadow and Act*, p. 252.

29. Sidran, *Black Talk*, p. 144. See also Haralambos, *Soul Music*, which treats soul music from a sociopolitical perspective. Soul music is believed to have originated in the mid-1950s, when Ray Charles began to sing secular versions of gospel tunes. It is an African-American vocal music that fuses gospel music and blues.

30. Merriam, *Anthropology*, pp. 259–276.

31. Feld, "Communication," pp. 7–8.

32. Lewis, "Urbanization," p. 158.

3. Jazz Styles

1. Before World War II, publications on jazz generally lacked scholarly focus. In fact, many harbored numerous inaccuracies as well as a bias against the music. After

the war, writers began to scrutinize more closely details, sources, and references. Today there are a number of textbooks on jazz from which to choose. For example, Gridley's work *Jazz Styles* provides a detailed discussion of the musical innovations leading to each substyle in the development of jazz.

2. Most substyles of jazz are still performed today. However, hard bop is currently considered at the forefront of the development of jazz.

3. Meyer, *Music*, p. 7.

4. Another term for the jazz continuum that is favored among jazz historians is *mainstream*. The term was first coined in 1958 by writer and producer Stanley Dance to refer to several musicians whom he recorded on the Felsted record label, which British Decca established between 1958 and 1959. Most of these musicians shared a common background in the swing era style of jazz. Artists featured on these recordings included Dicky Wells, Rex Stewart, Buster Bailey, Budd Johnson, Coleman Hawkins, and Buddy Tate. Since then, the term *mainstream* has been broadened to include more recent styles such as hard bop.

5. Morgenstern, "Ornette Coleman," p. 17.

6. Rivelli and Levin, *Giants*, p. 54.

7. One of the first significant studies of African music is Jones, *Studies in African Music*. In his book *Early Jazz*, pp. 10–15 and 40–62, Schuller bases his discussion of the African influences in early jazz on Jones's study. See also Waterman, "African Influence," pp. 207–218.

8. See Tallmadge, "Blue Notes," pp. 155–165. Tallmadge discusses the origins of blue tonality in African-American folk music and the extent to which the use of neutral pitches in white folksongs and Native American music may have influenced African-American usage.

9. Collier, "Jazz," p. 582.

10. Ibid.

11. This was after musicians left New Orleans to live and work either in Chicago or New York City.

12. In early New Orleans jazz the trombone functions more as an accompaniment instrument than a melody instrument, since it outlines the main chords of the tune.

13. However, in early recordings such as "Dippermouth Blues" the drums were excluded because they made the needle skip on the recording devices.

14. Certainly Louis Armstrong's 1927 Hot Five recording "Hotter than That" can be considered an exception.

15. Big bands also maintain a separate function for the accompaniment or rhythm section.

16. Rivelli and Levin, *Giants*, p. 120.

17. Spellman, *Four Lives*, p. 72.

18. See Owens, "Charlie Parker," 1: 28 and 2: 1.

19. Parker is regarded mostly as a vertical improviser; that is, he shapes his improvisations according to the chord changes. On occasions, however, Parker chooses to play in a more linear fashion and to develop motives borrowed from the theme to construct lyrically stable improvisations. To begin his solo in the first take of the

tune "Embraceable You" (recorded October 28, 1947), for example, Parker plays a brief motive extracted from the original Gershwin melody and reshapes it three additional times over the next three measures. Soon afterward he abandons the formulaic-thematic approach in favor of his usual means to construct the remainder of his solo.

20. Big bands of the 1930s and 1940s usually featured only a few soloists who were considered advanced enough to take long solos. In order to display or improve upon their skills, the other sidemen in the band often attended jam sessions after their performances, or they sat in with groups in the small club jazz scene on 52nd Street in Manhattan. The perceived need among some jazz musicians to increase solo time was one of many factors that led to the development of bebop in the 1940s. The recording industry also played an indirect role in increasing solo time. By replacing the 78 RPM record with the 33 1/3 LP record, jazz musicians could play longer solos without having to worry about time constraints.

21. Drummer Zutty Singleton, an exponent of early New Orleans jazz, is one of the earliest precursors of varied meters. See Gridley, *Jazz Styles*, pp. 253–256, for further discussion on the emancipation in the styles of musical performance among rhythm section instruments in modern jazz combos.

22. Rivelli and Levin, *Giants*, p. 63.

23. Gridley, *Jazz Styles*, p. 163.

24. Blake, "Thelonious Monk," p. 122.

25. See Chevan, "The Double Bass." The author convincingly argues that some of the innovations in bass playing usually credited to Jimmy Blanton are evident at an earlier date in the style of Leroy ("Slam") Stewart (p. 86).

26. This is especially noted in the recordings that mark the early development of bebop. As bebop progressed into the 1950s and was revitalized under the label hard bop, melodic phrases began to sound more connected and coherent. This was a matter of degree, however, and it does not represent a full solution to the problem of building melodic coherence among phrases of a solo improvisation.

27. Not all the performers on Davis's 1959 recording of "So What" observe this modal scheme. During his solo, John Coltrane, for instance, frequently sharpens the Dorian mode's seventh degree to C♯. It sounds dissonant against Bill Evans's piano accompaniment, which stays mostly in the Dorian mode. Thus Davis's approach is loosely defined as modal.

4. The Founders of Out Jazz

1. For further discussion on the backgrounds and music of Albert Ayler and out musicians from Chicago, see Litweiler, *The Freedom Principle*, pp. 151–200, and Jost, *Free Jazz*, pp. 121–132, 163–179.

2. An alternate take of *Free Jazz* was recorded and released as a separate LP recording entitled *Twins* (1959–1961, Atlantic 1588).

3. Rusch, *Jazztalk*, p. 21.

4. In a sense this may foreshadow Coleman's later interest in "harmolodics," which writers have found difficult to interpret. It seems to refer to a situation in which each of Coleman's sidemen plays the same basic melody line. However, each part may be transposed to a different key, resulting in polyphony.

5. Two takes of "Ascension" were recorded the same day. My analysis is of the first take.

6. In his analysis of "Ascension," Jost incorrectly posits only three modes in the collectively improvised sections. See his work *Free Jazz*, p. 88.

7. Rusch, *Jazztalk*, pp. 21–22.

8. Simosko and Tepperman, *Eric Dolphy*, p. 24.

9. Ibid., pp. 10–11.

10. Jones, *Black Music*, pp. 151–152.

11. Taylor's approach to shifting units of texture is perhaps best illustrated in Jost's analysis of "Unit Structures." In his work *Free Jazz*, p. 78, he says, "*Unit Structures* evolves from short self-contained models (structural units), some of which last just a few seconds. Their formation and gradual dissociation comprise the first part of the piece. This is followed by 'Area'—freely and in part soloistically improvised—where according to Taylor the known material is formed into a whole."

12. Frank Lowe, interview held June 29, 1983, at his apartment in New York City.

13. John Coltrane and Ornette Coleman are the two innovators most cited among second-generation performers as having the most influence.

14. Dewey Johnson claims that he has two sets of "chops." One set is for playing "inside" (bebop) and the other is for playing "out" (avant-garde). He is able to switch from one approach to the other like a bilingual person is able to speak in one language and then in another.

15. Similarly, much of the early stages of the development of bebop were never documented on recordings.

16. Moondoc's style of performance on the alto sax sometimes reflects the influence of Eric Dolphy and John Coltrane as well. During the later choruses of his solo, he plays a series of rapidly trilled notes that blend together in one long stream of sound. Similar to Coltrane's and Dolphy's technique (listen to Dolphy on "Woody'n You," from the recording *Copenhagen Concert*, 1961), the effect resembles individual notes tearing apart as they leave the alto saxophone.

17. Billy Bang, interview held January 11, 1984, at his apartment in New York City.

18. The didactic function of out jazz will be taken up later in greater detail.

19. Billy Bang, interview held January 11, 1984, at his apartment in New York City.

5. The Economics of Performing Out

1. To illustrate this point, consider a city of one million people. This large population is likely to contain enough people with similar interests in art, music, sports,

or any number of things who can join as a group, hold meetings, put on shows, and give workshops. In comparison, a city of only 50,000 inhabitants is less likely to have enough people with the same interests in such diverse fields to form organized groups. In the early 1800s, New Orleans may have been an exception. Despite its population of only about 50,000 people, it nurtured as many as three opera companies and several symphony orchestras, not to mention a large sampling of brass bands.

2. In the transition from rural to urban life, some sociologists assumed that urbanization precipitated the breakdown of social order and the moral and psychological make-up of individuals and, hence, the formation of "deviant" subcultures (see Wirth, "Urbanism," pp. 3–24). When bebop eventually gained the attention of the American public in the 1940s, for instance, the music as well as the musicians' unusual styles of dress, behavior, and speech were spurned as a significant threat to American middle-class values and the welfare of its teenagers and young adults (see Jones, *Blues People*, pp. 181–182, and Miller and Skipper, "Sounds of Black Protest," pp. 26–28). Such criticism was in no way limited exclusively to African-American performers, since white musicians who performed Dixieland in the 1920s also met with opposition from the dominant society. From a more objective perspective, so-called deviant subcultures are not the result of a breakdown of morality. They form because enough people with the same interests assemble together as a group and express themselves in modes of behavior that they find acceptable.

3. This is a tendency among club owners that also affected musicians such as Lennie Tristano, Charlie Parker, Dizzy Gillespie, and others whose styles of performing, at one time or another, were considered to be unusual.

4. Charles Tyler, interview held July 11, 1983, at his home in Brooklyn, New York.

5. Spellman, *Black Music*, p. 8.

6. These include Albert Ayler, Milford Graves, Noah Howard, Sunny Murray, Paul Bley, Ornette Coleman, Henry Grimes, Frank Wright, Sun Ra, Marion Brown, Marzette Watts, Burton Greene, and the New York Art Quartet.

7. Lyons, *The 101 Best*, pp. 375–376.

8. Jones, *Black Music*, p. 93.

9. I have observed occasions when musicians were recruited right off the streets. The leader or organizer of a loft performance would go around the streets of the Lower East Side and Greenwich Village seeking out musicians. He or she would then have them sign their names to a paper or flyer that advertised the performance and that would be photocopied and distributed by hand throughout the Village. Sometimes there were no rehearsals, and musicians simply had to be there the day of the concert and ready to perform.

10. Precedents for collectivity in African-American music are found among African-American gospel quartets, which formed unions in the late 1920s and early 1930s. These unions functioned to help find work for the different quartets. See Lornell, *Happy in the Service*, pp. 81–84. In the 1930s and 1940s, American folk singers also formed collectives. The Almanac Singers, for example, consisted of several performing groups which appeared simultaneously before different audiences.

The overall goal of the collective was to increase consciousness of the plight of American laborers and to support the American labor movement of the 1930s and 1940s. See Denisoff, *Great Day Coming*, pp. 77–105.

11. Backus, *Fire Music*, p. 68.

12. Levin, "The Jazz Composers Guild," p. 17.

13. Backus, *Fire Music*, pp. 66–83.

14. Mandel, "Musicians," p. 73.

15. Milford Graves, interview held January 25, 1984, at his home in Jamaica, New York.

16. Lewis Porter, discussion held January 29, 1990, over the telephone.

17. This was told to Lewis Porter during a conversation he had with the drummer in question who will remain anonymous. Porter conveyed the quotation to me during a telephone conversation held January 29, 1990.

18. Bob Rusch, interview held January 20, 1990, over the telephone.

19. Frank Lowe, interview held June 29, 1983, at his apartment in New York City.

20. Baker, *New Perspectives*, p. 109.

6. Perceiving Out Music

1. The history of black dialectology is summarized in Smith, "Research Perspectives," pp. 24–39. See also Mitchell-Kernan, "Signifying and Marking," pp. 161–179, and Abrahams, *Talking Black*, pp. 1–92.

2. Abrahams, *Deep Down*, pp. 39–43.

3. Daniels, "Lester Young," p. 314.

4. Gold, *A Jazz Lexicon*, p. 223.

5. Ibid., p. xxii.

6. The notion of "swing" feeling is problematic in many ways. Listeners often disagree over which performances swing and which do not. It is not necessarily a feeling limited to the rhythm, since melodic lines can also be rhythmic and produce either a swing feeling or create a kind of tension against the drumming, which also contributes to swing feeling. Since general rhythmic concepts change from one style of jazz to another, different swing feelings exist.

7. Gold, *A Jazz Lexicon*, pp. 223–224.

8. Among African-American groups, the practice of altering critical lexes into positive referents dates back to an era of sung ballads and folktales of the 1890s whose heroes, often called "bad men," included Railroad Bill, Stagolee, and others. Though deemed bad, their deeds were nevertheless admired by the African-American community, for they challenged the conventions of the dominant society. The ballad "Railroad Bill" (see Laws, Jr., *Native American Balladry*, p. 252), for example, recounts the criminal exploits of the main character, who is depicted as a "bad man." Since it challenged some of the values of the dominant society, Railroad Bill's criminal behavior gained him the stature of a folk hero among the African-American community; hence, in this case, bad is good.

9. This is sometimes called the "interaction approach."

10. See Black, "More about Metaphor," pp. 28–31. Proponents of "comparison theory" generally oppose the interaction approach. They posit that metaphors do not involve thought and action; hence, they are incapable of creating in the hearer new ideas. See also Lakoff and Johnson, *Metaphors*, p. 153.

11. Whereas some approaches to metaphor rely on the comparison of actual properties of objects in a literal manner ("comparison theory"), Black's interaction model focuses directly on what the terms of the metaphor call to mind in the perceiver. Hence, it is more sensitive to the pressures and dynamics of the context in which a metaphor is used.

12. Metaphors can be grouped into broadly defined categories, including structural, conduit, orientational, ontological, and personification metaphors. Structural metaphors are metaphors in which one concept is metaphorically structured in terms of another. In their book *Metaphors*, pp. 3–6, Lakoff and Johnson suggest that phrases such as "his criticisms were right on target" and "he shot down my argument" are related in meaning to the conceptual metaphor ARGUMENT IS WAR. The intent of the first metaphor is coherent with and partially derived from the conceptual metaphor, which is culturally and socially based. In other words, in our society the activity of arguing is structured along the same lines in which war is pursued. In a battle, strategies, attacks, and defenses are carefully planned, and winners and losers both emerge. Thus conceptual metaphors lie at the root of how we perceive objects, events, situations, and people in terms of something else.

13. Though I borrow from Lakoff and Johnson's model for interpreting metaphors, their approach fails to account for the various usages of a single expression in different contexts or their ability to alter or create new meanings for the listener. In this regard, the model is static and is not sufficiently sensitive to the complexities of the contextual environment.

14. Such, "'Out There,'" p. 84.

15. A few of my male students occasionally use the expression "out there" to refer to an attractive female. Like many other expressions, it is slowly filtering into other segments of the dominant society.

16. Williams, *Jazz Masters*, p. 249.

17. Ken McIntyre, interview held October 14, 1985, at his loft in New York City.

18. The source of the quotation wishes to remain anonymous, since he feels that this study does not sufficiently reflect the oppression and alienation that African-American jazz artists are made to suffer. It has been my opinion, throughout my entire association with out performers, that there are several other important aspects in the lives of these musicians which deserve attention as well.

19. Milford Graves, interview held January 25, 1984, at his home in Jamaica, New York.

20. Earl Cross, interview held January 31, 1984, at the author's apartment.

21. Daniel Carter, interview held June 22, 1983, at a park in the Lower East Side of Manhattan.

22. Frank Lowe, interview held June 29, 1984, at his apartment in New York City.

23. Coldlight, interview held January 10, 1984, at the author's apartment in New York City. "Up there" can also mean a musician who is playing in the extended ranges of his or her instrument, which listeners and performers usually regard as a very expressive moment in the performance. It is possible that Johnson was using "up there" in both a metaphoric sense and to mean playing in the higher registers of the instrument.

24. One is perhaps reminded of the problems Cecil Taylor faced early in his career. He discovered that his music evolved into areas incompatible with the isometric rhythms of his former drummer, Dennis Charles. Some out drummers like Andrew Cyrille, Milford Graves, Sunny Murray, and Paul Murphy, for example, have learned to internalize the main beat and to develop fluid patterns around the off beat.

7. Communicating Out Worldviews

1. In his book *Philosophy and the Analysis of Music*, pp. xiii-xxi, Ferrara points out that the listener engages a work of music on both the intrinsic and referential levels. For instance, while perceiving musical syntax, the listener may also reflect upon the music as a product of the historical epoch in which the work was created. Ferrara is critical of current methods of formal musical analysis that fail to consider both the intrinsic and referential meaning of music.

2. Ibid., p. 4. See also Hanslick, *The Beautiful in Music*, and Gurney, *The Power of Sound*. Both Hanslick and Gurney forward methodologies for analyzing absolute music, that is, music not having predetermined emotional or referential meaning.

3. For a detailed overview of the ancient Greek practice of assigning mathematical ratios to pitch intervals, see Walker, *Musical Beliefs*, chap. 3.

4. Ibid., pp. xi, 86–89.

5. For a detailed discussion and critique of these approaches, see Serafine, *Music as Cognition*, pp. 18–23.

6. Cook, *Music*, p. 3. Cook effectively argues in favor of bridging the gap between formal musical analysis and what the average listener actually perceives (pp. 5–7).

7. Ibid., pp. 146–147.

8. Meyer, *Music*, p. 8.

9. Ibid., pp. 170–232.

10. Ibid., pp. 6–12.

11. For meaning to be transmitted and comprehended, a plethora of cognitive processes are set into motion that may be so complex that they elude identification. Relatively new disciplines, such as psychobiology, have recently emerged and attempt to isolate these physical and mental processes and explain their operations.

12. It seems possible for a listener to adjust his or her mood to fit the perceived mood of the music. This may enable him or her to relieve stress caused by negative emotions, such as remorse.

13. Kivy, *Music Alone*, pp. 30–41, 42–48.

14. Kaufmann, *The Ragas*, pp. 10–20.

15. Walker, *Musical Beliefs*, pp. 189–190.

16. Merriam, *The Anthropology*, pp. 243–245

17. Geertz, *The Interpretation*, pp. 129–130.

18. Rusch, *Jazztalk*, p. 62.

19. Primack, "Sun Ra," p. 41.

20. Fiofori, "Sun Ra's Space Odyssey," p. 15.

21. Ibid., p. 14.

22. Townley, "Sun Ra," p. 38.

23. A religious cult based on Coltrane's spiritual and philosophical beliefs is reported to have originated in San Francisco.

24. "Musicians Talk about John Coltrane," p. 38.

25. Ibid.

26. Abrams, Baker, and Ellison, "The Social Role," p. 102.

27. Sidran, *Black Talk*, p. 148.

28. Coltrane explored multiphonics (i.e., tones in which several different harmonics or frequencies become audible) as early as 1959 when he recorded "Harmonique" (*Coltrane Jazz*). It was during the mid-1960s on recordings such as *Meditations, Expression*, and *Live in Seattle* that he incorporated this technique into playing controlled screeches. See Gridley, *Jazz Styles*, p. 281.

29. By extension, one may also perceive life as beautiful but fraught with danger and risk, as suggested by rose thorns. Like a garden, life also needs to be cultivated to produce fruits (the "fruits of life").

30. In these approaches to performing music, preperformance roles and statuses are dissolved. Parallel occurrences of this phenomenon in the trance-induced music and dance rituals of non-Western societies (e.g., the Vodun people) have been reported by Rouget, *Music and Trance*, p. 56. Rouget, however, defines trance as an altered, transitory state of consciousness conforming to a cultural model. This implies that music, dance, and the trance-induced states which result in certain cultures vary little from performance to performance. In comparison, it is interesting to note that the musical content of out performances differs significantly in each performance. The reasons for these differences are of course rooted in the specific meanings that music and trance have in a particular culture.

31. Pharoah Sanders, interview held January 23, 1990, over the telephone.

32. In 1986, Dr. Roger Kendall (Department of Music, UCLA) and I videotaped a live performance by pianist Horace Tapscott and his quartet. On the videotape, we localized points of structural differentiation and peak levels of heightened interaction that performers, in part, agreed had occurred after they reviewed the performance. The videotape was then shown to a sampling of students drawn from the Development of Jazz course, which I taught that year at UCLA (each quarter, the course invariably draws an enrollment well over five hundred students). Students were divided into test groups based on modality (i.e., some groups attended the live performance, whereas others saw only the videotaped performance) and factor (i.e., some groups had training in music and interest in jazz, whereas others did not). While watching the videotape, students responded to a questionnaire that measured

certain dependent variables, including activity, potency, and evaluation, along an eight-point scale. In this manner, they responded to a total of seven localized sections of the performance, which was eight minutes and eight seconds in duration. Once all the data have been analyzed, we intend to publish the results as an article in a suitable journal.

33. Other visionaries, according to Parker, include Ornette Coleman, Albert Ayler, Cecil Taylor, Bill Dixon, Milford Graves, Don Cherry, and Daniel Carter.

34. During a performance, Parker's emotions may vary, but often they include compassion, love, and sincerity. His values include high regard for freedom of expression, alternative ways of thinking and perceiving, and brotherhood.

35. Other out jazz musicians have attested to the occurrence of this phenomenon during their performances.

36. Parker, *Document Humanum*, pp. 13, 16.

37. Dewey Johnson, interview held July 3, 1983, at Columbia University.

38. Ibid.

39. Those who view out jazz as protest music might tend to imagine that the aggressive manner of the performance is the result of anger. From the perspective presented here, the free-form, collectively improvised approach enables out performers to express a wide range of emotions, including just feeling good.

40. This performance took place in February 1984. The recording has not been commercially marketed and is not available to readers.

41. I do not entirely agree with Carter on this issue, since in most forms of Western music tension-release frameworks are common. The tonic of a particular melody, for instance, is used to resolve tension that may result from dissonant relationships among other notes. In Carter's performance, a similar tension was created when the trumpet and saxophone played polyphonically, sometimes in unrelated keys, and was resolved when both sustained a common note. This tendency, therefore, is not a genetic response.

42. Interview with Daniel Carter, October 14, 1985, at a park in the Lower East Side of Manhattan.

43. Peikoff, *The Ominous Parallels*, pp. 119–127.

44. Furthermore, Carter's unconventional usages of language function in a similar manner, since they allow him to recreate relationships among external phenomena using intuitive modes of cognition.

45. Woodward, *The Myths*, p. xix.

46. See also Brown, *Recollections*, pp. 127–151.

8. The Implications of Fusing Out Jazz and Culture

1. Anthropologists first expressed interest in the notion of culture as early as the mid-1800s. Since then other social science disciplines have widely adopted the term as a key conceptual component for understanding human behavior. As a result, a

variety of definitions of culture coexist. For a brief overview of some of these definitions of culture, see Lett, *The Human Enterprise.*

2. Berliner, *The Soul of Mbira*, p. 48.

3. Ibid., pp. 201–202.

4. See D'Andrade, "Cultural Meaning Systems," pp. 88–119.

5. William Parker, interview held June 21, 1983, at his apartment in New York City.

6. Several studies, including the present one, which look closely at the relationships between music and culture do not radically depart from Alan Merriam's tripartite model involving conceptualization about music, behavior in relation to music, and music sound itself. So it would seem, as Tim Rice suggests, that all ethnomusicological investigation and methodology could perhaps fit under one roof (see his article "Toward the Remodeling of Ethnomusicology," pp. 469–488). Rice envisions a disciplinary model that reconstructs the history of music (i.e., those pressures over time effecting change or promoting stability), that assesses processes of social maintenance (e.g., the role of supportive belief systems), and that determines the role of the individual as a listener or performer (p. 480). This model expands upon Merriam's view of music as a product directly or indirectly resulting from interrelated human, social, and cultural processes. It accounts for our universal tendency to relate to music and our environment through a complex web of symbols and meanings. Of course, it is debatable whether ethnomusicologists should confine their researches within the framework of a single model.

7. Levels or degrees of abstraction of music are also suggested in Alan Merriam's model for the study of music and culture (see his book *The Anthropology of Music*, p. 232). He identifies four levels (the level of signing, affective meaning, music as a reflection of social organization, and music as a universal) for the study of music as a "'symbolic' part of life." These levels are organized in an ascending order, whereby the symbolic relationships between music and life or culture become more abstract (pp. 229–258). Timothy Rice's model for ethnomusicology is also organized with this kind of hierarchy in mind. See also Mantle Hood's notion of the G-S line, which he explains in his book *The Ethnomusicologist*, p. 303. Refer also to Béhague, *Performance Practice*; Stone, *Let the Inside Be Sweet*, pp. 2, 20–27; Herndon and McCleod, *Music as Culture*, pp. 26–30; Blacking, "The Problem," pp. 184–194; Feld, "Communication," pp. 1–18; Roseman, "The Social Stucturing of Sound," pp. 411–445; and Herndon, "Analysis," pp. 219–262.

8. It is useful to consider that meaning does not reside entirely in a sign. It involves the interplay of an interpreter who perceives the sign and conceptualizes its meaning. Hence, signs are perhaps better imagined as having the "capacity" or "potential" to communicate.

9. Michael Keith, interview held July 7, 1983, at a friend's apartment.

10. See Stone, *Let the Inside Be Sweet*, p. xv. See also Spradley, *Culture and Cognition*, pp. 18–35, and Giddins, *Central Problems*, pp. 2–8.

11. The notion of whether human behavior is free or determined is a point of

contention among sociologists and symbolic interactionists. Refer to Meltzer, Petras, and Reynolds, *Symbolic Interactionism*, pp. 61–66.

12. Folklorists played an important role in establishing a precedent for looking at the individual and the context of performance. In general, their studies demonstrated how expressive behavior is shaped by human psychological and biological factors such as cognition, aesthetic response, motivations, creativity, and beliefs. For example, see Ben-Amos, *Folklore Genres*, pp. xxxvi–xxxix; Bronner, *American Folk Art*; and Caravelli, "The Symbolic Village." Jones, in his study *The Hand Made Object and Its Maker*, focuses on an individual chairmaker living in southeastern Kentucky and the ways in which the chairmaker's experiences influenced certain designs.

13. The notion of causal relationships between the musical and cultural is rooted in a structural-functionalist view of culture, which perceives culture as a number of highly integrated parts that function to maintain the equilibrium of the whole and to reinforce social organization. Though they can be studied separately or together, they are considered to be static over time.

14. Written in 1911 and published in 1921, sociologist Max Weber's work *Die rationalen und soziologischen Grundlagen der Musik* (The rational and social foundations of music) was one of the first to explore causal relationships between the musical and social. It attempts to trace the influence of social factors (e.g., the highly rational mind of Westerners) on the development of Western music. Causal relationships between the social and musical are abundantly found in more recent studies conducted by various ethnomusicologists. These generally focus upon one or more topics, including music as a social class phenomenon (see Feld, "Sound Structure," p. 384, and Roseman, "The Social Structuring of Sound," p. 411), as a reflection of gender-role distinctions (Campbell and Eastman, "Ngoma," p. 467), and as something determined by socioeconomic conditions (Turino, "The Urban-Mestizo Charango Tradition," p. 253) or sociopolitical attitudes (DjeDje, "Change and Differentiation," p. 241).

15. These include diffusion, urbanization, acculturation (to which syncretism is closely related), Westernization, and modernization (see Nettl, *The Western Impact on World Music*). In his book *The Music of Africa*, Nketia attributes several variables (e.g., political formations, trade, religion, geography, and cultural contact with Islam and Europe) that account for the diversity of music found in Africa (pp. 3–20).

16. Coplan, "Go to My Town," pp. 96–114.

17. Blacking, "Some Problems," p. 1.

18. This suggests a view of the city in which small primary groups are not weakened by urbanization. Instead, bonds are created among members of such groups which function as buffers against anomie. This contrasts with Louis Wirth's negative view of urbanization, which he believes is the main cause for the breakdown of primary groups ("Urbanism as a Way of Life," pp. 3–24).

19. Berger and Luckman, *The Social Construction of Reality*, p. 32. "Typification" is a term I have borrowed and reshaped from Berger's discussion of how face-to-face interaction is influenced by individuals who perceive in other individuals

certain traits, such as "man," "European," "jovial type," etc. (pp. 29–32). Social structure, according to Berger, is the sum total of these typifications and the patterns of behavior with which they are associated.

20. Keil, *Tiv Song*, pp. 25–52.

21. This raises the possibility, however, for multiple interpretations of the same culture to exist among anthropologists, much like the principles of hermeneutics. That is, culture resembles an assemblage of texts to be interpreted. Because no one interpretation is absolute, all are valid. It remains to be seen to what degree multiple interpretations of the same culture by anthropologists would differ in comparison to the multiple interpretations among literary critics who for instance study Shakespeare.

22. Wachsmann, "The Changeability," pp. 207–211; Zemp, "'Are' are Classification," pp. 37–67.

23. Feld, "Sound Structure," p. 390.

24. Some resemblance is noted between out worldviews that integrate music and the supernatural and some non-Western rituals involving the same concepts.

25. Some musicians may base their aesthetic preferences for music on personal choice or upon things other than the social or ritual functions which scholars of music have often regarded as crucial to the modeling of music in culture. When Shona *mbira* players, for example, play in nonritual contexts, selection and the length of pieces they perform are determined in part by personal factors, such as mood (Berliner, *The Soul of Mbira*, pp. 52–53).

26. Meyer holds the position that "musical meaning lies exclusively within the context of the work itself" (*Emotion and Meaning in Music*, p. 1). To assume, like Meyer, that music is nonreferential is a mistake, since it is possible for listeners to superimpose their own images and emotional response upon music, which of course may vary among listeners. These views have led Meyer to conclude that aleatory music is meaningless, which is an unproven assumption (see also Sherburne, "Meaning and Music," p. 579).

27. Starr, *Red and Hot*, pp. 316–321.

28. Ken McIntyre, interview held October 14, 1985, at his apartment in New York City.

29. John Zorn, interview held October 16, 1985, at his apartment in New York City.

30. Simosko and Tepperman, *Eric Dolphy*, p. 26.

31. Seeger, *Studies in Musicology*, pp. 42–52.

32. The emphasis upon the aural-oral mode of communication in these groups is not only an important reason for the continuing survival of an African-American culture but no doubt is partly the reason why slang and metaphoric expressions enter easily into African-American speech patterns.

33. Csikszentmihalyi, "Phylogenetic and Ontogenetic Functions," pp. 123–124.

34. Ibid., p. 124.

selected discography

Abrams, Richard. *Levels and Degrees of Light* (1968). Delmark 413.

Allen, Byron. *The Byron Allen Trio* (1965). ESP 1005.

Art Ensemble of Chicago. *A Jackson in Your House* (1969). BYG Actuel 2 (529.302).

Ayler, Albert. *New York Eye and Ear Control* (1964). ESP 1061.

———. *Vibrations* (1964). Arista-Freedom AL 1000.

———. *New Grass* (1968). Impulse AS-9175.

———. *Music Is the Healing Force of the Universe* (1969). Impulse AS-9191.

Bang, Billy. *Changing Seasons* (1980). Bellows 004.

———. *Untitled Gift* (1982). Anima 3BG9.

———. *Outline No. 12* (1982). Cell 5004.

Bang, Billy, with Charles, Dennis. *Bangception* (1982). Hat Musics 3512.

Bley, Paul. *Barrage* (1964). ESP 1008.

———. *Closer* (1965). ESP 1021.

Bluiett, Hamiet. *Endangered Species* (1976). India Navigation IN1025.

Bowie, Lester. *Numbers 1 and 2* (1967). Nessa n-1.

Braxton, Anthony. *Three Compositions of New Jazz* (1968). Delmark 415.

Brown, Marion. *Afternoon of a Georgia Faun* (1970). ECM 1004.

Cherry, Don. *Complete Communion* (1965). Blue Note 84226.

———. *Symphony for Improvisers* (1966). Blue Note 84247.

Coleman, Ornette. *Something Else* (1958). Contemporary S 7551.

———. *Change of the Century* (1959). Atlantic 1327.

———. *The Shape of Jazz to Come* (1959). Atlantic 1317.

———. *Tomorrow Is the Question* (1959). Contemporary S 7569.

———. *The Best of Ornette Coleman* (1959–1961). Atlantic SD 1558.

———. *Free Jazz* (1960). Atlantic 1364.

Coleman, Ornette, with Schuller, Gunther. *John Lewis Presents Gunther Schuller, Jazz Abstractions* (1960). Atlantic 1365.

Coltrane, John. *Coltrane Jazz* (1959). SD-1354

———. *Impressions* (1961/62/63). Impulse AS-42.

———. *A Love Supreme* (1964). Impulse AS-66.

———. *Ascension* (1965). Impulse AS-95.

———. *Om* (1965). Impulse AS-9140.

———. *Meditations* (1966). Impulse AS-9110.

———. *The Best of John Coltrane*, vol. 2. Impulse 9223-2.

Corea, Chick, with Braxton, Anthony, and Circle. *Circling In* (1968–1970). BN-LA472-H2.

Cyrille, Andrew, and Maono. *Metamusician's Stomp* (1978). BSR 0025.

Davis, Miles. *Milestones* (1958). Columbia CL 1193.

———. *Kind of Blue* (1959). CBS 62066.

Dixon, Bill. *Bill Dixon Septet* (1963). Savoy MG-12184.

———. *Thoughts* (1985). SN 1111.

Dixon, Bill, with Shepp, Archie. *Archie Shepp—Bill Dixon Quartet* (1962). Savoy 12178.

Dolphy, Eric. *Outward Bound* (1960). NewJ 8236.

———. *Copenhagen Concert* (1961). Prestige 24027.

———. *The Eric Dolphy Memorial Album* (1961). Prst. 7334.

———. *Conversations* (1963). FM 308.

———. *Out to Lunch* (1964). Blue Note BST84163.

Energy Essentials: A Developmental and Historical Introduction to the New Music. Impulse ASD 9228.

Evans, Bill. *Portrait in Jazz* (1959). Riverside RLP12-315.

———. *Bill Evans Trio: Sunday at the Village Vanguard* (1961). OJC-140 (RLP-9376).

Giuffre, Jimmy. *Free Fall* (1962). Columbia CL1964.

Graves, Milford. *Percussion Duo* (1964). ESP 1015.

———. *You Never Heard Such Sounds in Your Life: Milford Graves Percussion Ensemble with Sonny Morgan* (1965). ESP 1015.

Graves, Milford, with Cyrille, Andrew. *Dialogue of the Drums* (1974). IPS 001.

Graves, Milford, with Pullen, Don. *Nommo—In Concert at Yale University*, vol. 2 (1966). SRP Records PG290.

Haden, Charlie. *Liberation Suite* (1969). Impulse AS-9183.

Hill, Andrew. *Judgment* (1964). Blue Note 4159.

———. *Point of Departure* (1964). Blue Note BST84167.

Ibrahim, Abdullah [Dollar Brand]. *The Journey* (1977). Chiaroscuro CR 187.

Jarman, Joseph. *Song For* (1967). Delmark 410.

Jazz Composers' Orchestra. *The Jazz Composers' Orchestra* (1968). JCOA1001/2.

Lowe, Frank. *Black Beings* (1973). ESP 3013.

———. *The Flam* (1976). BSR 0005.

———. *The Frank Lowe Orchestra: Lowe and Behold* (1977). Music Works 3002.

———. *Exotic Heartbreak* (1981). SN 1032.

Lowe, Frank, with Ali, Rashied. *Duo Exchange* (1973). Survival 101.

Lyons, Jimmy. *Other Afternoons* (1969). BYG 529309.

———. *Push Pull* (1978). HH YZZ.

———. *Jump Up/What to Do About* (1980). HH21.

———. *Wee Sneezawee* (1983). BS 0067.

———. *Give It Up* (1985). BS 0087.

Mingus, Charles. *Jazz Experiment* (1954). Bethlehem BCP65.

———. *Pithecanthropus Erectus* (1956). Atlantic 1237.

———. *Stormy Weather* (1960). Barnaby (GRT Canada) 2-6015.

———. *Black Saint and Sinner Lady* (1963). Impulse S-35.

———. *Mingus*. Prestige 24010.

Mirage: Avant-garde and Third-stream Jazz. New World Records NW 216.

Mitchell, Roscoe. *Sound* (1966). Delmark 408.

Monk, Thelonious. *At the Five Spot* (with Johnny Griffin, 1957). M-47043.

———. *The Complete Blue Note Recordings of Thelonious Monk*. Mosaic MR4-101.

Moondoc, Jemeel. *Judy's Bounce* (1981). Soulnote 1051.

Morris, Butch. *Current Trends in Racism in Modern America (A Work in Progress)* (1985). Sound Aspects 4010.

Murray, David. *Interboogieology* (1978). BSR 0018.

———. *David Murray Octet: New Life* (1985). Black Saint BSR 0100.

Murray, Sunny. *Sunny Murray Quintet* (1966). ESP 1032.

———. *Homage to Africa* (1969). BYG 529303.

———. *Sunshine* (1969). BYG 529348.

———. *Never Give a Sucker an Even Break* (1969). BYG 529332.

———. *Apple Cores* (1978). Philly Jazz 1004.

New Music: Second Wave (1962–1964). Savoy 2235.

New Thing. Actuel BYG 23.

Newton, James. *Romance and Revolution* (1986). Blue Note BT 85134.

New York Contemporary Five. *New York Contemporary Five at Jazzhus Montmartre* (1963). Sonet SLP 51.

Outstanding Jazz Compositions of the 20th Century. C2L31/C2S 831.

Parker, William, Matsuura, Takeshi Zen, Hwang, Jason, and Connell, Will. *Commitment* (1980). C1001.

Rivers, Sam. *The Live Trios: Dedication Series*, vol. 12 (1973). JA-9352-2.

Roach, Max. *We Insist!: Max Roach and Oscar Brown, Jr.'s Freedom Now Suite* (1960). AMLP 810.

Rollins, Sonny. *Sonny Rollins: The Blue Note Re-issue Series* (1956–57). BN-LA401-H2-0798.

———. *Freedom Suite* (1959). Riverside RLP1Z-258.

———. *The Bridge* (1962). RCA LSP2527.

Russell, George. *The Jazz Workshop* (1956). RCA LPM2534.

———. *Brandeis University 1957 Festival of the Arts Jazz Concert* (1957). Columbia WL127.

———. *Jazz in the Space Age* (1960). Decca DL9219.

———. *Ezz-thetics* (1961). Riverside RLP375.

———. *Outer Thoughts* (1962). Prestige M-47027.

Shepp, Archie. *Peace* (1962). Savoy MG 12178.

———. *New York Contemporary Five* (1963). Fontana 881013 ZY.

———. *New York Contemporary Five* (1964). Savoy/CBS 52422.

———. *Four for Trane* (1964). Impulse AS-71.

———. *Fire Music* (1965). Impulse AS-86.

Silva, Alan. *Luna Surface* (1969). BYG 529-312.

Sun Ra. *The Futuristic Sounds of Sun Ra* (1961). Savoy MG 12138.

———. *Sun Song* (1965). Delmark 411.

———. *The Heliocentric Worlds of Sun Ra*, vol. 1 (1965). ESP 1014.

————. *Sun Ra and His Arkestra: Live at Montreux* (1976). Inner City IC 1039.

Taylor, Cecil. *Looking Ahead* (1958). Contemporary 3562.

————. *Into the Hot* (1961). Impulse A-9.

————. *Conquistador* (1966). Blue Note 84260.

————. *Unit Structures* (1966). Blue Note 84237.

Tchicai, John, Shepp, Archie, Moses, J. C., and Moore, Don. *Rufus* (1963). Fontana 881 014 ZY.

Threadgill, Henry, Hopkins, Fred, and McCall, Steve. *Air: Air Lore* (1979). Arista AN 3014.

Tristano, Lennie, with Dameron, Tadd. *Crosscurrents* (1949). Affinity 149.

Tyler, Charles. *Charles Tyler Live in Europe* (1975). AK-BA 1010.

————. *Saga of the Outlaws* (1976). Nessa 16.

————. *Definite* (1981). Sto. 4098-9.

Wildflowers: The New York Loft Jazz Sessions, vols. 1−5 (1976). Casablanca Records and Filmworks Inc./Douglas NBLP 7045-NBLP 7049.

The World Saxophone Quartet. *Steppin'* (1978). BSR 0027.

Wright, Frank. *Uhuru Na Umoja* (1970). America 30AM6104.

The Young Lions: A Concert of New Music Played by Seventeen Exceptional Young Musicians (The Kool Jazz Festival, June 30, 1982). Musician 9 60196-1.

selected bibliography

Abrahams, Roger D. *Deep Down in the Jungle: Negro Narrative Folklore from the Streets of Philadelphia*. Chicago: Aldine, 1970.

———. *Talking Black*. Rowley, Mass.: Newbury House Publishers, 1976.

Abrams, Richard, Baker, David N., and Ellison, Charles. "The Social Role of Jazz." In *Reflections on Afro-American Music*, pp. 101–110. Ed. Dominique-René de Lerma. Kent, Ohio: Kent State University Press, 1973.

Armstrong, Robert Plant. *The Affecting Presence: An Essay in Humanistic Anthropology*. Chicago: University of Illinois Press, 1971.

Asch, Michael I. "Social Context and the Musical Analysis of Slavey Drum Dance Songs." *Ethnomusicology* 19 (1975): 245–257.

Attali, Jacques. *Noise: The Political Economy of Music*. Trans. Brian Massumi; foreword by Frederic Jameson; afterword by Susan McClary. Theory and History of Literature, vol. 16. Minneapolis: University of Minnesota Press, 1985.

Backus, Rob. *Fire Music: A Political History of Jazz*. Chicago: Vanguard Books, 1976.

Baker, David N., ed. *New Perspectives on Jazz*. Report on a National Conference Held at Wingspread, Racine, Wisconsin, Sept. 8–10, 1986. Washington, D.C.: Smithsonian Institution Press, 1990.

Baker, David N., Belt, Lida M., and Hudson, Herman C., eds. *The Black Composer Speaks: A Project of the Afro-American Arts Institute, Indiana University*. Metuchen, N.J.: Scarecrow Press, 1978.

Balliet, Whitney. *Such Sweet Thunder: Forty-nine Pieces on Jazz*. Indianapolis: Bobbs-Merrill, 1966.

Baron, Robert. "Syncretism and Ideology: Latin New York Salsa Musicians." *Western Folklore* 36 (1977): 209–225.

Barth, Fredrik, ed. *Ethnic Groups: The Social Organization of Culture Difference*. Little, Brown Series in Anthropology. Boston: Little, Brown, 1969.

Basso, Ellen B. "A 'Musical View of the Universe': Kalapalo Myth and Ritual as Religious Performance." *Journal of American Folklore* 94 (1981): 273–291.

Basso, Keith H., and Selby, Henry A., eds. *Meaning in Anthropology*. School of American Research Advanced Seminar Series. Albuquerque: University of New Mexico Press, 1976.

Bauman, Richard. "Conceptions of Folklore in the Development of Literary Semiotics." *Semiotica* 39, no. 1/2 (1982): 1–20.

———. "Differential Identity and the Social Base of Folklore." *Journal of American Folklore* 84 (1971): 31–42.

———. *Verbal Art as Performance*. Series in Sociolinguistics. Rowley, Mass.: Newbury House, 1977.

Bauman, Richard, and Sherzer, Joel. *Explorations in the Ethnography of Speaking*. New York: Cambridge University Press, 1974.

Becker, A. L., and Yengoyan, Aram A., eds. *The Imagination of Reality: Essays in Southeast Asian Coherence Systems.* Norwood, N.J.: Ablex, 1979.

Becker, Howard S. *The Outsiders: Studies in the Sociology of Deviance.* New York: Free Press, 1973.

———. "The Professional Jazz Musician and His Audience." In *The Sounds of Social Change: Studies in Popular Culture*, pp. 248–260. Ed. R. Serge Denisoff and Richard A. Peterson. Rand McNally Sociology Series. Chicago: Rand McNally, 1972.

Béhague, Gerard, ed. *Performance Practice: Ethnomusicological Perspectives: Contributions in Intercultural and Comparative Studies, Number 12.* Westport, Conn.: Greenwood Press, 1984.

Ben-Amos, Dan. "Toward a Definition of Folklore in Context." *Journal of American Folklore* 84 (1971): 3–15.

———, ed. *Folklore Genres.* Publications of the American Folklore Society, Bibliographical and Special Series, vol. 26. Austin: University of Texas Press, 1976.

Ben-Amos, Dan, and Goldstein, Kenneth, eds. *Folklore: Performance and Communication.* Approaches to Semiotics 40. The Hague: Mouton, 1975.

Berendt, Joachim E. *The Jazz Book: From Ragtime to Fusion and Beyond.* Trans. H. and B. Bredigkeit with Dan Morgenstern. Westport, Conn.: L. Hill, 1982.

Berger, Peter L., and Luckmann, Thomas. *The Social Construction of Reality: A Treatise in the Sociology of Knowledge.* Garden City, N.Y.: Doubleday, 1966.

Berliner, Paul. *The Soul of Mbira: Music and Traditions of the Shona People of Zimbabwe.* Berkeley: University of California Press, 1978.

Berlyne, D. E. *Aesthetics and Psychobiology.* Century Psychology Series. New York: Appleton-Century-Crofts, 1971.

Black, Max. "More about Metaphor." In *Metaphor and Thought*, pp. 19–43. Ed. Andrew Ortony. New York: Cambridge University Press, 1979.

Blacking, John. *How Musical Is Man?* John Danz Lecture. Seattle: University of Washington Press, 1973.

———. "The Problem of 'Ethnic' Perceptions in the Semiotics of Music." In *The Sign in Music and Literature*, pp. 184–194. Ed. Wendy Steiner. Austin: University of Texas Press, 1981.

———. "Some Problems of Theory and Method in the Study of Musical Change." *Yearbook of International Folk Music Council* 9 (1977): 1–26.

———. "The Structure of Musical Discourse: The Problem of the Song Text." *Yearbook for Traditional Music* 14 (1982): 15–23.

Blacking, John, and Kealiinohomoku, Joann W., eds. *The Performing Arts: Music and Dance.* The Hague, New York: Mouton, 1979.

Blancq, Charles. *Sonny Rollins: The Journey of a Jazzman.* Boston: Twayne Publishers, 1983.

Blauner, Robert. "Black Culture: Myth or Reality?" In *Afro-American Anthropology: Contemporary Perspectives*, pp. 347–366. Ed. Norman E. Whitten, Jr., and John F. Szwed. New York: Free Press, 1970.

Blesh, Rudi. *Shining Trumpets: A History of Jazz.* New York: Alfred A. Knopf, 1958; 2d ed., revised and enlarged. New York: Da Capo Press, 1975.

Blumer, Herbert. *Symbolic Interactionism: Perspective and Method.* Englewood Cliffs, N.J.: Prentice-Hall, 1969.

Boilés, Charles L. "Processes of Musical Semiosis." *Yearbook for Traditional Music* 14 (1982): 24–44.

———. "Tepehua Thought-Song: A Case of Semantic Signaling." *Ethnomusicology* 11 (1967): 267–292.

Boon, James A. *From Symbolism to Structuralism: Lévi-Strauss in a Literary Tradition.* Explorations in Interpretive Sociology. Oxford: Blackwell, 1972.

Borneman, Ernest. "Black Light and White Shadow: After Black Power, What?" *Jazzforschung* 3/4 (1971/72): 11–34.

Bronner, Simon J., ed. *American Folk Art: A Guide to Sources.* Garland Reference Library of the Humanities, vol. 464. New York: Garland, 1984.

Brook, Barry S., Downes, Edward O. D., and Solkema, Sherman van. *Perspectives in Musicology: The Inaugural Lectures of the Ph.D. Program in Music at the City University of New York.* New York: W. W. Norton, 1972.

Brown, Marion. "Improvisation and the Aural Tradition in Afro-American Music." *Black World* 23 (1973): 14–19.

———. *Recollections: Essays, Drawings, Miscellanea.* Frankfurt, Germany: Juergen A. Schmitt, 1984.

Budd, Malcolm. *Music and the Emotions: The Philosophical Theories.* Boston: Routledge and Kegan Paul, 1985.

Budds, Michael J. *Jazz in the Sixties: The Expansion of Musical Resources and Techniques.* An expanded edition, 1st ed. Iowa City: University of Iowa Press, 1990.

Byrnside, Ronald. "The Performer as Creator: Jazz Improvisation." In *Contemporary Music and Music Cultures,* pp. 223–251. Ed. Charles Hamm, Bruno Nettl, and Ronald Byrnside. Englewood Cliffs, N.J.: Prentice-Hall, 1975.

Cage, John. *Silence.* Cambridge: Massachusetts Institute of Technology Press, 1966.

Campbell, Carol A., and Eastman, Carol M. "Ngoma: Swahili Adult Song Performance in Context." *Ethnomusicology* 28 (1984): 467–493.

Caravelli, Anna. "The Symbolic Village: Community Born in Performance." *Journal of American Folklore* 98 (1985): 259–286.

Carles, Philippe, and Comolli, Jean-Louis. *Free Jazz/Black Power.* Paris: Editions Champ Libre, 1971.

Chevan, David. "The Double Bass as a Solo Instrument in Early Jazz." *Black Perspective in Music* 17 (1989): 72–91.

Cohen, Abner. "Drama and Politics in the Development of a London Carnival." *Journal of the Royal Anthropological Institute* 15 (1980): 65–88.

———. *Two-dimensional Man: An Essay on the Anthropology of Power and Symbolism in Complex Society.* Berkeley: University of California Press, 1974.

————, ed. *Urban Ethnicity*. ASA Monographs, vol. 12. New York: Tavistock Publications, 1974.

Coker, Jerry. *Improvising Jazz*. Englewood Cliffs, N.J.: Prentice-Hall, 1964.

Collier, James Lincoln. "Jazz." In *The New Grove Dictionary of Jazz*, pp. 580–606. Ed. Barry Kernfeld. New York: Macmillan, 1988.

————. *The Making of Jazz: A Comprehensive History*. New York: Dell, 1978.

Cone, James H. *The Spirituals and the Blues*. New York: Seabury Press, 1972.

Cook, Bruce. *The Beat Generation*. New York: Scribner's, 1971.

Cook, Nicholas. *Music, Imagination, and Culture*. Oxford: Clarendon Press, 1990.

Cope, David H. *New Directions in Music*. 4th ed. Dubuque, Iowa: W. C. Brown, 1984.

Coplan, David. "Go to My Town, Cape Coast!: The Social History of Ghanaian Highlife." In *Eight Urban Musical Cultures: Tradition and Change*, pp. 96–114. Ed. Bruno Nettl. Chicago: University of Illinois Press, 1978.

————. *In Township Tonight!: South Africa's Black City Music and Theatre*. New York: Longman, 1985.

Courlander, Harold. *Negro Folk Music, U.S.A.* New York: Columbia University Press, 1963.

Crook, Rodney. "Observers as Participants: A Note in Anthropology and Social Theory." *Yearbook of Symbolic Anthropology* 1 (1978): 31–36.

Crouch, Stanley. "The Avant-garde's Lost Patrols." *Village Voice*, June 28, 1983, p. 68.

Csikszentmihalyi, Mihaly. "Phylogenetic and Ontogenetic Functions of Artistic Cognition." In *The Arts, Cognition, and Basic Skills*, pp. 114–127. Ed. Stanley S. Madeja. Yearbook on Research in Arts and Aesthetics Education, vol. 2. St. Louis, Mo.: CEMREL, 1978.

D'Andrade, Roy G. "Cultural Meaning Systems." In *Culture Theory: Essays on Mind, Self, and Emotion*, pp. 88–119. Ed. Richard A. Shweder and Robert A. LeVine. New York: Cambridge University Press, 1984.

Daniels, Douglas. "Lester Young: Master of Jive." *American Music* 3 (1985): 312–328.

De Arce, Daniel Mendoza. "Contemporary Sociological Theories and the Sociology of Music." *International Review of the Aesthetics and Sociology of Music* 5 (1974): 231–248.

DeMicheal, Don. "John Coltrane and Eric Dolphy Answer the Jazz Critics." *Down Beat* 46 (1979): 16, 52.

DeMicheal, Don, and Coltrane, John. "Coltrane on Coltrane." *Down Beat* 47 (1979): 17.

Denisoff, R. Serge. *Great Day Coming: Folk Music and the American Left*. Urbana: University of Illinois Press, 1971.

Dillard, J. L. *American Talk: Where Our Words Came From*. New York: Random House, 1976.

————. *Lexicon of Black English*. New York: Seabury Press, 1977.

DjeDje, Jacqueline Cogdell. "Change and Differentiation: The Adoption of Black

American Gospel Music in the Catholic Church." *Ethnomusicology* 30 (1986): 223–252.

Dorson, Richard. "Is There a Folk in the City?" In *The Urban Experience and Folk Tradition*, pp. 21–64. Ed. Américo Paredes and Ellen J. Stekert. Publications of the American Folklore Society Bibliographical and Special Series, vol. 22. Austin: University of Texas Press, 1971.

Douglas, Mary. *Implicit Meanings: Essays in Anthropology*. London: Routledge and Kegan Paul, 1975.

Dowling, Jay, and Harwood, Dane L. *Music Cognition*. Academic Press Series in Cognition and Perception. Orlando, Fla.: Academic Press, 1986.

Dumas, Bethany K., and Lighter, Jonathan. "Is Slang a Word for Linguistics?" *American Speech: A Quarterly of Linguistic Usage* 53 (1978): 5–39.

Dundes, Alan. "Folk Ideas as Units of World View." *Journal of American Folklore* 84 (1971): 93–104.

Dundes, Alan, and Pagter, Carl R. *Urban Folklore from the Paperwork Empire*. Publications of the American Folklore Society, Memoir Series, vol. 62. Austin: American Folklore Society, 1975.

Eisenberg, Evan. *The Recording Angel: Explorations in Phonography*. New York: McGraw-Hill, 1987.

Eisenstadt, S. N. *Social Differentiation and Stratification*. Glenview, Ill.: Scott, Foresman, 1971.

Ekwueme, Lazarus E. "African Music Retentions in the New World." *Black Perspective in Music* 2 (1974): 128–144.

Ellison, Ralph. *Shadow and Act*. New York: Random House, 1964.

Epstein, Dena J. *Sinful Tunes and Spirituals: Black Folk Music to the Civil War*. Music in American Life. Urbana: University of Illinois Press, 1977.

Essien-Udom, E. U. *Black Nationalism: A Search for an Identity in America*. Chicago: University of Chicago Press, 1962.

Evans, David. "African Elements in Twentieth-Century United States Black Folk Music." In *Report of the Twelfth Congress, Berkeley, 1977*, pp. 54–66. Ed. Daniel Heartz and Bonnie Wade. Philadelphia: American Musicological Society, 1981. Reprinted in *Jazzforschung* 10 (1978): 85–110.

———. *Big Road Blues: Tradition and Creativity in the Folk Blues*. Berkeley: University of California Press, 1982.

Feather, Leonard. *The Encyclopedia of Jazz in the '60s*. New York: Da Capo, 1966.

Feld, Steven. "Communication, Music, and Speech about Music." *Yearbook for Traditional Music* 16 (1984): 1–18.

———. "Linguistic Models in Ethnomusicology." *Ethnomusicology* 18 (1974): 197–217.

———. "Sound Structure as Social Structure." *Ethnomusicology* 28 (1984): 383–409.

Fernandez, James W. "Persuasions and Performances: Of the Beast in Every Body . . . and the Metaphors of Everyman." In *Myth, Symbol, and Culture*, pp. 39–60. Ed. Clifford Geertz. New York: W. W. Norton, 1971.

Ferrara, Lawrence. *Philosophy and the Analysis of Music: Bridges to Musical Sound, Form, and Reference.* New York: Greenwood Press, 1991.

Fiofori, Tam. "Sun Ra's Space Odyssey." *Down Beat,* May 14, 1970, pp. 14–17.

Fisch, Max Harold, ed. *Writings on Charles S. Peirce: A Chronological Edition.* Bloomington: Indiana University Press, 1982.

Fischer, Claude S. *The Urban Experience.* New York: Harcourt, Brace, Jovanovich, 1976.

Folb, Edith A. *Runnin' Down Some Lines: The Language and Culture of Black Teenagers.* Cambridge, Mass.: Harvard University Press, 1980.

Foster, Mary LeCron, and Brandes, Stanley H., eds. *Symbol as Sense: New Approaches to the Analysis of Meaning.* New York: Academic Press, 1980.

Fujie, Linda. "Effects of Urbanization on Matsuri-Bayashi in Tokyo." *Yearbook for Traditional Music* 15 (1983): 38–44.

Gans, H. J. *The Urban Villagers: Group and Class in the Life of Italian-Americans.* Foreword by Erich Lindmann. New York: Free Press, 1962; updated and expanded ed., New York: Free Press, 1982.

Gardner, Howard. "The Development of Competence in Culturally Defined Domains: A Preliminary Framework." In *Culture Theory: Essays on Mind, Self, and Emotion,* pp. 257–275. Ed. Richard A. Shweder and Robert A. LeVine. New York: Cambridge University Press, 1984.

Geertz, Clifford. "From the Native's Point of View: On the Nature of Anthropological Understanding." In *Culture Theory: Essays on Mind, Self, and Emotion,* pp. 123–136. Ed. Richard A. Shweder and Robert A. LeVine. New York: Cambridge University Press, 1984.

———. *The Interpretation of Cultures: Selected Essays.* New York: Basic Books, 1973.

———, ed. *Myth, Symbol, and Culture.* New York: W. W. Norton, 1971.

Giddins, Anthony. *Central Problems in Social Theory: Action, Structure and Contradiction in Social Analysis.* Berkeley: University of California Press, 1979.

Giddins, Gary. *Rhythm-a-ning: Jazz Tradition and Innovation in the '80s.* New York: Oxford University Press, 1985.

Giglioli, Pier Paolo, ed. *Language and Social Context: Selected Readings.* Penguin Modern Sociology Readings. Baltimore: Penguin Books, 1972.

Gillespie, Dizzy, with Fraser, Al. *To Be, or Not . . . to Bop: Memoirs.* Garden City, N.Y.: Doubleday, 1979.

Gitler, Ira. *Swing to Bop: An Oral History of the Transition in Jazz in the 1940s.* New York: Oxford University Press, 1985.

Glazer, Nathan, and Moynihan, Daniel Patrick. *Beyond the Melting Pot: The Negroes, Puerto Ricans, Jews, Italians, and Irish of New York City.* 2d ed. Cambridge: Massachusetts Institute of Technology Press, 1963.

Goffman, Erving. *Behavior in Public Places: Notes on the Social Organization of Gatherings.* New York: Free Press of Glencoe, 1963.

———. *The Presentation of Self in Everyday Life.* New York: Doubleday, 1959.

Gold, Robert S. *A Jazz Lexicon.* New York: Alfred A. Knopf, 1964.

————. *Jazz Talk*. Indianapolis: Bobbs-Merrill, 1975.

Gossen, Gary H. "To Speak with a Heated Heart: Chamula Canons of Style and Good Performance." In *Explorations in the Ethnography of Speaking*, pp. 389–413. Ed. Richard Bauman and Joel Sherzer. New York: Cambridge University Press, 1974.

Gray, Herman. *Producing Jazz: The Experience of an Independent Record Company*. Philadelphia: Temple University Press, 1988.

Gray, John, comp. *Fire Music: A Bibliography of the New Jazz, 1959–1990*. Foreword by Val Wilmer. New York: Greenwood Press, 1991.

Gregerson, Edgar A. "Linguistic Models in Anthropology." In *Language and Thought: Anthropological Issues*. World Anthropology. Ed. William C. McCormack and Stephen A. Wurm. The Hague: Mouton, 1977.

Gridley, Mark C. *Jazz Styles: History and Analysis*. 3d ed. Englewood Cliffs, N.J.: Prentice-Hall, 1988.

Gumperz, John J. "Types of Linguistic Communities." In *Readings in the Sociology of Language*, pp. 460–472. Ed. Joshua A. Fishman. The Hague: Mouton, 1968.

Gurney, Edmund. *The Power of Sound*, 1880. With an introductory essay by Edward T. Cone. New York: Basic Books, 1966.

Hall, Edward T. *Beyond Culture*. Garden City, N.Y.: Anchor Press, 1976.

Halliday, M. A. K. *Language as a Social Semiotic: The Social Interpretation of Language and Meaning*. Baltimore: University Park Press, 1978.

Hallowell, Irving A. *Culture and Experience*. Pennsylvania Paperback, 39. Philadelphia: University of Pennsylvania Press, 1974.

Hamm, Charles, Nettl, Bruno, and Byrnside, Ronald. *Contemporary Music and Music Cultures*. Englewood Cliffs, N.J.: Prentice-Hall, 1975.

Hanslick, Edward. *The Beautiful in Music*, 1891. Trans. Gustave Cohen. Ed. and with an introduction by Morris Weitz; 8th ed., New York: Liberal Arts Press, 1957.

Haralambos, Michael. *Soul Music: The Birth of a Sound in Black America*. New York: Da Capo Press, 1974.

Harrison, Frank. "Traditions and Acculturation: A View of Some Musical Processes." In *Essays on Music for Charles Warren Fox*, pp. 114–125. Ed. Jerald C. Graue, introduction by Edward G. Evans, Jr., foreword by Robert S. Freeman. New York: Eastman School of Music Press, 1979.

Harrison, Max. *A Jazz Retrospect*. Boston: Crescendo, 1976.

Harrison, Max, Morgan, Alun, Atkins, Ronald, James, Michael, and Cooke, Jack. *Modern Jazz: The Essential Records*. London: Aquarius Books, 1975.

Harvey, Edward. "Social Change and the Jazz Musician." *Social Forces* 46 (1967): 34–42.

Hastrup, Kirsten. "The Post-Structuralist Position of Social Anthropology." *Yearbook of Symbolic Anthropology* 1 (1978): 123–147.

Hatch, Elvin. *Theories of Man and Culture*. New York: Columbia University Press, 1973.

Hatten, Robert. "Nattiez's Semiology of Music: Flaws in the New Science." *Semiotica* 31, no. 1/2 (1980): 139–155.

Hawkes, Terence. *Metaphor*. Critical Idiom, 25. London: Methuen, 1972.

———. *Structuralism and Semiotics*. Berkeley: University of California Press, 1977.

Heartz, Daniel, and Wade, Bonnie, eds. *Reports of the Twelfth Congress, Berkeley, 1977*. Philadelphia: American Musicological Society, 1981.

Hentoff, Nat. *The Jazz Life*. New York: Da Capo Press, 1975.

Hentoff, Nat, and McCarthy, Albert J., eds. *Jazz: New Perspectives on the History of Jazz by Twelve of the World's Foremost Jazz Critics and Scholars*. New York: Rhinehart, 1959; reprint ed., New York: Da Capo Press, 1959.

Herndon, Marcia. "Analysis: The Herding of Sacred Cows?" *Ethnomusicology* 28 (1974): 219–262.

Herndon, Marcia, and McLeod, Norma. *Music as Culture*. Darby, Pa.: Norwood Editions, 1980.

Herskovits, Melville J. *The Myth of the Negro Past*. Boston: Beacon Press, 1958.

Hodeir, André. "Free Jazz." *World of Music* 10 (1968): 20–29.

Hood, Mantle. *The Ethnomusicologist*. New York: McGraw-Hill, 1971.

Hopkins, Pandora. "Individual Choice and the Control of Musical Change." *Journal of American Folklore* 89 (1976): 449–463.

Horowitz, Irving Louis. "Authenticity and Originality in Jazz: Toward a Paradigm in the Sociology of Music." *Journal of Jazz Studies* 1 (1973): 57–64.

Hughes, Phillip S. "Jazz Appreciation and the Sociology of Jazz." *Journal of Jazz Studies* 1 (1974): 79–96.

Hurley, Neil P. "Toward a Sociology of Jazz." *Thought* 44 (1969): 219–246.

Hymes, Dell. "Models of the Interaction of Language and Social Life." In *Directions in Sociolinguistics: The Ethnography of Communication*, pp. 35–71. Ed. John J. Gumperz and Dell Hymes. New York: Holt, Rinehart and Winston, 1972.

———. "Ways of Speaking." In *Explorations in the Ethnography of Speaking*, pp. 433–451. Ed. Richard Bauman and Joel Sherzer. New York: Cambridge University Press, 1974.

Jackson, Bruce. "Folkloristics." *Journal of American Folklore* 98 (1985): 95–101.

Jackson, George. *White and Negro Spirituals, Their Life Span and Kinship: Tracing 200 Years of Untrammeled Song Making and Singing among Our Country Folk; with 116 Songs as Sung by Both Races*. New York: J. J. Augustin, 1943; reprint ed., New York: Da Capo Press, 1975.

———. *White Spirituals in the Southern Uplands: The Story of the Fasola Folk, Their Songs, Singings, and "Buckwheat Notes."* Chapel Hill: University of North Carolina Press, 1933; reprint ed., 1964.

Jairazbhoy, Nazir A. "The 'Objective' and Subjective View in Music Transcription." *Ethnomusicology* 31 (1977): 263–273.

Johnson, Mark, ed. *Philosophical Perspectives on Metaphor*. Minneapolis: University of Minnesota Press, 1981.

Jones, A. M. *Studies in African Music*, 2 vols. New York: Oxford University Press, 1959.

Jones, LeRoi [Amiri Baraka]. *Black Music*. New York: William Morrow, 1967.

————. *Blues People: Negro Music in White America*. New York: William Morrow, 1963.

Jones, Michael Owen. *The Hand Made Object and Its Maker*. Berkeley: University of California Press, 1975.

Jost, Ekkehard. *Free Jazz*. Graz, Austria: Universal Edition, 1974.

————. "Free Jazz und die Musik der dritten Welt." *Jazzforschung* 3/4 (1971/72): 141–154.

————. "Zum Problem des politischen Engagements im Jazz." *Jazzforschung* 5 (1973): 33–43.

Joyce, James. *Finnegan's Wake*. London: Faber and Faber, 1939.

Kaplan, David, and Manners, Robert A. *Culture Theory*. Foundations of Modern Anthropology Series. Englewood Cliffs, N.J.: Prentice-Hall, 1972.

Karp, David A., Stone, Gregory P., and Yoels, William C. *Being Urban: A Social Psychological View of City Life*. Lexington, Mass.: Heath, 1977.

Kauffman, Robert. "Multi-part Relationships in the Shona Music of Rhodesia." Ph.D. diss., University of California, Los Angeles, 1970.

Kaufmann, Walter. *The Ragas of North India*. Bloomington: Indiana University Press, 1968.

Keil, Charles. *Tiv Song*. Chicago: University of Chicago Press, 1979.

————. *Urban Blues*. Chicago: University of Chicago Press, 1966.

————. "Who Needs 'the Folk' ?" *Journal of the Folklore Institute* 15 (1978): 263–265.

Keil, Charles, and Keil, Angeliki. "Musical Meaning: A Preliminary Report." *Ethnomusicology* 10 (1966): 153–173.

Kennington, Donald, and Read, Danny L. *The Literature of Jazz: A Critical Guide*. 2d ed. Chicago: American Library Association, 1980.

Kernfeld, Barry Dean. "Adderley, Coltrane, and Davis at the Twilight of Bebop: The Search for Melodic Coherence (1958–59)." 2 vols. Ph.D. diss., Cornell University, 1981.

Kerouac, Jack. *On the Road*. New York: Viking Press, 1979.

Kirshenblatt-Gimblett, Barbara. "The Future of Folklore Studies in America: The Urban Frontier." *Folklore Forum* 16 (1983): 175–234.

Kivy, Peter. *Music Alone: Philosophical Reflections on the Purely Musical Experience*. Ithaca: Cornell University Press, 1990.

Kochman, Thomas, ed. *Rappin' and Stylin' Out: Communication in Urban Black America*. Urbana: University of Illinois Press, 1972.

Kofsky, Frank. *Black Nationalism and the Revolution in Music*. New York: Pathfinder Press, 1970.

————. "Elvin Jones, Part I: Rhythmic Innovator." *Journal of Jazz Studies* 4 (1976): 3–24.

————. "Elvin Jones, Part II: Rhythmic Displacement in the Art of Elvin Jones." *Journal of Jazz Studies* 4 (1977): 11–32.

Kraków, Roman Kowal. "New Jazz and Some Problems of Its Notation." *Jazzforschung* 3/4 (1971/72): 180–193.

Krehbiel, Henry Edward. *Afro-American Folk Songs: A Study in Racial and National Music.* New York: F. Ungar, 1962.

Laba, Martin. "Urban Folklore: A Behavioral Approach." *Western Folklore* 38 (1979): 158–169.

Lakoff, George, and Johnson, Mark. *Metaphors We Live By.* Chicago: University of Chicago Press, 1980.

Lang, Iain. *Jazz in Perspective: The Background of the Blues.* New York: Da Capo Press, 1976.

Langness, L. L. *The Study of Culture.* San Francisco: Chandler and Sharp, 1974.

Laws, Malcolm G., Jr. *Native American Balladry: A Descriptive Study and a Bibliographical Syllabus.* Publications of the American Folklore Society Bibliographical and Special Series, vol. 1, rev. ed. Philadelphia: American Folklore Society, 1964.

Leeds, Morton. "The Process of Cultural Stripping and Reintegration: The Rural Migrants in the City." In *The Urban Experience and Folk Tradition,* pp. 165–173. Ed. Américo Paredes and Ellen J. Stekert. Publications of the American Folklore Society Bibliographical and Special Series, vol. 22. Austin: University of Texas Press, 1971.

Leonard, Neil. *Jazz and the White Americans: The Acceptance of a New Art Form.* Chicago: University of Chicago Press, 1962.

Lett, James. *The Human Enterprise: A Critical Introduction to Anthropological Theory.* Boulder, Colo.: Westview Press, 1987.

Levin, Robert. "The Jazz Composers Guild: An Assertion of Dignity." *Down Beat,* May 6, 1965, p. 17.

Levine, Lawrence. *Black Culture and Black Consciousness: Afro-American Folk Thought from Slavery to Freedom.* New York: Oxford University Press, 1977.

LeVine, Robert A. "Properties of Culture: An Ethnographic View." In *Culture Theory: Essays on Mind, Self, and Emotion,* pp. 67–87. Ed. Richard A. Shweder and Robert A. LeVine. New York: Cambridge University Press, 1984.

Lewis, Alan. "The Social Interpretation of Modern Jazz." *Canadian University Music Review* 2 (1981): 138–165.

Lewis, Oscar. "Urbanization without Breakdown." *Scientific Monthly* 75 (July 1952): 31–41.

Lidov, David. "Musical and Verbal Semantics." *Semiotica* 31, no. 3/4 (1980): 369–391.

Lincoln, Eric C. *The Black Muslims in America.* Foreword by Gordon W. Allport. Rev. ed. Westport, Conn.: Greenwood Press, 1973.

Litweiler, John. *The Freedom Principle: Jazz after 1958.* New York: William Morrow, 1984.

———. "Shepp: An Old Schoolmaster in Brown Suit." *Down Beat,* November 7, 1974, pp. 15–17, 44.

Lomax, Alan. *Cantometrics: An Approach to the Anthropology of Music.* Berkeley: University of California Extension Media Center, 1976.

———. *Folk Song Style and Culture: With Contributions by the Cantometrics Staff and with the Editorial Assistance of Edwin E. Erickson*. Publication (American Association for the Advancement of Science), no. 88. Washington, D.C.: American Association for the Advancement of Science, 1968.

Lord, Albert B. *The Singer of Tales*. Harvard Studies in Comparative Literature, 24. Cambridge: Harvard University Press, 1960.

Lornell, Kip. *Happy in the Service of the Lord: Afro-American Gospel Quartets in Memphis, Tennessee*. Urbana: University of Illinois Press, 1988.

Lyons, Len. *The 101 Best Jazz Albums: A History of Jazz on Records*. New York: William Morrow, 1980.

McCleod, Norma, and Herndon, Marcia, comps. *The Ethnography of Musical Performance*. Norwood, Pa.: Norwood Editions, 1980.

McDonough, John, Haden, Charlie, and Litweiler, John. "30 Years of Free." *Down Beat* (January 1992): 29–31.

Mandel, Howard. "Musicians of Brooklyn Initiative: Infant Steps." *Village Voice*, October 8, 1985, p. 73.

Marcuse, Herbert. *The Aesthetic Dimension: Toward a Critique of Marxist Aesthetics*. Boston: Beacon Press, 1978.

Martin, Henry. *Enjoying Jazz*. New York: Schirmer Books, 1986.

Meltzer, Bernard N., Petras, John W., and Reynolds, Larry T. *Symbolic Interactionism: Genesis, Varieties and Criticism*. Boston: Routledge and Kegan Paul, 1975.

Merriam, Alan P. *The Anthropology of Music*. Evanston, Ill.: Northwestern University Press, 1964.

———. "Ethnomusicology: Discussion and Definition of the Field." *Ethnomusicology* 4 (1960): 107–114.

———. "Ethnomusicology Today." *Current Musicology* 20 (1975): 50–66.

———. "Richard Waterman, 1914–1971." *Ethnomusicology* 17 (1973): 72–94.

Merriam, Alan P., and Garner, Fradley H. "Jazz—The Word." *Ethnomusicology* 12 (1968): 373–396.

Merriam, Alan P., and Mack, Raymond. "The Jazz Community." *Social Forces* 38 (1960): 211–222.

Merton, Robert K. *Social Theory and Social Structure*. Revised and enlarged edition. Glencoe, Ill.: Free Press, 1957.

Meyer, Leonard B. *Emotion and Meaning in Music*. Chicago: University of Chicago Press, 1956.

———. *Music, the Arts, and Ideas: Patterns and Predictions in Twentieth-Century Culture*. Chicago: University of Chicago Press, 1967.

Miller, Loyd, and Skipper, James K. "Sounds of Black Protest in Avant-garde Jazz." In *The Sounds of Social Change: Studies in Popular Culture*, pp. 26–36. Ed. Serge Denisoff and Richard A. Peterson. Chicago: Rand McNally, 1972.

Mitchell-Kernan, Claudia. "Signifying and Marking: Two Afro-American Speech Acts." In *Directions in Sociolinguistics: The Ethnography of Communication*, pp. 161–179. Ed. John J. Gumperz and Dell Hymes. New York: Holt, Rinehart and Winston, 1972; reprint ed., New York: B. Blackwell, 1986.

Moles, Abraham. *Information Theory and Esthetic Perception.* Trans. Joel F. Cohen. Urbana: University of Illinois Press, 1966.

Molino, Jean. "Fait musicale et sémiologie de la musique." *Musique en Jeu* 17 (1975): 37–62.

Moore, Sally Falk, and Myerhoff, Barbara B. *Symbol and Politics in Communical Ideology: Cases and Questions.* Ithaca: Cornell University Press, 1975.

Morgenstern, Dan. "Ornette Coleman: From the Heart." *Down Beat*, April 8, 1965, p. 17.

Morris, Ronald L. "Themes of Protest and Criminality in American Recorded Jazz, 1945–1975." *Annual Review of Jazz Studies* 3 (1985): 147–166.

"Musicians Talk about John Coltrane: Still a Force in '79." *Down Beat*, July 12, 1979, pp. 20, 38, 45.

Nanry, Charles, and Berger, Edward. *The Jazz Text.* New York: D. Van Norstrand Reinhold, 1979.

Nattiez, Jean-Jacques. *Fondements d'une sémiologie de la musique.* Paris: Union Générale d'Editions, 1976.

Nettl, Bruno. "Persian Classical Music in Tehran: The Processes of Change." In *Eight Urban Musical Cultures: Tradition and Change*, pp. 146–185. Ed. Bruno Nettl. Urbana: University of Illinois Press, 1978.

———. "The State of Research in Ethnomusicology and Recent Developments." *Current Musicology* 20 (1975): 67–78.

———. *The Study of Ethnomusicology: Twenty-nine Issues and Concepts.* Urbana: University of Illinois Press, 1983.

———. *Theory and Method in Ethnomusicology.* New York: Free Press of Glencoe, 1964.

———. "Thoughts on Improvisation: A Comparative Approach." *Musical Quarterly* 60 (1974): 1–19.

———. *The Western Impact on World Music: Change, Adaptation, and Survival.* New York: Schirmer Books, 1985.

The New Grove Dictionary of Jazz. Ed. Barry Kernfeld. 2 vols. New York: Macmillan, 1988.

New York Times, December 25, 1966, p. 10.

Newton, Francis. *The Jazz Scene.* New York: Monthly Review Press, 1960.

Nketia, J. H. Kwabena. "The Juncture of the Social and the Musical: The Methodology of Cultural Analysis." *World of Music* 23 (1981): 22–35.

———. "Multi-Part Organization in the Music of the Gogo of Tanzania." *Journal of International Folk Music Council* 19 (1967): 79–88.

———. *The Music of Africa.* New York: W. W. Norton, 1974.

Noske, Frits. *The Signifier and the Signified: Studies in the Operas of Mozart and Verdi.* The Hague: Nijhoff, 1977.

Oliver, Paul. *The Meaning of the Blues.* Foreword by Richard Wright. New York: Collier Books, 1972.

Oliver, Paul, Harrison, Max, and Bolcom, William. *The New Grove Gospel, Blues and Jazz with Spirituals and Ragtime.* New York: W. W. Norton, 1986.

Ortony, Andrew, ed. *Metaphor and Thought*. New York: Cambridge University Press, 1979.

Owens, Thomas. "Charlie Parker: Techniques of Improvisation." 2 vols. Ph.D. diss., University of California, Los Angeles, 1974.

Paredes, Américo, and Bauman, Richard, eds. *Toward New Perspectives in Folklore*. Publications of the American Folklore Society Bibliographical and Special Series, vol. 23. Austin: University of Texas Press, 1972.

Paredes, Américo, and Stekert, Ellen J., eds. *The Urban Experience and Folk Tradition*. Publications of the American Folklore Society Bibliographical and Special Series, vol. 22. Austin: University of Texas Press, 1971.

Parker, William. *Document Humanum*. N.p.: Centering, 1980.

Pearlman, Alan, and Greenblatt, Daniel. "Miles Davis Meets Noam Chomsky: Some Observations in Jazz Improvisation and Language Structure." In *The Sign in Music and Literature*, pp. 169–183. Ed. Wendy Steiner. Dan Danciger Publication Series. Austin: University of Texas Press, 1981.

Peikoff, Leonard. *The Ominous Parallels: The End of Freedom in America*. New York: Stein and Day, 1982.

Peña, Manuel. "From *Ranchero* to *Jaitón*: Ethnicity and Class in Texas-Mexican Music (Two Styles in the Form of a Pair)." *Ethnomusicology* 29 (1985): 29–55.

Pentikainen, Juha. "Life History and World View." *Temenos* 13 (1977): 146–153.

Perkins, David, and Leondar, Barbara, eds. *The Arts and Cognition*. Baltimore: Johns Hopkins University Press, 1977.

Peterson, Richard A. "Audiences—and All that Jazz." *Transaction* 1 (1964): 31–32.

Peterson, William, Novak, Michael, and Gleason, Philip. *Concepts of Ethnicity*. A Series of Selections from the Harvard Encyclopedia of American Ethnic Groups. Cambridge, Mass.: Belknap Press of Harvard University Press, 1982.

Porter, James. "Jeannie Robertson's My Son David." *Journal of American Folklore* 89 (1976): 7–26.

Porter, Lewis R. "John Coltrane's Music of 1960 through 1967: Jazz Improvisation as Composition." Ph.D. diss., Brandeis University, 1983.

———. *Lester Young*. Boston: Twayne Publishers, 1985.

Primack, Bret. "Sun Ra: Captain Angelic." *Down Beat*, May 14, 1978, pp. 14–16, 40–41.

Racy, Jihad Ali. "Musical Change and Commercial Recording in Egypt, 1904–1932." Ph.D. diss., University of Illinois at Urbana-Champaign, 1976.

Radano, Ronald M. "The Jazz Avant-garde and the Jazz Community: Action and Reaction." *Annual Review of Jazz Studies* 3 (1985): 71–79.

Rahn, Jay. *A Theory for All Music: Problems and Solutions in the Analysis of Non-Western Forms*. Toronto: University of Toronto Press, 1983.

Read, Herbert. *Art and Alienation: The Role of the Artist in Society*. New York: Horizon Press, 1967.

Reed, Harry A. "The Black Bar in the Making of a Jazz Musician: Bird, Mingus, and Stan Hope." *Journal of Jazz Studies* 5 (1979): 76–90.

Reisner, Robert George. *Bird: The Legend of Charlie Parker.* New York: Bonanza Books, 1962; reprint ed., Quartet Books, 1974.

Rice, Timothy. "Aspects of Bulgarian Musical Thought." *Yearbook of the International Folk Music Council* 12 (1980): 43–66.

———. "Toward the Remodeling of Ethnomusicology." *Ethnomusicology* 31 (1987): 469–488.

Rivelli, Pauline, and Levin, Robert, eds. *Giants of Black Music.* New York: Da Capo Press, 1979; originally published as *The Black Giants,* New York: World Publishing, 1970.

Roberts, John Storm. *Black Music of Two Worlds.* New York: Praeger, 1972.

Rogers, Robert. *Metaphor: A Psychoanalytic View.* Berkeley: University of California Press, 1978.

Roseman, Marina. "The Social Structuring of Sound: The Temiar of Peninsular Malaysia." *Ethnomusicology* 28 (1984): 411–445.

Roszak, Theodore. *The Making of a Counter Culture: Reflections on the Technocratic Society and Its Youthful Opposition.* Garden City, N.Y.: Doubleday, 1969.

Rouget, Gilbert. *Music and Trance: A Theory of the Relations between Music and Possession.* Trans. Derek Coltman; revised trans. Brunhilde Biebuyck. Chicago: University of Chicago Press, 1985.

Rusch, Robert D. *Jazztalk: The* Cadence *Interviews.* Secaucus, N.J.: Lyle Stuart, 1984.

Salzman, Eric. *Twentieth-Century Music: An Introduction.* 2d ed. Englewood Cliffs, N.J.: Prentice-Hall, 1967.

Sapir, David J., and Crocker, J. Christopher, eds. *The Social Use of Metaphor: Essays on the Anthropology of Rhetoric.* Philadelphia: University of Pennsylvania Press, 1977.

Saussure, Ferdinand de. *Course in General Linguistics.* Trans. W. Baskin. New York: McGraw-Hill, 1966.

Schramm, Adelaida Reyes. "Explorations in Urban Ethnomusicology: Hard Lessons from the Spectacularly Ordinary." *Yearbook for Traditional Music* 14 (1982): 1–14.

Schuller, Gunther. *Early Jazz: Its Roots and Musical Development.* History of Jazz, vol. 1. New York: Oxford University Press, 1968.

———. *The Swing Era: The Development of Jazz 1930–1945.* History of Jazz, vol. 2. New York: Oxford University Press, 1989.

Seeger, Charles. "Music as a Tradition of Communication, Discipline and Play." *Ethnomusicology* 6 (1962): 156–163.

———. *Studies in Musicology 1935–1975.* Berkeley: University of California Press, 1977.

Serafine, Mary Louise. *Music as Cognition: The Development of Thought in Sound.* New York: Columbia University Press, 1988.

Shapiro, Nat, and Hentoff, Nat, eds. *Hear Me Talkin' to Ya: The Story of Jazz as Told by the Men Who Made It.* New York: Dover, 1955; reprint ed., 1966.

Shepherd, John. "A Theoretical Model for the Sociomusicological Analysis of Popular Musics." *Popular Music: Theory and Method* 2 (1982): 145–177.

Shepp, Archie. "A View from the Inside." *Down Beat's Music '66* 11 (1966). 39–42, 44.

Sherburne, Donald W. "Meaning and Music." *Journal of Aesthetics and Art Criticism* 24 (1966): 579–583.

Shweder, Richard A., and LeVine, Robert A., eds. *Culture Theory: Essays on Mind, Self, and Emotion.* New York: Cambridge University Press, 1984.

Sidran, Ben. *Black Talk.* New York: Holt, Rinehart and Winston, 1971; reprint ed., New York: Da Capo Press, 1981.

Simosko, Vladimir, and Tepperman, Barry. *Eric Dolphy: A Musical Biography and Discography.* New York: Da Capo Press, 1971.

Simpkins, Cuthbert Ormond. *Coltrane: A Biography.* New York: Herndon House, 1975.

Sinclair, John, and Levin, Robert. *Music and Politics.* New York: World Publishing, 1971.

Slater, Phillip E. "Role Differentiation in Small Groups." *American Sociological Review* 20 (1955): 300–310.

Smith, Riley B. "Research Perspectives on American Black English: A Brief Historical Sketch." *American Speech: A Quarterly of Linguistic Usage* 49 (1974): 24–39.

Southern, Eileen. *The Music of Black Americans: A History.* 2d ed. New York: W. W. Norton, 1983.

Spellman, A. B. *Four Lives in the Bebop Business.* New York: Pantheon, 1966. Reprinted as *Black Music: Four Lives in the Bebop Business.* New York: Schocken, 1970.

Spradley, James P., ed. *Culture and Cognition: Rules, Maps, and Plans.* San Francisco: Chandler, 1972.

Stahl, Sandra. "Personal Narrative as Folklore." *Journal of the Folklore Institute* 14 (1977): 9–30.

Starr, Frederick S. *Red and Hot: The Fate of Jazz in the Soviet Union, 1917–1980.* New York: Oxford University Press, 1983.

Stearns, Marshall W. *The Story of Jazz.* New York: Oxford University Press, 1956; reprint ed., 1972.

Stebbins, Robert A. "Role Distance, Role Distance Behaviour and Jazz Musicians." *British Journal of Sociology* 20 (1969): 406–415.

———. "A Theory of the Jazz Community." *Sociological Quarterly* 9 (1968): 318–331.

Stewart, Milton. "Some Characteristics of Clifford Brown's Improvisational Style." *Jazzforschung/Jazz Research* 11 (1979): 135–164.

Stone, Kurt. "Problems and Methods of Notation." In *Perspectives on Notation and Performance*, pp. 9–31. Perspectives of New Music Series. Ed. Benjamin Boretz and Edward T. Cone. New York: W. W. Norton, 1976.

Stone, Ruth. *Let the Inside Be Sweet: The Interpretation of Musical Event among the Kpelle of Liberia.* Bloomington: Indiana University Press, 1982.

———. "Toward a Kpelle Conceptualization of Music Performance." *Journal of American Folklore* 94 (1981): 188–206.

Strunk, Steven. "Bebop Melodic Lines: Tonal Characteristics." *Annual Review of Jazz Studies* 3 (1985): 97–120.

Sturman, Janet L. "Zarzuela Productions in New York." *Yearbook for Traditional Music* 18 (1986): 103–113.

Such, David G. "Music, Metaphor and Values among Avant-garde Jazz Musicians Living in New York City." Ph.D. diss., University of California, Los Angeles, 1985.

———. "'Out There': A Metaphor of Transcendence among New York City Avant-garde Jazz Musicians." *New York Folklore* 7 (1981): 83–95.

———. Review of *The Freedom Principle: Jazz after 1958* by John Litweiler. *Pacific Review of Ethnomusicology* 2 (1985): 120–123.

———. Review of *Sounds So Good to Me: The Bluesman's Story* by Barry Lee Pearson. *Journal of American Folklore* 101 (1988): 99–100.

Such, David G., and Jairazbhoy, Nazir A. "Manifestations of Cyclic Structures in Indian Classical Music." *Journal of Asian Culture* 6 (1982): 104–117.

Tagg, Phillip. "Analysing Popular Music: Theory, Method, and Practice." *Popular Music: Theory and Method* 2 (1982): 37–68.

Taggart, James M. "Animal Metaphors in Spanish and Mexican Oral Tradition." *Journal of American Folklore* 95 (1982): 280–303.

Tallmadge, William H. "The Black in Jackson's White Spirituals." *Black Perspective in Music* 9 (1981): 139–160.

———. "Blue Notes and Blue Tonality." *Black Perspective in Music* 12 (1984): 155–165.

Tamony, Peter. "Funky." *American Speech: A Quarterly of Linguistic Usage* 55 (1980): 210–213.

———. "Jazz, the Word." *Jazz: A Quarterly of American Music* 1 (1958): 33–39, 42.

Taylor, Arthur. *Notes and Tones: Musician-to-Musician Interviews.* New York: Coward, McCann and Geoghegan, 1977.

Taylor, John E. "Somethin' on My Mind: A Cultural and Historical Interpretation of Spiritual Texts." *Ethnomusicology* 19 (1975): 387–399.

Thomas, J. C. *Chasin' the Trane: The Music and Mystique of John Coltrane.* New York: Doubleday, 1975.

Tirro, Frank. *Jazz: A History.* New York: W. W. Norton, 1977.

Titon, Jeff Todd. *Early Downhome Blues: A Musical and Cultural Analysis.* Music in American Life. Urbana: University of Illinois Press, 1977.

Touma, Habib Hassan. "The Maqam Phenomenon: An Improvisation Technique in the Music of the Middle East." *Ethnomusicology* 15 (1971): 38–48.

Townley, Ray. "Sun Ra." *Down Beat,* December 20, 1973, pp. 18, 38.

Turino, Thomas. "The Urban-Mestizo Charango Tradition in Southern Peru: A Statement of Shifting Identity." *Ethnomusicology* 28 (1984): 253–270.

Turner, Victor. *Dramas, Fields, and Metaphors: Symbolic Action in Human Society.* Symbol, Myth and Ritual Series. Ithaca, N.Y.: Cornell University Press, 1974.

———. *The Ritual Process: Structure and Anti-Structure.* Symbol, Myth and Ritual Series. Ithaca, N.Y.: Cornell University Press, 1969.

Tynan, John. "Take 5." *Down Beat*, November 23, 1961, pp. 29–31.

Uribe-Villegas, Oscar, ed. *Issues in Sociolinguistics.* The Hague: Mouton, 1977.

Vico, Giambattista. *The New Science.* Trans. from the 3d ed. (1744) Thomas Goddard Bergin and Max Harold Fisch. Ithaca, N.Y.: Cornell University Press, 1948.

Wachsmann, Klaus. "The Changeability of Musical Experience." *Ethnomusicology* 26 (1982): 197–215.

Wallaschek, Richard. *Primitive Music: An Inquiry into the Origin and Development of Music, Songs, Instruments, Dances, and Pantomime of Savage Races.* New York: Longmens, Green, 1893; reprint ed., New York: Da Capo Press, 1970.

Walker, Robert. *Musical Beliefs: Psychoacoustic, Mythical, and Educational Perspectives.* New York: Teachers College Press, 1990.

Warshaver, Gerald. "Urban Folklore." In *Handbook of American Folklore.* Ed. Richard M. Dorson; introduction by W. Edson Richmond. Bloomington: Indiana University Press, 1983.

Waterman, Richard Alan. "African Influence on the Music of the Americas." In *Acculturation in the Americas: Proceedings and Selected Papers of the XXIXth International Congress of Americanists.* Ed. Sol Tax. New York: Cooper Square Publishers, 1952; reprint ed., 1967.

Weber, Max. *The Rational and Social Foundations of Music.* Carbondale: Southern Illinois University Press, 1958. First published in German, 1921.

Wentworth, Harold, and Flexner, Stuart Berg. *Dictionary of American Slang.* New York: Crowell, 1960.

White, Andrew. "The Coltrane Legacy." *Down Beat* (September 1986): 63, 61, 48.

White, Newman Ivey. *American Negro Folk Songs.* Hatboro, Pa.: Folklore Associates, 1928; reprint ed., 1965.

Whitehead, Kevin. "Steve Lacy: The Interview." *Down Beat* (December 1987): 24–26, 62.

Wilgus, D. K. *Anglo-American Folksong Scholarship since 1898.* New Brunswick, N.J.: Rutgers University Press, 1959.

Williams, Martin T. *Jazz Masters in Transition, 1957–69.* New York: Da Capo, 1970; reprint ed., 1982.

Wilmer, Valerie. *As Serious as Your Life: The Story of the New Jazz.* Westport, Conn.: L. Hill, 1977.

Wilson, Olly. "The Significance of the Relationship between Afro-American Music and West African Music." *Black Perspective in Music* 1 (1973): 3–22.

Winter, Keith. "Communication Analysis in Jazz." *Jazzforschung* 11 (1979): 93–134.

Wirth, Louis. "Urbanism as a Way of Life." *American Journal of Sociology* 44 (1938): 3–24. Reprinted in *Urban Life: Readings in Urban Anthropology*, pp. 9–25. Ed. George Gmelch and Walter P. Zenner. New York: St. Martin's Press, 1980.

Woodward, Kathleen, ed. *The Myths of Information: Technology and Postindustrial Culture*. Theories of Contemporary Culture, vol. 2. Madison, Wis.: Coda Press, 1980.

Zemp, Hugo. "'Are' are Classification of Musical Types and Instruments." *Ethnomusicology* 22 (1978): 37–67.

———. "Aspects of 'Are' are Musical Theory." *Ethnomusicology* 23 (1979): 6–48.

index